Fifth Grade Math with Confidence

Student Workbook

Part A

KATE SNOW

WELL-TRAINED MIND PRESS

Names: Snow, Kate (Teacher), author.
Title: Fifth grade math with confidence. Student workbook part A / Kate Snow.
Other titles: Student workbook part A
Description: [Charles City, Virginia] : Well-Trained Mind Press, [2025] | Series: Snow, Kate (Teacher). Math with confidence. | Interest grade level: 5.
Identifiers: ISBN: 9781944481759 (paperback)
Subjects: LCSH: Mathematics--Study and teaching (Elementary) | LCGFT: Problems and exercises. | BISAC: JUVENILE NONFICTION / Mathematics / Algebra. | JUVENILE NONFICTION / Mathematics / Fractions.
Classification: LCC: QA107.2 .S665 2025 | DCC: 372.7--dc23

Reprinted July 2026 at Versa Press.

3 4 5 6 7 8 9 Versa 30 29 28 27 26

Fifth Grade Math with Confidence

Student Workbook

Part A

Table of Contents

Author's Note

You'll need three books to teach *Fifth Grade Math with Confidence*. All three books are essential for the program.

- The Instructor Guide contains the scripted lesson plans for the entire year.
- Student Workbook Part A contains the workbook pages for the first half of the year (Units 1–7).
- Student Workbook Part B contains the workbook pages for the second half of the year (Units 8–16).

The Student Workbooks are not meant to be used as stand-alone workbooks. The hands-on teaching activities in the Instructor Guide are an essential part of the program. You'll need the directions in the Instructor Guide to guide your child through the Lesson Activities pages. The icon with two heads means that your child should complete these pages with you, and that she is not expected to complete these pages on her own.

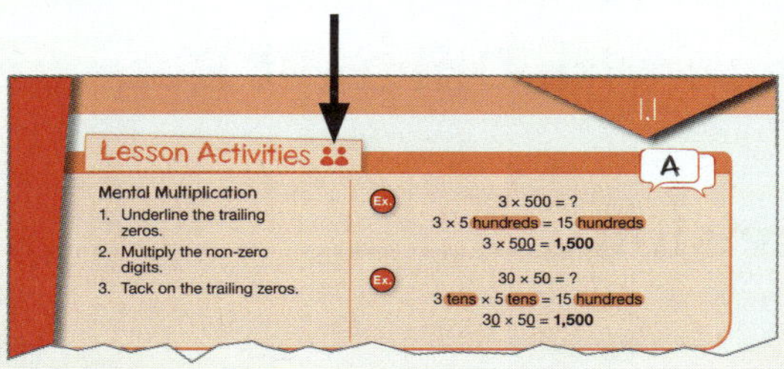

The Practice and Review pages give your child practice with new concepts and review previously-learned skills. The icon with one head means that your child may complete these pages on his own. Most fifth-graders will be able to complete these pages independently, and it's fine if your child sometimes needs a little extra support or coaching.

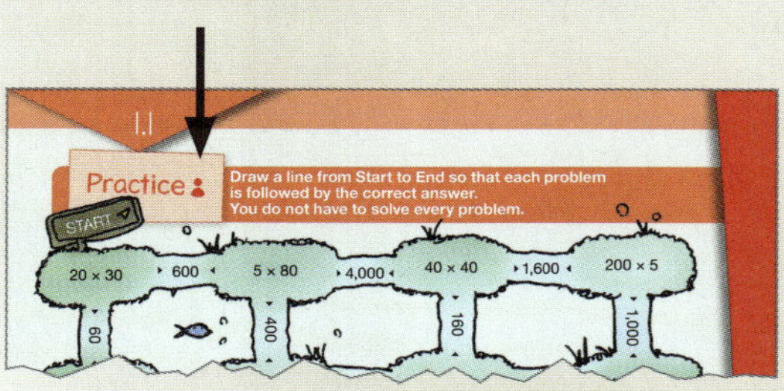

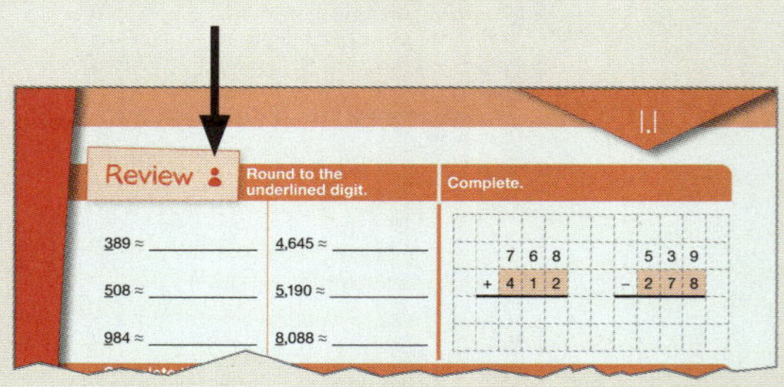

Lesson Activities

A

Mental Multiplication

1. Underline the trailing zeros.
2. Multiply the non-zero digits.
3. Tack on the trailing zeros.

Ex.

3 × 500 = ?

3 × 5 hundreds = 15 hundreds

3 × 500 = **1,500**

Ex.

30 × 50 = ?

3 tens × 5 tens = 15 hundreds

30 × 50 = **1,500**

6 × 70 = ________

60 × 70 = ________

6,000 × 7 = ________

6 × 700 = ________

500 × 8 = ________

5 × 80 = ________

50 × 80 = ________

5 × 8,000 = ________

8 × 800 = ________

80 × 8 = ________

80 × 80 = ________

8,000 × 8 = ________

B

Theme Park Vacation Costs

Round-trip plane tickets:
$319 per person

Hotel:
$176 per night

Rental car:
$83 per day

Park tickets:
$119 per person per day

Dining plan:
$68 per person per day

Estimated Budget

Plane tickets	
5 nights at the hotel	
Rental car for 5 days	
Park tickets for 5 days	
Food for 5 days	
Total cost	

Practice

Draw a line from Start to End so that each problem is followed by the correct answer. You do not have to solve every problem.

Review

Round to the underlined digit.

389 ≈ ______ (3 underlined)

508 ≈ ______ (5 underlined)

984 ≈ ______ (9 underlined)

4,645 ≈ ______ (4 underlined)

5,190 ≈ ______ (5 underlined)

8,088 ≈ ______ (8 underlined)

Complete.

$$\begin{array}{r} 768 \\ +\ 412 \\ \hline \end{array} \qquad \begin{array}{r} 539 \\ -\ 278 \\ \hline \end{array}$$

Complete the chart.

Hours	1	2	3	4	5	6
Minutes	*60*					

Complete the missing fractions on the number lines.

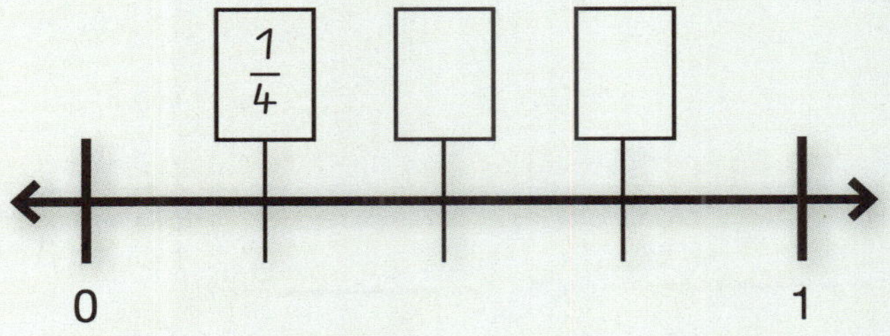

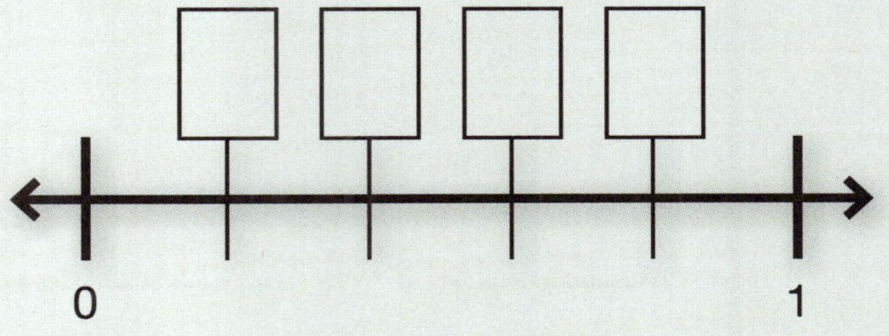

Use the clues to complete the chart.

- Julia is 11 years old.
- Sam is 3 years younger than Julia.
- Mom is 4 times as old as Julia.
- Dad is 5 times as old as Sam.
- Great-grandpa is 10 times as old as Sam.

Name	Age
Julia	
Sam	
Mom	
Dad	
Great-grandpa	

1.2

Lesson Activities

A

1. Multiply 5 ones by 3.
2. Multiply 4 tens by 3. Add 1 ten.
3. Multiply 2 hundreds by 3. Add 1 hundred.

Ex.

$$\begin{array}{r} {\scriptstyle 1} \\ 245 \\ \times \quad 3 \\ \hline 5 \end{array} \longrightarrow \begin{array}{r} {\scriptstyle 11} \\ 245 \\ \times \quad 3 \\ \hline 35 \end{array} \longrightarrow \begin{array}{r} {\scriptstyle 11} \\ 245 \\ \times \quad 3 \\ \hline 735 \end{array}$$

	4	1	7
×			4

Estimate

× ______

	2,	9	8	1
×				5

Estimate

× ______

B

Multiplication War

(2-Player Game)

Player 1

Round 1	Round 2	Round 3	
☐☐☐ × ☐	☐☐☐ × ☐	☐☐☐ × ☐	Round 1
			Round 2
			Round 3
			Total

Player 2

Round 1	Round 2	Round 3	
☐☐☐ × ☐	☐☐☐ × ☐	☐☐☐ × ☐	Round 1
			Round 2
			Round 3
			Total

Practice

Find the products.

$$\begin{array}{r} 41 \\ \times \quad 6 \\ \hline \end{array} \qquad \begin{array}{r} 73 \\ \times \quad 5 \\ \hline \end{array} \qquad \begin{array}{r} 93 \\ \times \quad 4 \\ \hline \end{array} \qquad \begin{array}{r} 86 \\ \times \quad 3 \\ \hline \end{array} \qquad \begin{array}{r} 99 \\ \times \quad 6 \\ \hline \end{array}$$

$$\begin{array}{r} 343 \\ \times \quad 2 \\ \hline \end{array} \qquad \begin{array}{r} 216 \\ \times \quad 4 \\ \hline \end{array} \qquad \begin{array}{r} 1,027 \\ \times \quad 3 \\ \hline \end{array} \qquad \begin{array}{r} 2,680 \\ \times \quad 5 \\ \hline \end{array}$$

Use the price list to answer the questions.
Write the equations you use in the work space.

WORK SPACE

How much do 3 tickets to St. Louis cost?

How much do 6 tickets to Boston cost?

How much do 4 tickets to Miami cost?

How much do 9 tickets to Seattle cost?

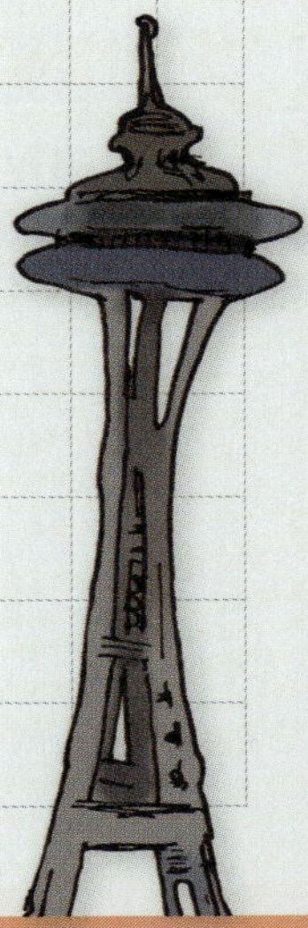

Review

Complete.

6 × 6 = ______ 9 × 4 = ______ 6 × 9 = ______

9 × 3 = ______ 7 × 4 = ______ 8 × 6 = ______

7 × 6 = ______ 8 × 9 = ______ 5 × 8 = ______

4 × 8 = ______ 8 × 8 = ______ 9 × 7 = ______

Complete the chart.

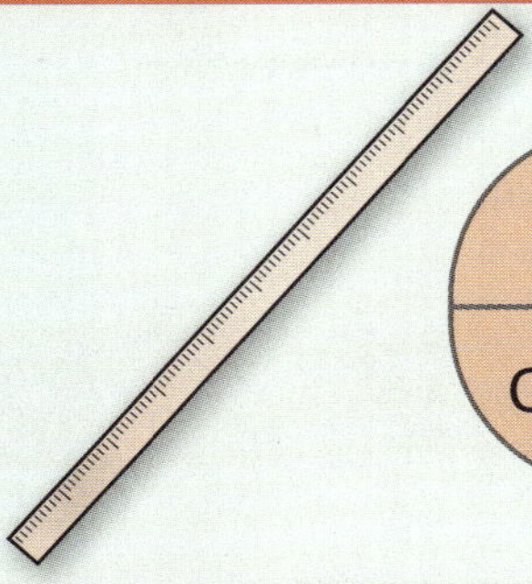

Meters	1	2	3	4	5	6
Centimeters	*100*					

Find the area and perimeter.

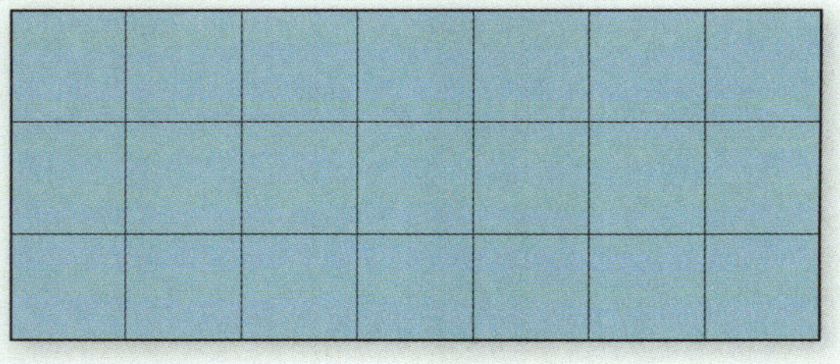

Perimeter: ______________ cm

Area: ______________ sq. cm

Write each number in expanded form.

789 = *700 + 80 + 9*

708 = ______________

7,080 = ______________

7,890 = ______________

Solve. Write the equations you use.

Harmony buys 3 tacos for $6 each and 2 burritos for $8 each.
How much does she spend?

Watson has $20.
He buys 4 drinks for $3 each.
How much money does he have left?

Lesson Activities

A

Two Ways to Understand Division

Ex. I have 10 in. of ribbon. I cut the ribbon into 2 equal pieces. How long is each piece?

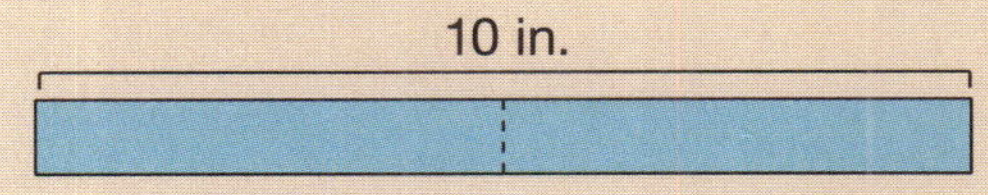

10 ÷ 2 = **5 in.**

total → 10; number of groups → 2; size of each group → 5 in.

Ex. I have 10 in. of ribbon. I cut the ribbon into pieces that are each 2 in. long. How many pieces do I make?

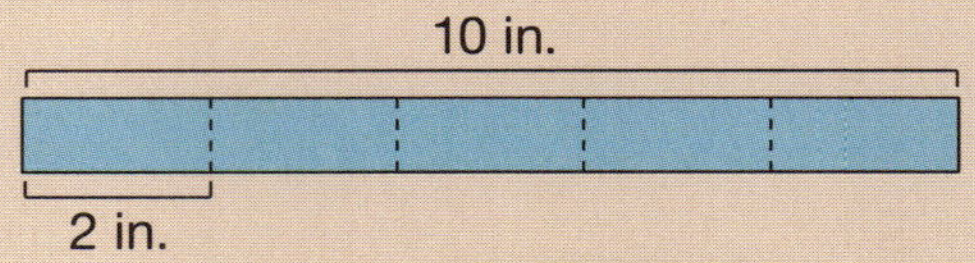

10 ÷ 2 = **5 pieces**

total → 10; size of each group → 2; number of groups → 5 pieces

B

Mental Division

1. Underline the trailing zeros.
2. Divide the other digits.
3. Tack on the underlined trailing zeros.

Ex.

18,000 ÷ 6 = ?

18 thousands ÷ 6 = 3 thousands

18,000 ÷ 6 = **3,000**

If the non-zero digits aren't divisible by the divisor, try underlining fewer zeros.

Ex.

200 ÷ 4 = ?

2 hundreds ÷ 4 = ?

2 isn't divisible by 4. Try underlining only one zero.

200 ÷ 4 = ?

20 tens ÷ 4 = 5 tens

200 ÷ 4 = **50**

350 ÷ 7 = ________

3,500 ÷ 7 = ________

35,000 ÷ 7 = ________

6,400 ÷ 8 = ________

640 ÷ 8 = ________

64,000 ÷ 8 = ________

400 ÷ 5 = ________

40,000 ÷ 5 = ________

4,000 ÷ 5 = ________

Practice

Complete.

420 ÷ 7 = ______	4,800 ÷ 6 = ______	81,000 ÷ 9 = ______
4,200 ÷ 7 = ______	48,000 ÷ 6 = ______	810 ÷ 9 = ______
6,400 ÷ 8 = ______	490 ÷ 7 = ______	54,000 ÷ 6 = ______
640 ÷ 8 = ______	49,000 ÷ 7 = ______	5,400 ÷ 6 = ______
720 ÷ 9 = ______	56,000 ÷ 8 = ______	6,300 ÷ 7 = ______
7,200 ÷ 9 = ______	5,600 ÷ 8 = ______	630 ÷ 7 = ______
★ 450 ÷ ______ = 90	★ ______ ÷ 4 = 800	★ ______ ÷ 5 = 5,000

Solve. Write the equations you use.

Wyatt earns $160 for 8 hours of work. How much does he earn for each hour of work?

Katelyn bakes 80 cupcakes. She puts 4 cupcakes in each box. How many boxes does she fill?

Valentina has 40 cm of string. She cuts the string into pieces that are each 8 cm long. How many pieces of string does she make?

Swim camp costs $200 for 5 days. How much does each day of camp cost?

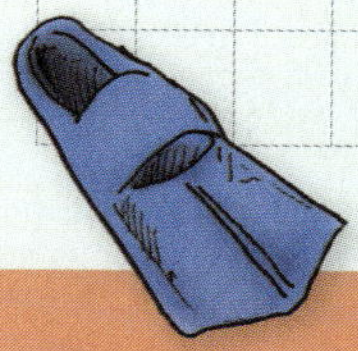

Review

Use mental math to complete.

35 + 5 = ______
35 + 6 = ______
35 + 7 = ______

48 + 20 = ______
48 + 22 = ______
48 + 25 = ______

65 + 15 = ______
65 + 25 = ______
65 + 35 = ______

73 – 3 = ______
73 – 4 = ______
73 – 5 = ______

86 – 3 = ______
86 – 13 = ______
86 – 23 = ______

91 – 90 = ______
91 – 89 = ______
91 – 88 = ______

Label the numbers on the number line.

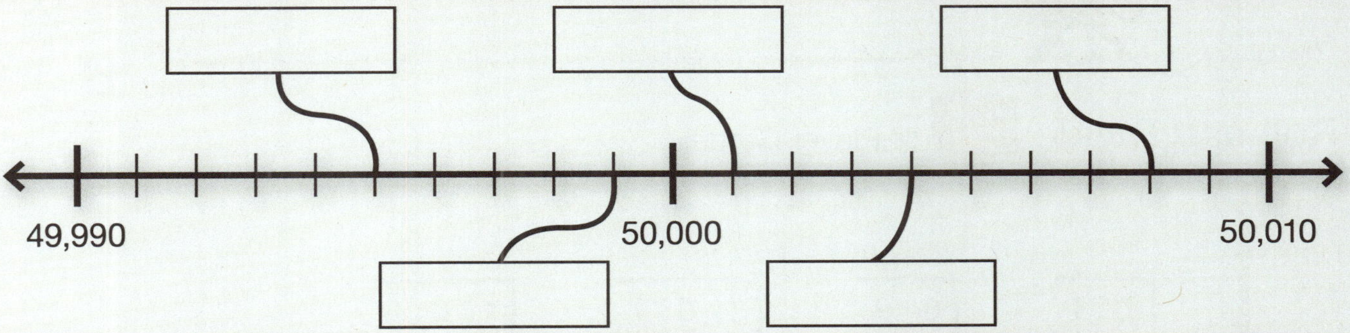

Complete the chart.

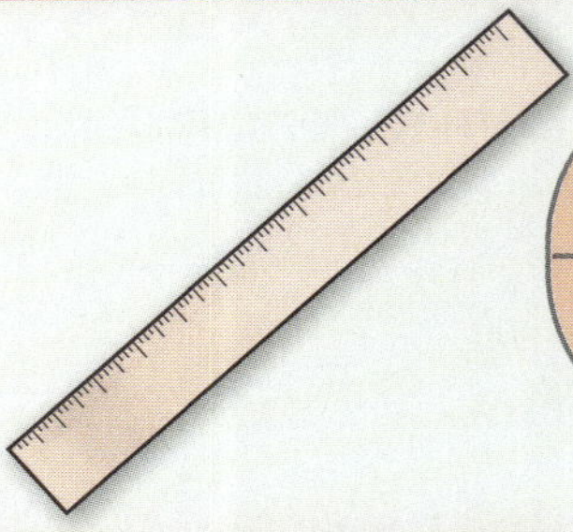

Feet	1	2	3	4	5	6	7	8
Inches	12							

Complete.

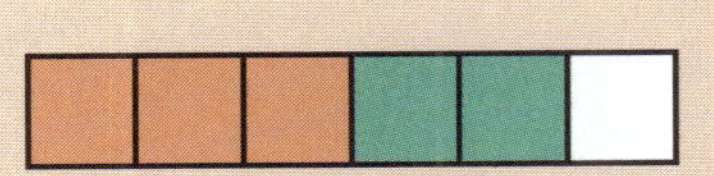

$\frac{3}{6} + \frac{2}{6} = \frac{5}{6}$

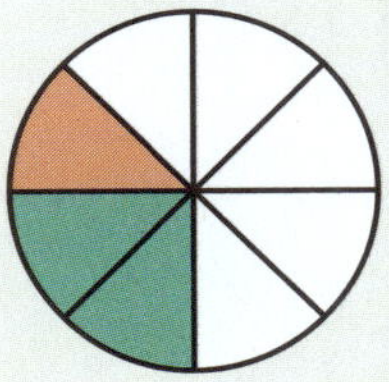

$\frac{1}{8} + \frac{2}{8} =$

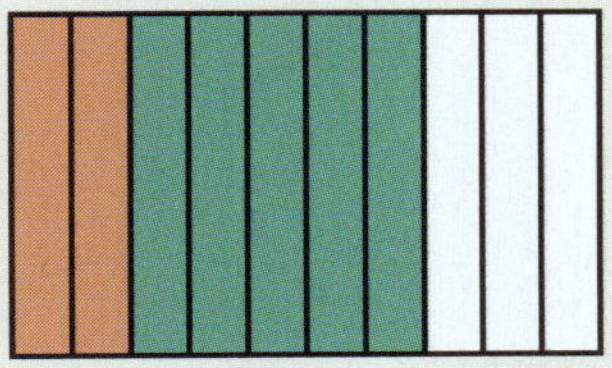

$\frac{2}{10} + \frac{5}{10} =$

Lesson Activities

A

Repeat if needed

1. Divide
2. Multiply
3. Subtract
4. Bring down the next digit (if needed)

Ex.

```
    2                28
 3 | 85           3 | 85
   - 6↓      →      - 6↓
    25               25
                   - 24
                      1
```

Ex.

```
     2                 23
 5 | 115           5 | 115
   - 10↓      →      - 10↓
     15                15
                      -15
                        0
```

B

Roll and Divide  (2-Player Game)

Player 1

⟌ 7 1	⟌ 8 9	⟌ 1 0 7	⟌ 1 6 3

Sum of remainders

Player 2

⟌ 7 1	⟌ 8 9	⟌ 1 0 7	⟌ 1 6 3

Sum of remainders

Practice

Solve.

$2\overline{)93}$ $3\overline{)67}$ $4\overline{)253}$ $3\overline{)658}$ $5\overline{)706}$

$5\overline{)89}$ $6\overline{)80}$

Use long division to solve. Write the equations you use in the work space.

How much does the Alaska cruise cost per day?

How much does the Greece cruise cost per day?

WORK SPACE

Review

Round to the underlined digit.

$5\underline{3}9 \approx$ ____________

$\underline{5}39 \approx$ ____________

$1{,}\underline{5}08 \approx$ ____________

$\underline{1}{,}508 \approx$ ____________

Complete the missing factors in the factor pairs.

Factors of 24	Factors of 40
1 × 24	1 × ____
2 × ____	2 × ____
3 × ____	4 × ____
4 × ____	5 × ____

Choose the more reasonable measurement for each angle.

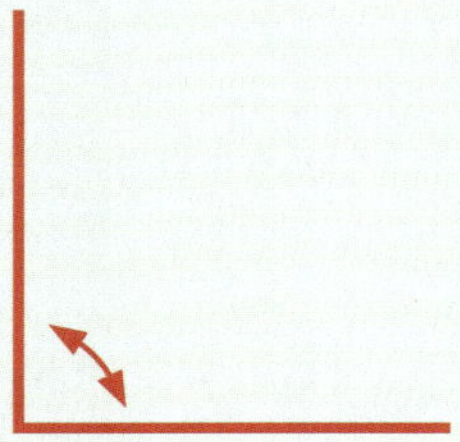

10° | 90°

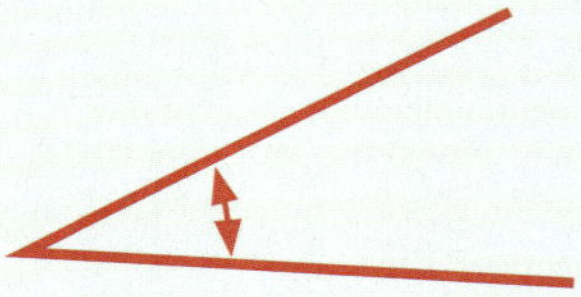

30° | 130°

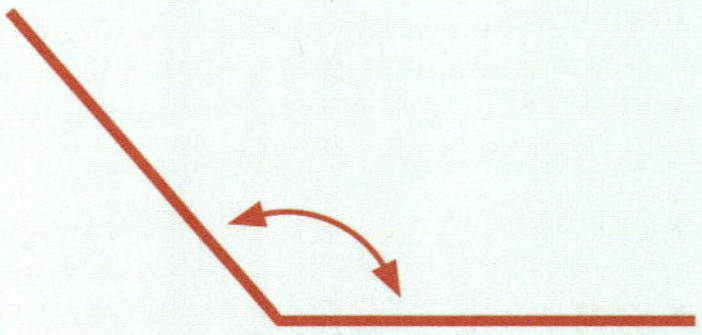

30° | 130°

Complete the chart.

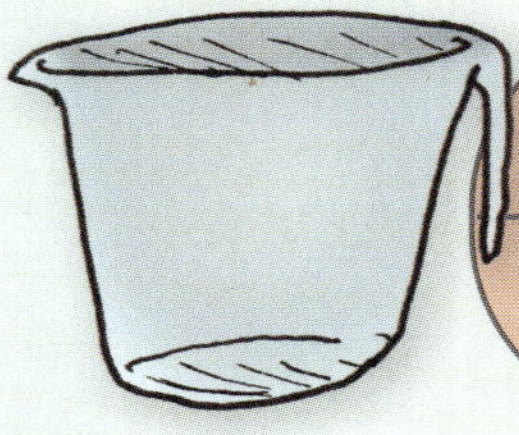

Cups	1	2	3	4	5	6	7	8
Fluid Ounces	8							

Solve. Write the equations you use.

Gwen has 32 fl. oz. of juice.
She pours 6 fl. oz. into each glass.
How many glasses does she fill?
How many fluid ounces does she have left?

Charlie fills his water bottle with 24 fl. oz. of water. He drinks some water, and then he has 17 fl. oz. left.
How many fluid ounces did he drink?

Lesson Activities

A

Line Plots

A line plot is a graph made from X's and part of the number line.

The number of X's above each value tells how many times that value occurred in the data set.

Ex. How many baskets of apples weigh 6 lb.?

Weights of Baskets of Apples

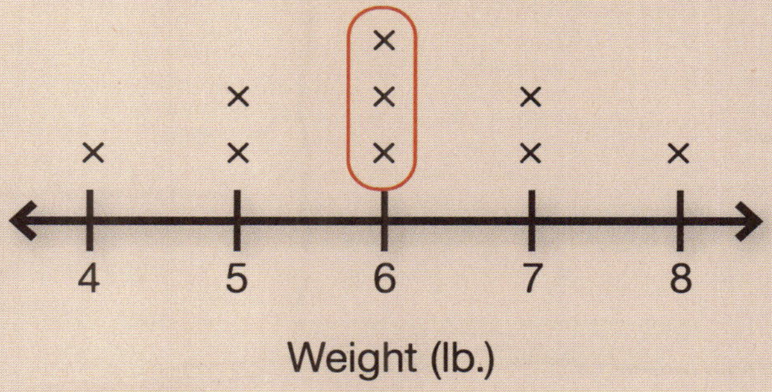

3 baskets weigh 6 lb.

Averages

The average is one way to describe the "center" of a data set. To find the average:

1. Add up all the values in the data set.
2. Divide by the number of values in the data set.

Ex. What's the average weight of the baskets of apples?

4 + 5 + 5 + 6 + 6 + 6 + 7 + 7 + 8 = 54
54 ÷ 9 = **6 lb.**

If you split all the apples evenly into 9 baskets, each basket would weigh 6 lb.

Pumpkins' Weights (lb.)

9	13
12	12
13	9
14	13
11	14
12	12

Pumpkins' Weights

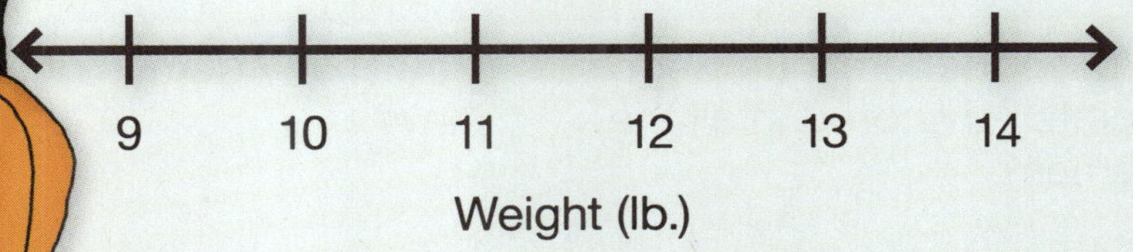

What's the total weight of all the pumpkins?

How many pumpkins' weights are represented in the data set?

What's the average weight of the pumpkins?

Practice

Elisha and AJ are on different basketball teams. They kept track of how many points they scored in each game. Make a line plot for each data set. Then, answer the questions.

Elisha's Points

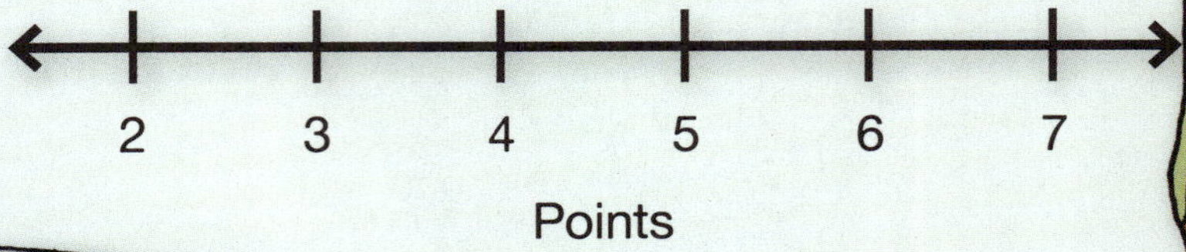

What's the total number of points Elisha scored in all the games?	How many games did Elisha play?	What's the average number of points Elisha scored per game?

AJ's Points

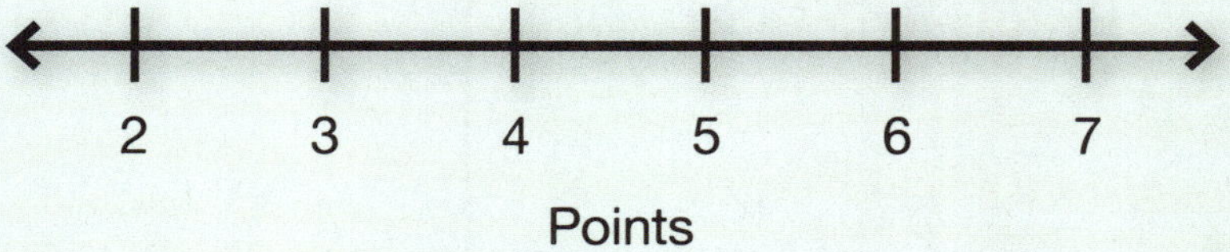

What's the total number of points AJ scored in all the games?	How many games did AJ play?	What's the average number of points AJ scored per game?
Who scored more points in all?	Who played more games?	Who had the higher average number of points per game?

Review

Match.

two hundred thousand five hundred	200,050
two hundred thousand fifty	250,000
two hundred five thousand	200,500
two hundred fifty thousand	205,000

Use the pictures to complete the equivalent fractions.

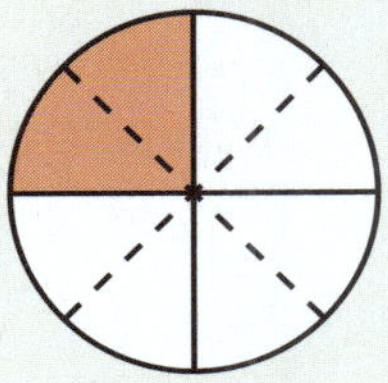

$\frac{1}{4} = \frac{}{8}$

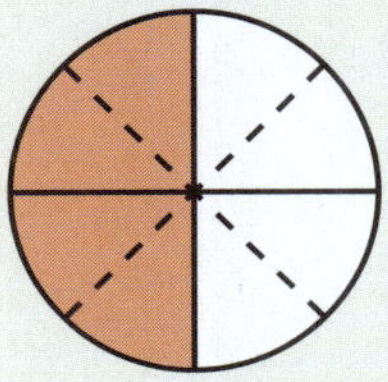

$\frac{2}{4} = \frac{}{8}$

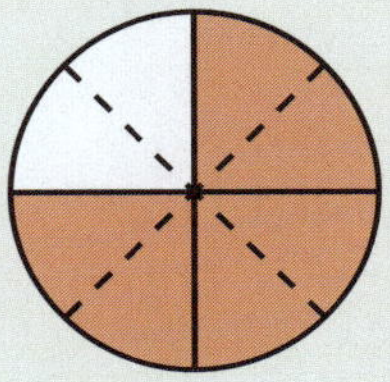

$\frac{3}{4} = \frac{}{8}$

Complete the chart.

Liters	1	2	3	4	5	6
Milliliters	1,000					

Solve. Write the equations you use.

Ryan buys a bottle of soda with 2 L.
He divides it equally into 4 glasses.
How many milliliters are in each glass?

Cora fills her water bottle with 1 L of water.
She drinks 300 mL.
How many milliliters does she have left?

1.6

Lesson Activities

A

Measurement Scavenger Hunt

About 1 foot long	About 1 inch long	About 1 yard long	* About 1 mile long
Weighs about 1 pound	Weighs about 1 ounce	Holds about 1 fluid ounce	Holds about 1 cup
About 1 meter long	About 1 centimeter long	About 1 millimeter long	* About 1 kilometer long
Weighs about 1 gram	Weighs about 1 kilogram	Holds about 1 milliliter	Holds about 1 liter

B

Multiply or Divide to Convert Measurements

To convert from a larger unit to a smaller unit, multiply by the conversion factor. Add on any extra smaller units.

Ex. 4 yd. 1 ft. = _____ ft.

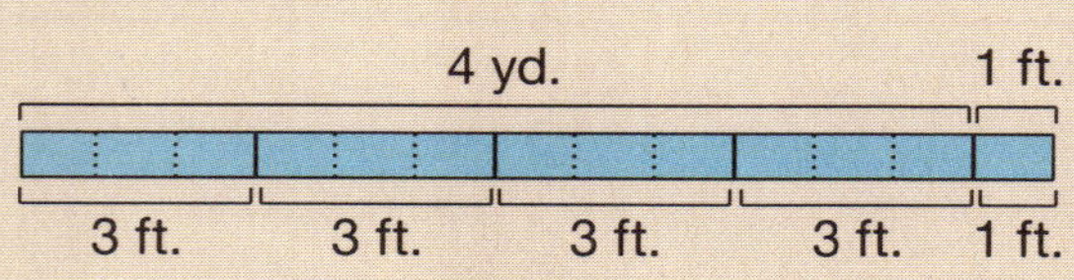

4 × 3 = 12
12 + 1 = 13
4 yd. 1 ft. = **13 ft.**

Whole to parts? Multiply to start!

To convert from a smaller unit to a larger unit, divide by the conversion factor.

Ex. 37 mm = _____ cm

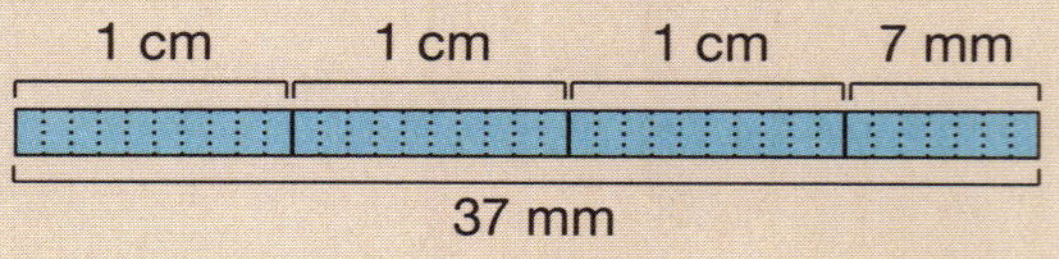

37 ÷ 10 = 3 R7
37 mm = **3 cm 7 mm**

Parts to whole? Division's in control!

5 c. = ______________ fl. oz.

2 kg 150 g = ___________ g

20 oz. = _____ lb. _____ oz.

Practice

Match each unit with its abbreviation.

Unit	Abbreviation	Unit	Abbreviation
meter	km	yard	in.
millimeter	cm	foot	ft.
centimeter	m	mile	lb.
kilometer	mL	inch	yd.
liter	kg	pound	mi.
milliliter	mm	ounce	c.
gram	L	fluid ounce	oz.
kilogram	g	cup	fl. oz.

Complete.

1 km = ______________ m

1 m = ______________ cm

1 cm = ______________ mm

1 L = ______________ mL

1 kg = ______________ g

1 mi. = ______________ ft.

1 yd. = ______________ ft.

1 ft. = ______________ in.

1 lb. = ______________ oz.

1 c. = ______________ fl. oz.

1 week = ______________ days

1 day = ______________ hr.

1 hr. = ______________ min.

1 min. = ______________ sec.

Complete. Write the equations you use.

3 hr. = ______________ min.

29 in. = ______ ft. ______ in.

1 mi. 10 ft. = ______________ ft.

235 cm = _____ m _____ cm

4,000 mL = ______________ L

1 km 250 m = ______________ m

Review

Complete the fact families.

7 + ______ = 13

______ + 7 = 13

13 − ______ = 7

______ − 7 = 6

7 × ______ = 63

______ × 7 = 63

63 ÷ ______ = 7

______ ÷ 7 = 9

Round to the underlined digit.

3$\underline{6}$,782 ≈ ______

8$\underline{9}$,905 ≈ ______

15$\underline{2}$,234 ≈ ______

47$\underline{6}$,500 ≈ ______

Match each fraction or mixed number to its place on the number line.

$\frac{3}{6}$ $\frac{1}{6}$ $\frac{5}{6}$ $1\frac{4}{6}$ $1\frac{2}{6}$ $1\frac{3}{6}$

Complete the chart.

Kilograms	1	2	3	4	5	6
Grams	1,000					

Solve. Write the equations you use.

Hattie has 1 kilogram of clay. She uses 800 grams to make a sculpture. How many grams of clay does she have left?

Whitman has 1 kilogram of gummy bears. He divides the gummy bears equally into 2 bags. How many grams of gummy bears are in each bag?

Lesson Activities

A

Find Missing Numbers in Addition or Subtraction Equations

Ex. 15 + _____ = 40

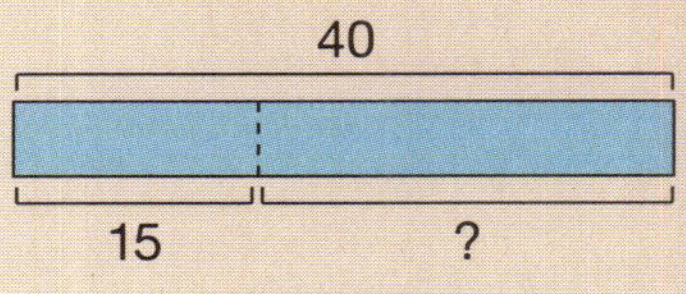

40 – 15 = 25

15 + **25** = 40

Ex. _____ – 30 = 40

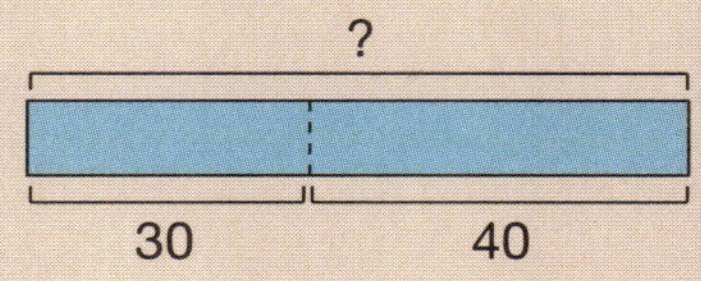

40 + 30 = 70

70 – 30 = 40

Ex. 50 – _____ = 30

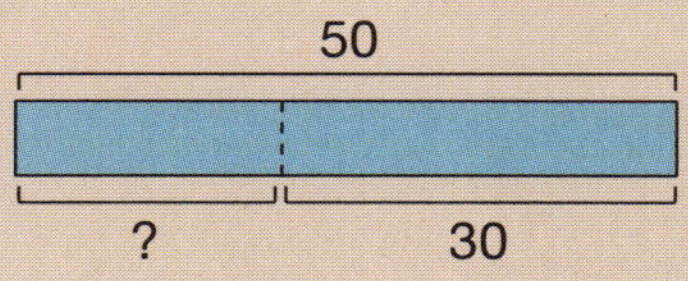

50 – 30 = 20

50 – **20** = 30

25 + _______ = 80

_______ – 14 = 22

57 – _______ = 15

B

Find Missing Numbers in Multiplication or Division Equations

Ex. 3 × _____ = 24

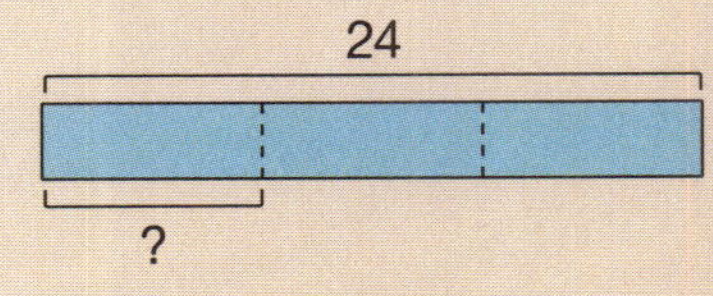

24 ÷ 3 = 8

3 × **8** = 24

Ex. 36 ÷ _____ = 4

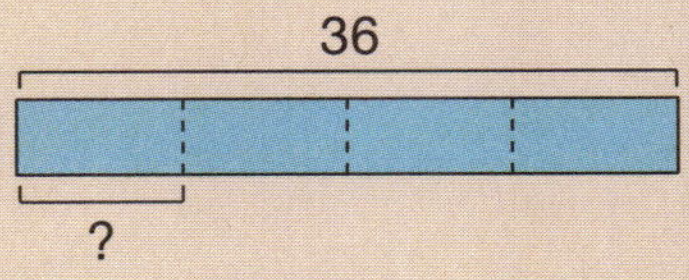

36 ÷ 4 = 9

36 ÷ **9** = 4

Ex. _____ ÷ 6 = 5

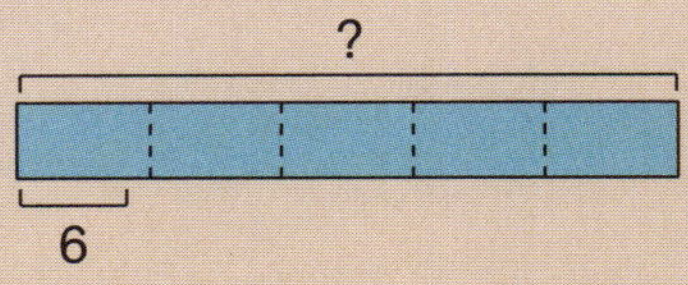

5 × 6 = 30

30 ÷ 6 = 5

4 × _______ = 92

63 ÷ _______ = 9

_______ ÷ 4 = 15

Practice

Circle the problem you can use to find the missing number. Then, solve the problem (with mental math or in the work space) to find the missing number.

78 – ______ = 52

- 78 + 52
- 78 – 52

______ – 36 = 54

- 36 + 54
- 54 – 36

88 ÷ ______ = 8

- 88 ÷ 8
- 88 × 8

______ ÷ 12 = 6

- 12 × 6
- 12 ÷ 6

WORK SPACE

Circle the equation that best matches the word problem. Then, use the equation to solve the word problem.

Theo had some money. He spent $16, and then he had $27 left. How much money did Theo start with?

- ___ – 16 = 27
- 27 – ___ = 16

Molly had $27. She spent some money, and then she had $16 left. How much money did Molly spend?

- ___ – 16 = 27
- 27 – ___ = 16

There are 20 children at astronomy camp. The leaders divide the children into equal groups. There are 4 children in each group. How many groups did the leaders make?

- 20 ÷ ___ = 4
- ___ ÷ 4 = 20

The gymnastics camp leaders divide the children into 4 equal groups. They put 20 children in each group. How many children are at gymnastics camp?

- 20 ÷ ___ = 4
- ___ ÷ 4 = 20

Review

Complete with <, >, or =.

43,560 ◯ 43,000

43,560 ◯ 43,500

43,560 ◯ 43,600

43,560 ◯ 45,460

43,560 ◯ 43,559

Complete.

450 + _______ = 500	999 + _______ = 1,000
350 + _______ = 500	899 + _______ = 1,000
250 + _______ = 500	799 + _______ = 1,000
150 + _______ = 500	699 + _______ = 1,000
50 + _______ = 500	599 + _______ = 1,000

Complete the chart.

Pounds	1	2	3	4	5	6
Ounces	16					

Use the line plot to answer the questions.

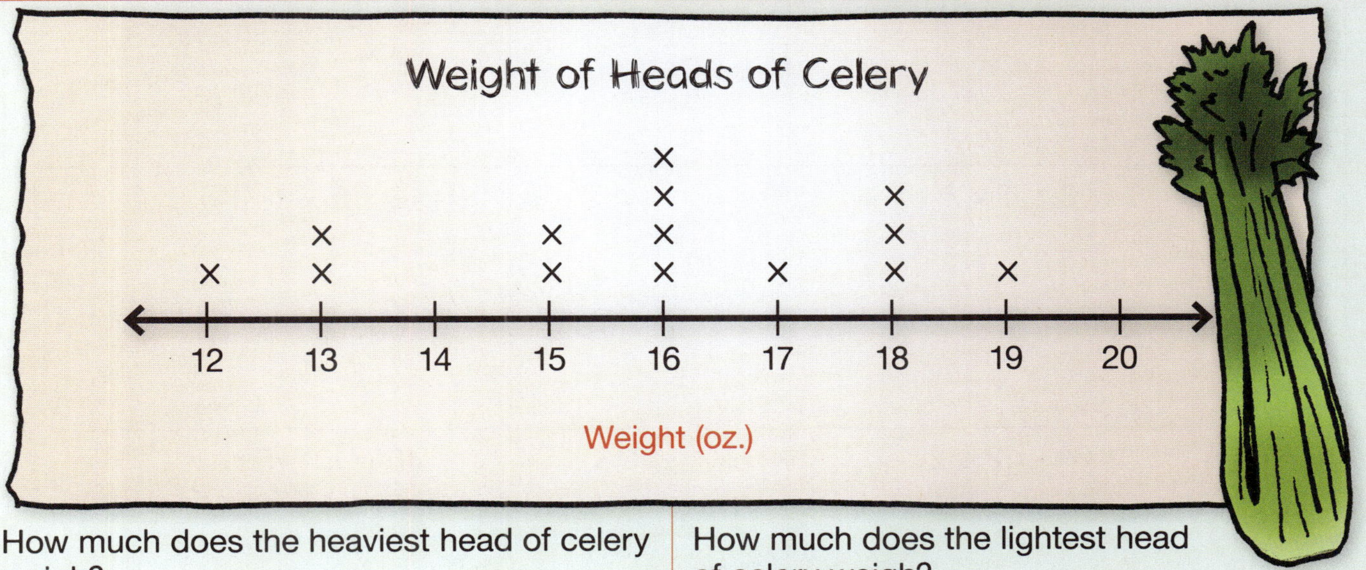

How much does the heaviest head of celery weigh?

How much does the lightest head of celery weigh?

How many heads of celery weigh exactly 1 pound (16 oz.)?

How many heads of celery weigh more than 1 pound (16 oz.)?

Lesson Activities

A

Parentheses

Parentheses mean "do this first!"

When you see an expression with parentheses, perform the operation in the parentheses before the other operations.

Ex. $7 + (4 \div 2)$ → $7 + 2$ → **9**

Ex. $(8 - 3) \times (6 - 4)$ → 5×2 → **10**

$6 - (8 \div 4)$	$(9 + 1) \times 6$	$(7 \times 2) - (3 + 1)$

B

Parentheses Power (1-Player Game)

$4 \times 3 + 2$	$30 - 8 + 2$
$8 \div 4 \times 2$	$2 \times 5 \times 4$
$24 - 12 \div 2$	$40 - 10 - 5$
Total Score: ____________________	

Scoring Guide

Math Master: **less than 120**

Math Whiz: **120-139**

Math Superstar: **140 or more**

Practice

Evaluate.

$4 + (6 \times 7)$

$3 \times (12 \div 4)$

$(4 \times 9) \div 9$

$8 \times (5 - 5)$

$(3 \times 8) + (7 \times 8)$

$(4 \times 7) - (6 \div 6)$

$(30 + 6) \div (8 - 4)$

$(17 - 7) \times (4 + 6)$

Circle the expression that best matches the word problem. Then, evaluate the expression to find the answer to the word problem.

Sarah's mom has $30. She buys a lamp at the garage sale for $12. Then, she splits the remaining money evenly between her 3 children. How much money does each child get?

$(30 - 12) \div 3$

$30 - (12 \div 3)$

Alex buys 5 mystery novels and 4 historical fiction novels at the garage sale. Each book costs $3. How much does he pay for all the books?

$5 + (4 \times 3)$

$(5 + 4) \times 3$

Review

Write the multiples of each number in order. Then, answer the questions.

Multiples of 3	3	6	9	___	___	___	___	___	___
Multiples of 6	6	12	___	___	___	___	___	___	___
Multiples of 9	9	___	___	___	___	___	___	___	___

Which numbers appear on the list of multiples of 3 and the list of multiples of 6?

Which numbers appear on the list of multiples of 6 and the list of multiples of 9?

Which numbers appear on the list of multiples of 3 and the list of multiples of 9?

Complete. Write the equations you use.

5 min. = ____________ sec.

4 km 75 m = __________ m

18 oz. = _____ lb. _____ oz.

Use long division to solve.

$7\overline{)257}$

$7\overline{)932}$

Find the average number of fish in the tanks at the pet store.

Number of Fish in Each Tank

7, 10, 9, 15, 6, 13, 3

Lesson Activities

A

$3 + 4 \times 5 = ?$

Sam's Answer

$3 + 4 \times 5$

$3 + 20$

23

Louisa's Answer

$3 + 4 \times 5$

7×5

35

B

Order of Operations

If there is more than one operation, we complete them in this order:

1. Multiply or divide, from left to right.
2. Add or subtract, from left to right.

Ex. $20 \div 4 \times 2$ → 5×2 → **10**

Ex. $2 + 12 \div 3 - 1$ → $2 + 4 - 1$ → $6 - 1$ → **5**

$20 - 10 + 3$

M or D →

A or S →

$5 \times 8 \div 10$

M or D →

A or S →

$15 - 2 \times 4$

M or D →

A or S →

$6 \div 2 + 8$

M or D →

A or S →

$3 + 9 - 3 - 9$

M or D →

A or S →

$7 \times 6 \div 7 \div 6$

M or D →

A or S →

$1 + 8 \times 3 \div 6$

M or D →

A or S →

$10 \times 4 - 2 \times 5$

M or D →

A or S →

Practice

Evaluate. Then, find the blank that matches the answer. Write the matching letter in the blank to solve the riddle.

(A) 35 + 5 − 10

M or D →
A or S →

(D) 32 ÷ 4 × 2

M or D →
A or S →

(R) 20 − 2 × 6 + 1

M or D →
A or S →

(E) 4 × 10 − 3 × 2

M or D →
A or S →

(A) 4 + 3 + 15 ÷ 3

M or D →
A or S →

(D) 16 ÷ 4 × 2 + 3

M or D →
A or S →

What do you call a snake that solves equations?

___	N	___	___	___	___	___
30		12	11	16	34	9

Complete the expression to match the word problem. Then, evaluate the expression to find the answer to the word problem.

Laura sells 40 trading cards at the garage sale. She sells the trading cards in packs of 5. She charges $3 for each pack. How much money does she earn in all?

☐ ÷ ☐ × ☐

Paul has $28. Then, he buys a skateboard for $9 and 2 board games for $4 each. How much money does he have left?

☐ − ☐ − ☐ × ☐

Review

Use the pictures to complete the equivalent fractions.

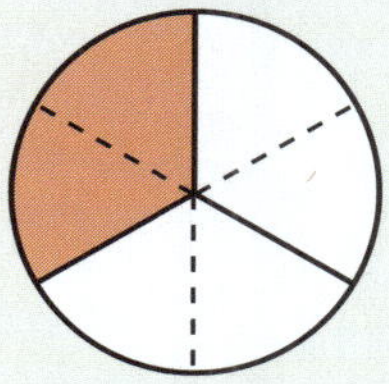

$\frac{1}{3} = \frac{}{6}$

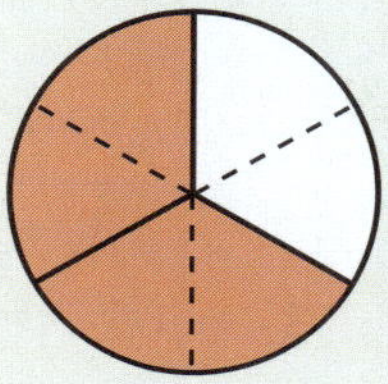

$\frac{2}{3} = \frac{}{6}$

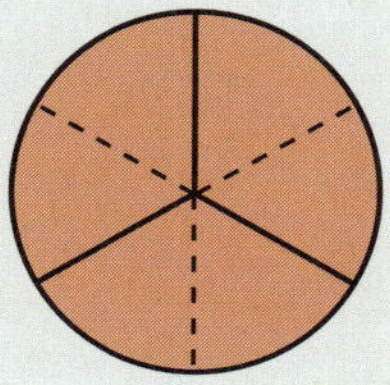

$\frac{3}{3} = \frac{}{6}$

Complete. Write the equations you use.

10 days = ____________ hr.

5 ft. 2 in. = ____________ in.

2,300 mL = ____ L ____ mL

Circle the better estimate for each product.

6 × 415

2,400 | 24,000

2,078 × 9

1,800 | 18,000

32 × 47

150 | 1,500

Circle the equation that best matches the word problem. Then, use the equation to solve the word problem.

I'm thinking of a number. The sum of my number and 47 is 93. What is my number?

____ − 47 = 93

____ + 47 = 93

★ I'm thinking of a number. If you divide my number by 6, you get 300. What is my number?

____ ÷ 6 = 300

300 ÷ 6 = ____

1.10

Lesson Activities

A

$8 + 3 \times 4$

M or D →

A or S →

$6 \div 3 \times 5 - 2$

M or D →

A or S →

B

Order of Operations with Parentheses

1. Complete operations in parentheses.
2. Multiply or divide, from left to right.
3. Add or subtract, from left to right.

Ex.

$7 + (5 - 3) \times 4$

$7 + 2 \times 4$

$7 + 8$

15

C

Order of Operations War (2-Player Game)

Player 1

P / M or D → / A or S →: ☐ + (☐ − ☐) × ☐

P / M or D → / A or S →: ☐ + ☐ + (☐ × ☐)

P / M or D → / A or S →: ☐ × (☐ + ☐) − ☐

Total Score

Player 2

P / M or D → / A or S →: ☐ + (☐ − ☐) × ☐

P / M or D → / A or S →: ☐ + ☐ + (☐ × ☐)

P / M or D → / A or S →: ☐ × (☐ + ☐) − ☐

Total Score

Practice

Evaluate.

$20 - (3 + 1) \times 2$

P
M or D →
A or S →

$15 - 3 \times 4 + 6$

P
M or D →
A or S →

$4 + 3 \times (5 + 2)$

P
M or D →
A or S →

$15 + 23 - (15 + 23)$

P
M or D →
A or S →

$7 - 6 \div 6 \times 2$

P
M or D →
A or S →

$7 \times (20 - 20) \times 12$

P
M or D →
A or S →

$(50 - 10) \div (3 + 5)$

P
M or D →
A or S →

$13 \times (2 \times 5)$

P
M or D →
A or S →

Circle the expression that best matches the word problem.
Then, evaluate the expression to find the answer to the word problem.

Mykah had $61. Then, she bought a movie ticket for $12 and a popcorn for $8. How much money does she have now?

$61 - 12 + 8$

$61 - (12 + 8)$

Charlie had $32. He spent $7, and then he earned $20. How much money does he have now?

$32 - 7 + 20$

$32 - (7 + 20)$

1.10

Review

Choose the more reasonable measurement for each angle.

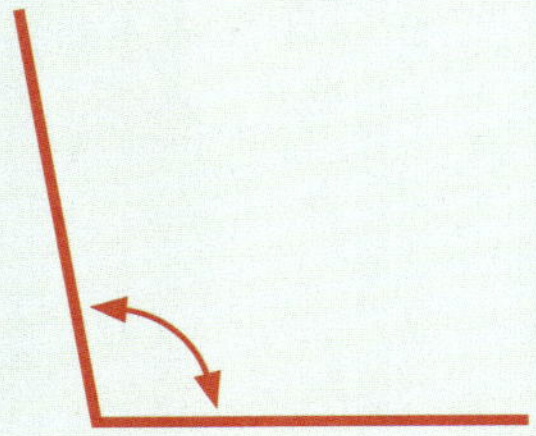

100° | 20°

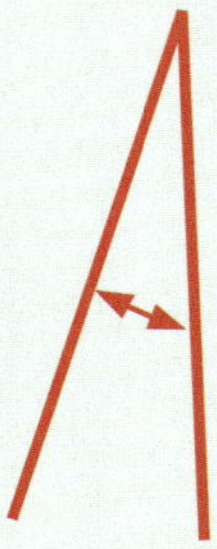

120° | 20°

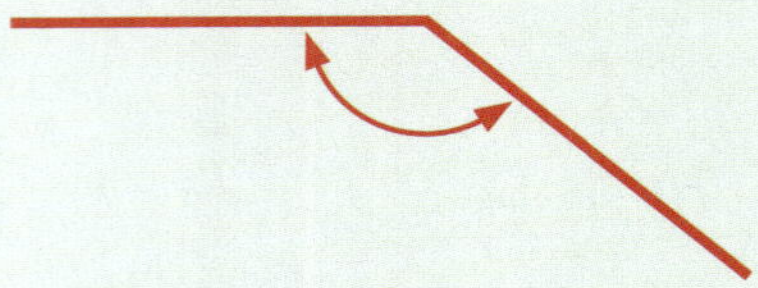

140° | 40°

Complete.

1 km = ______ m

1 m = ______ cm

1 cm = ______ mm

1 L = ______ mL

1 kg = ______ g

1 mi. = ______ ft.

1 yd. = ______ ft.

1 ft. = ______ in.

1 lb. = ______ oz.

1 c. = ______ fl. oz.

1 week = ______ days

1 day = ______ hr.

1 hr. = ______ min.

1 min. = ______ sec.

Complete. Write the equations you use.

2 hr. 15 min. = ______ min.

50 yd. = ______ ft.

17 kg = ______ g

Complete.

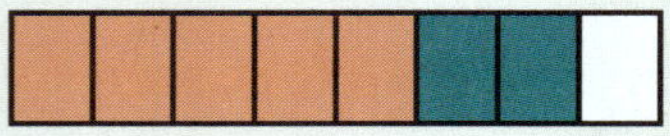

$\frac{5}{8} + \frac{2}{8} =$

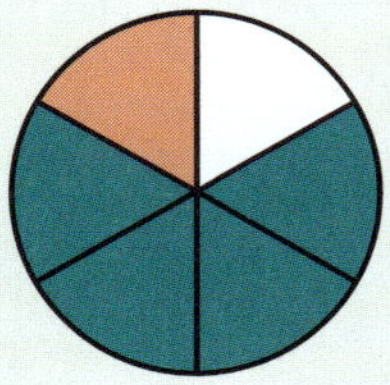

$\frac{1}{6} + \frac{4}{6} =$

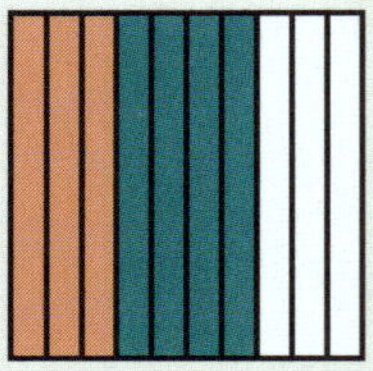

$\frac{3}{10} + \frac{4}{10} =$

Unit Wrap-Up

Circle the problems that equal the number in the star.

4,800	2,000	40	500
60 × 80	50 × 40	280 ÷ 7	300 ÷ 6
6 × 800	5 × 40	2,800 ÷ 7	3,000 ÷ 6
60 × 8	500 × 4	200 ÷ 5	450 ÷ 9
6,000 × 8	5 × 4,000	2,000 ÷ 5	4,500 ÷ 9

Solve. Write the equations you use.

Ryan and Tabitha sell bracelets at the craft fair. They keep track of how many bracelets they sell each day.

How many bracelets did they sell in all?

What's the average number of bracelets they sold each day?

Evaluate.

30 ÷ 2 + 3 × 3

P
M or D →
A or S →

10 − 3 × 2 ÷ 2

P
M or D →
A or S →

30 ÷ (2 + 3) × 3

P
M or D →
A or S →

(10 − 3) × 2 ÷ 2

P
M or D →
A or S →

Unit Wrap-Up

Use the ad to answer the questions. Write the equations you use in the work space.

Whitewater River Rafting Trips

4-hour trip (per person) $96

Lunch is not included in the 4-hour trip. You can buy lunch for an additional $12 per person.

3-day trip (per person) $1,347

Tents, camping supplies, and all meals are included in the 3-day trip.

WORK SPACE

James had some money. He bought 1 ticket for the 4-hour trip, and then he had $47 left. How much money did he have before he paid for the trip?

How much does it cost for 8 people to go on the 4-hour trip?

How much does it cost for 5 people to purchase lunch and go on the 4-hour rafting trip?

How much does it cost for 4 people to go on the 3-day trip?

How much does the 3-day trip cost per day for one person?

Lesson Activities

A

4,879 | 6,792 | 12,104 | 12,756

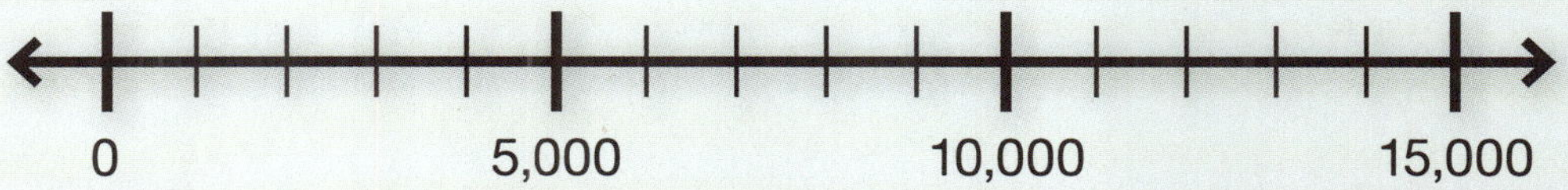

49,528 | 51,118 | 120,536 | 142,984

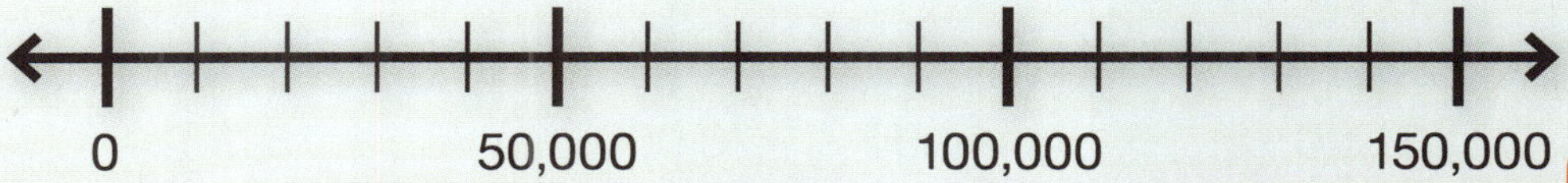

B

How to Round Numbers

1. Underline the digit in the place you are rounding to.
2. Look at the digit in the next-smaller place.
   - If the digit is less than 5, round down. Keep the underlined digit the same, and change all the digits after it to zeros.
   - If the digit is 5 or greater, round up. Increase the underlined digit by 1. Change all the digits after it to zeros.

Ex. Round 12,756 to the nearest thousand.

12,756 ≈ **13,000**

The digit in the next-smaller place is 7.
7 is greater than 5, so you round up.

Ex. Round 12,756 to the nearest ten-thousand.

12,756 ≈ **10,000**

The digit in the next-smaller place is 2.
2 is less than 5, so you round down.

C

Planet	Diameter (km)	Diameter Rounded to the Nearest Thousand (km)
Mercury	4,879	
Venus	12,104	
Earth	12,756	
Mars	6,792	
Jupiter	142,984	
Saturn	120,536	
Uranus	51,118	
Neptune	49,528	

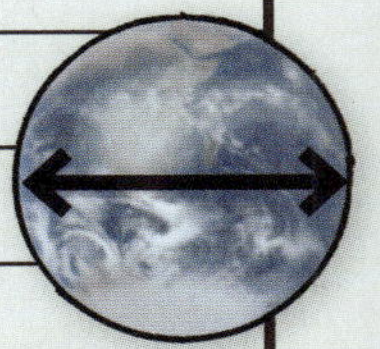

Practice

Label the number on the number line.

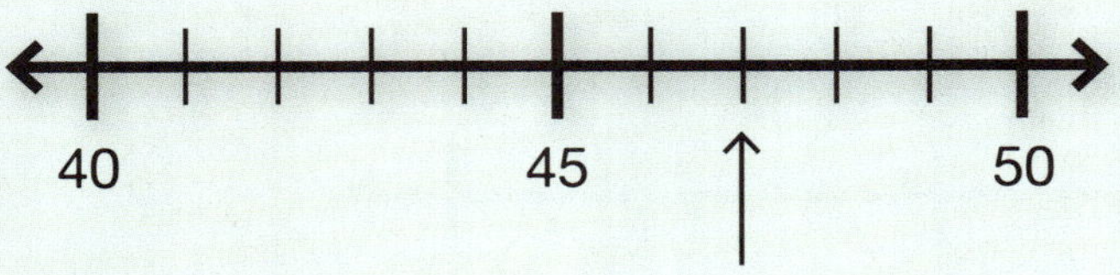

______

______

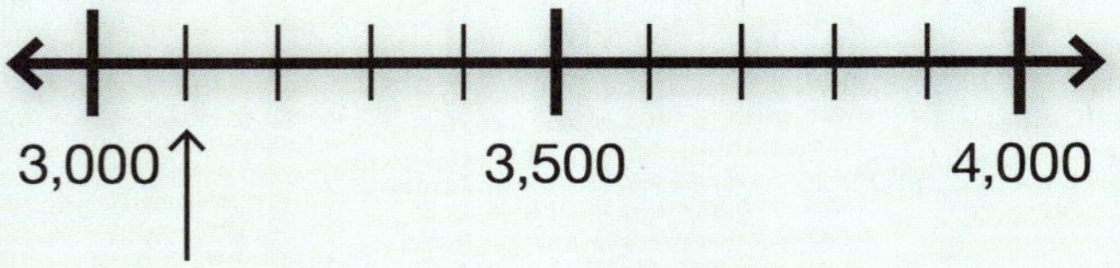

______

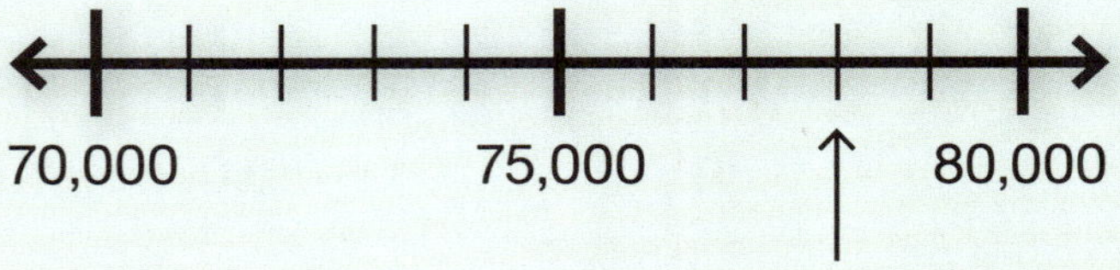

______

Circle the greatest number in each group.

57,498	283,791	47,890	99,909
56,921	280,791	4,789	99,990
58,001	282,791	478,900	99,900

Round to the underlined place.

$\underline{1}5{,}894 \approx$ ______

$1\underline{5}{,}894 \approx$ ______

$15{,}\underline{8}94 \approx$ ______

$15{,}8\underline{9}4 \approx$ ______

$\underline{3}29{,}708 \approx$ ______

$3\underline{2}9{,}728 \approx$ ______

$32\underline{9}{,}728 \approx$ ______

$329{,}\underline{7}28 \approx$ ______

Use the clues to solve the number riddle.

- I am greater than 520,000 and less than 530,000.
- The digit in my thousands-place is 4.
- The digit in my hundreds-place is the same as the digit in my hundred-thousands-place.
- The digit in my tens-place is 2 times the digit in my thousands-place.
- The digit in my ones-place is 4 less than the digit in my thousands-place.

☐☐☐,☐☐☐

Review

Complete the chart.

Standard Form	Expanded Form
4,291	4,000 + 200 + 90 + 1
3,685	
25,290	
30,018	

Color the squares to match the fractions.

$\frac{1}{10}$ $\frac{3}{10}$ $\frac{5}{10}$ $\frac{8}{10}$ $\frac{10}{10}$

Find the sum or difference.

248 + 379

379 – 166

508 – 149

Solve. Write the equations you use.

The bakery had some cookies. It sold 28 cookies and then had 54 cookies left. How many cookies were there at the start?

The bakery sold 16 chocolate chip cookies and 12 pumpkin spice cookies. Chocolate chip cookies cost $2 each. Pumpkin spice cookies cost $3 each. How much money did the bakery take in for all 28 cookies?

2.2

Lesson Activities

A

Diameter of the Sun:
1,391,400 km

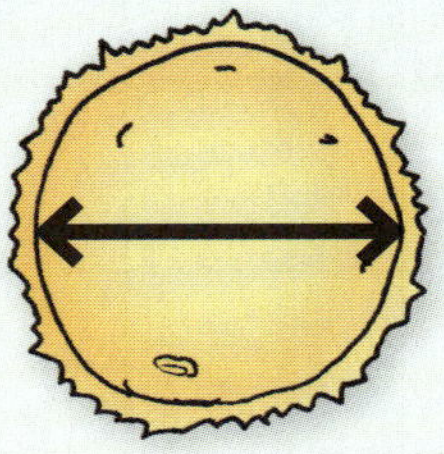

1,391,400 ≈ ____________

1,391,400 ≈ ____________

1,391,400 ≈ ____________

1,391,400 ≈ ____________

B

Distance from the Sun to Pluto:
7,304,326,000 km

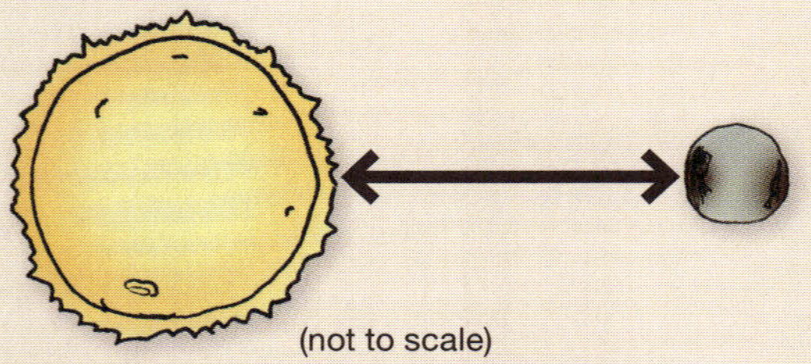

(not to scale)

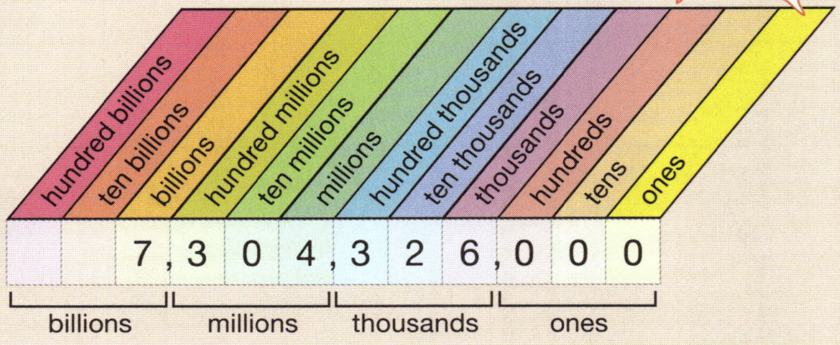

7,304,326,000 ≈ ____________

7,304,326,000 ≈ ____________

C

Planet	Distance from the Sun (km)	Distance from the Sun Rounded to the Nearest Ten Million (km)
Mercury	69,818,000	
Venus	108,941,000	
Earth	152,100,000	
Mars	249,261,000	
Jupiter	816,363,000	
Saturn	1,506,527,000	
Uranus	2,732,696,000	
Neptune	4,471,050,000	

Practice

Match.

4,000,000	four million forty thousand
4,000,000,000	four billion forty million
4,040,000	four million
4,040,000,000	four billion forty thousand
4,400,000	four billion
4,000,040,000	four million four hundred thousand

Circle the greatest number in each group.

4,067,208	1,567,893,200	7,650,800	25,567,432,891
2,999,999	1,567,704,500	70,650,800	25,567,432,894
3,878,078	1,567,635,900	7,650,800,000	25,567,432,893

Round to the underlined place.

$\underline{3}74,965,288 \approx$ ________________

$3\underline{7}4,965,288 \approx$ ________________

$37\underline{4},965,288 \approx$ ________________

$374,\underline{9}65,288 \approx$ ________________

$374,9\underline{6}5,288 \approx$ ________________

$374,96\underline{5},288 \approx$ ________________

$374,965,\underline{2}88 \approx$ ________________

Use the clues to solve the number riddle.

- I am greater than 367,000 and less than 368,000.
- The digit in my hundreds-place is 3 times the digit in my hundred-thousands-place.
- The digit in my tens-place is half of the digit in my ten-thousands-place.
- I am even.
- I am divisible by 10.

☐☐☐,☐☐☐

2.2

Review

Color the squares to match the fractions.

$\frac{9}{100}$ $\frac{50}{100}$ $\frac{99}{100}$ $\frac{90}{100}$ $\frac{76}{100}$

Complete. Write the equations you use.

3 hr. 15 min. = ______ min.

23 ft. = _____ yd. _____ ft.

4 L 200 mL = ________ mL

Complete the circles with +, −, ×, or ÷ to make the equations true.

★ (3 + 3) ◯ (3 ÷ 3) = 5

★ 3 + 3 + (3 ◯ 3) = 6

★ 3 + 3 + (3 ◯ 3) = 7

Solve. Write the equations you use in the work space.

Lukas' parents bought 6 dining chairs. They paid $1,128 in all for the chairs. Each chair had the same price. How much did each chair cost?

They also bought a dining table for $874 and a cabinet for $1,039. How much more did the cabinet cost than the table?

WORK SPACE

Lesson Activities

A

	Population (2023)	Population Rounded to the Nearest Million
China	1,411,750,000	
India	1,392,329,000	
United States	335,167,000	
Indonesia	277,750,000	
World	8,051,404,000	

B

About how many more people live in China than the United States? (Use the rounded numbers from part A.)

About how many fewer people live in India than China? (Use the rounded numbers from part A.)

What is the approximate combined population of both India and China? (Use the rounded numbers from part A.)

★ About how many people in the world do not live in India or China? (Use the rounded numbers from part A.)

Practice

Use the chart to answer the questions. Write the equations you use in the work space.

Continent	Area (square miles)
Africa	11,724,000
Antarctica	5,500,000
Asia	17,226,000
Europe	3,900,000
North America	9,360,000
Oceania	3,286,000
South America	6,878,000

WORK SPACE

Which continent has the largest area?

Which continent has the smallest area?

What's the total area of North America and South America?

How much larger is North America than South America?

How much larger is Africa than North America?

Review

Write each money amount with a decimal point.

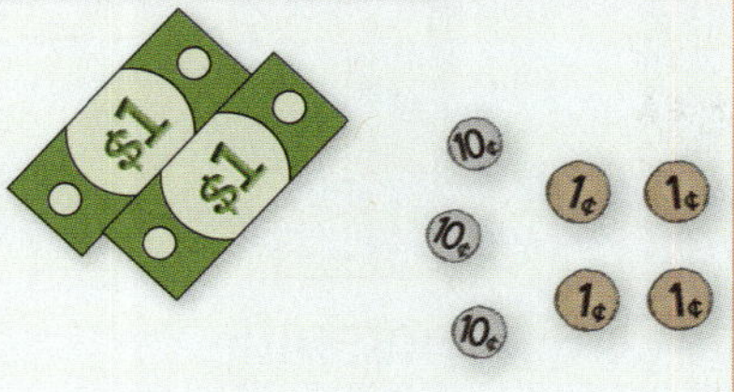

$2.34

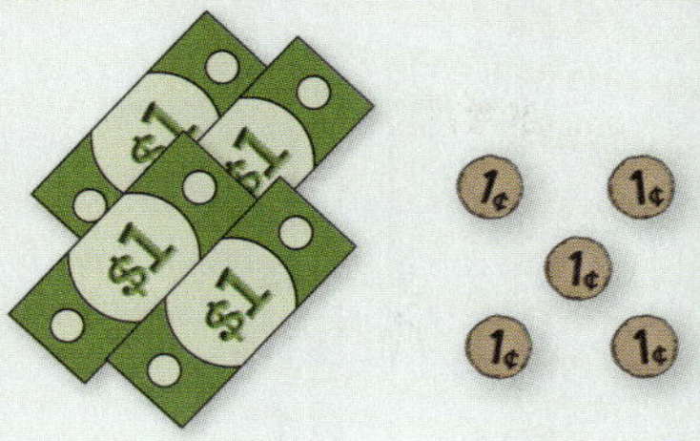

______

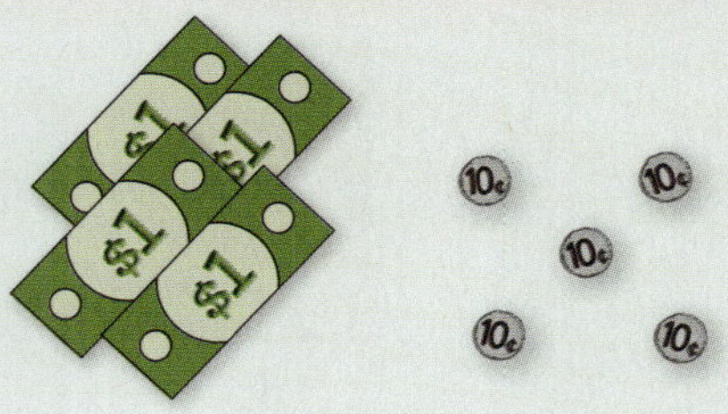

______

Complete.

7 × 70 = ______

70 × 70 = ______

7,000 × 7 = ______

600 × 8 = ______

6 × 80 = ______

60 × 80 = ______

9 × 900 = ______

9,000 × 9 = ______

90 × 90 = ______

Complete the chart.

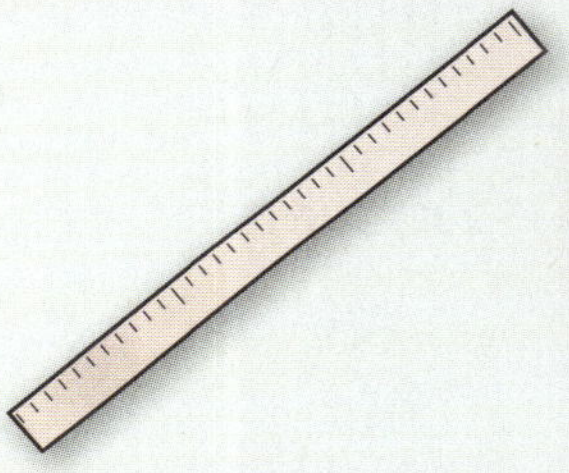

Yards	1	7	10	20	100	500
Feet	3					

Oscar counted how many letters are in his friends' names. Use his data to make a line plot.

Number of Letters in People's Names

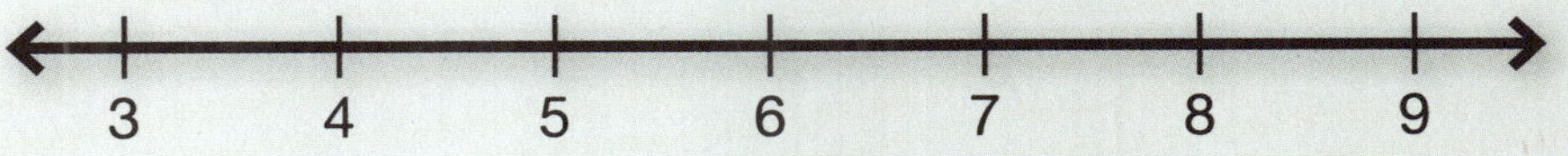

Lesson Activities

A

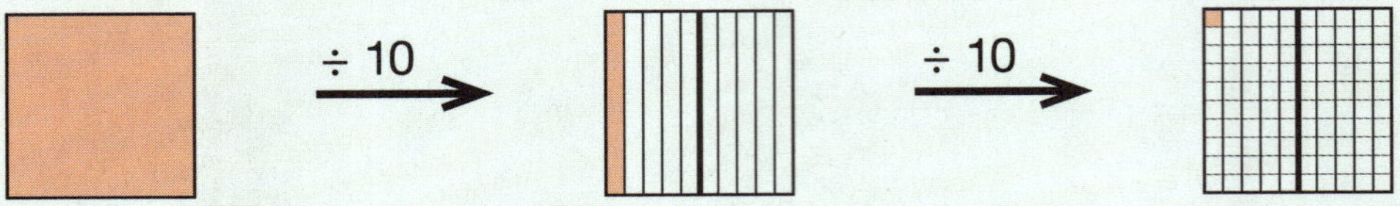

1 whole | 1 tenth | 1 hundredth
1 | 0.1 | 0.01

B

Decimals with Tenths and Hundredths

Ex. Write 1.7 in expanded form and as a mixed number.

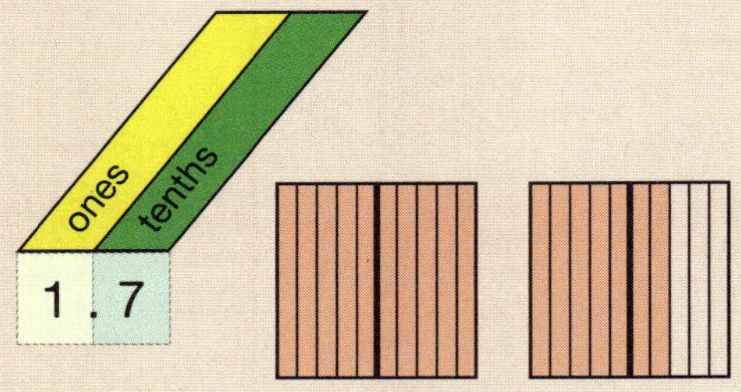

Expanded form: $1 + \frac{7}{10}$

Mixed number: $1\frac{7}{10}$

Ex. Write 0.63 in expanded form and as a fraction.

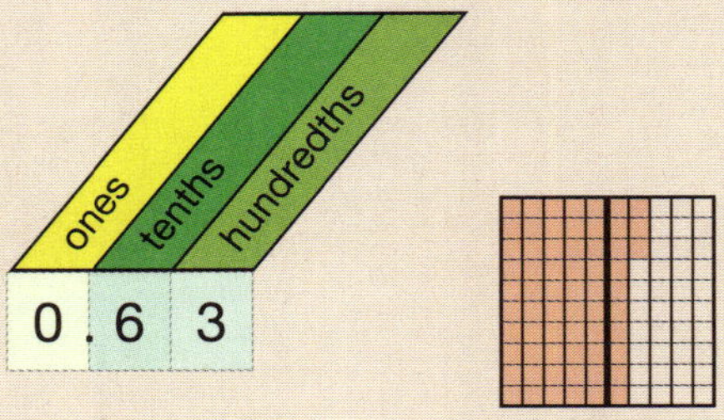

Expanded form: $\frac{6}{10} + \frac{3}{100}$

Fraction: $\frac{63}{100}$

Decimal	Decimal Squares	Expanded Form	Fraction or Mixed Number
0.27	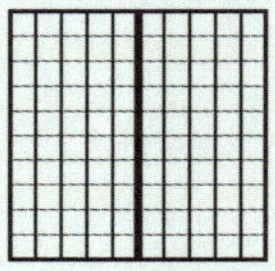		
1.3	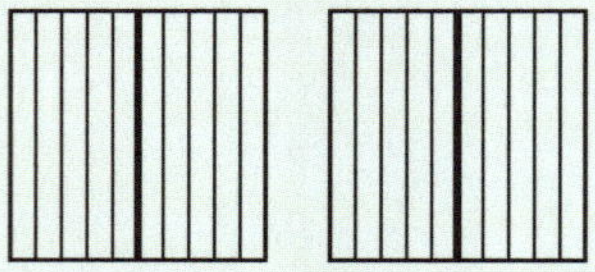		
1.45	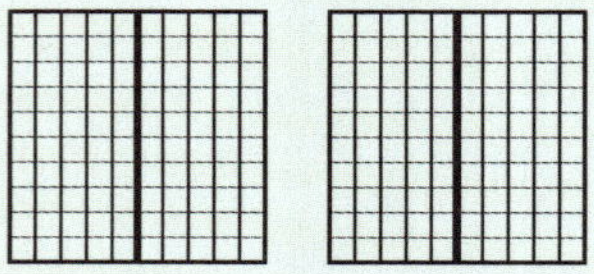		
1.06	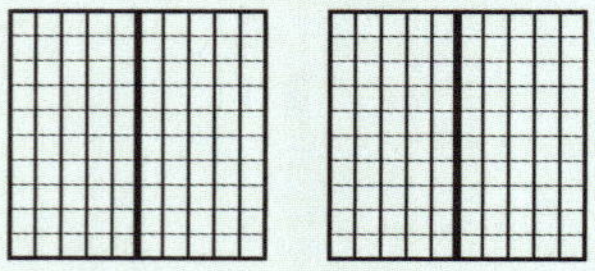		

Practice

Color the decimal squares to match. Then, write a fraction to match.

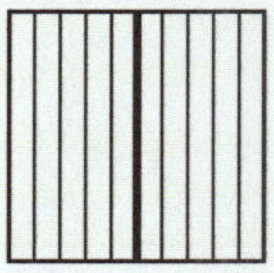

$0.1 = \frac{1}{10}$

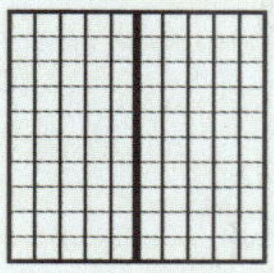

0.07 =

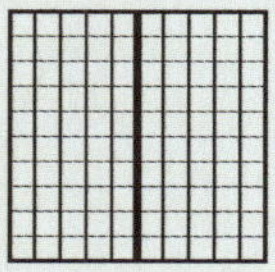

0.17 =

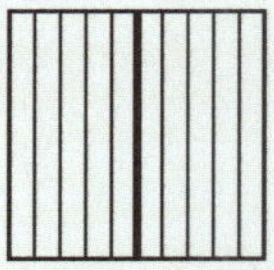

0.6 =

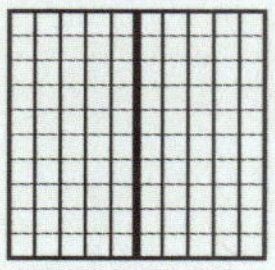

0.01 =

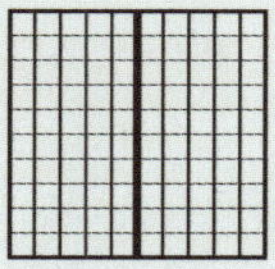

0.61 =

Color the decimal squares to match. Then, complete the circles with <, >, or =.

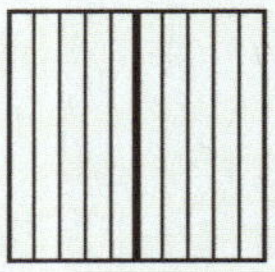

0.4

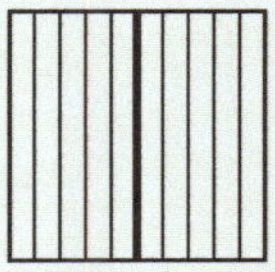

0.9

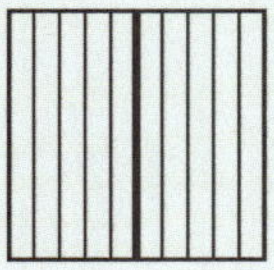

0.2

0.4 ◯ 0.9

0.9 ◯ 0.2

0.4 ◯ 0.2

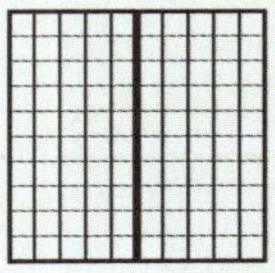

0.04

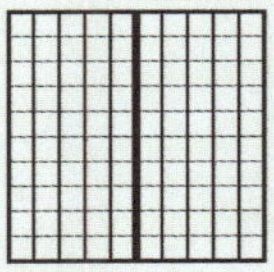

0.09

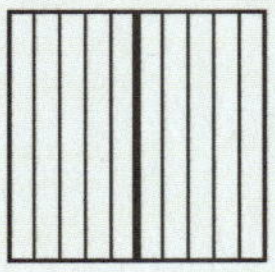

0.1

0.04 ◯ 0.09

0.09 ◯ 0.1

0.04 ◯ 0.1

Use the charts to answer the questions.

Trail	Length (km)
Pine	3.89
Cedar	4.1
Hemlock	4.05

Which trail is the longest?

Which trail is the shortest?

Name	Race Time (sec.)
Ravi	19.4
Emmy	18.72
Natasha	18.09

Whose time was shortest?

Whose time was longest?

2.4

Review

Complete the chart.

Minutes	1	5	10	30	60	90
Seconds	60					

Complete.

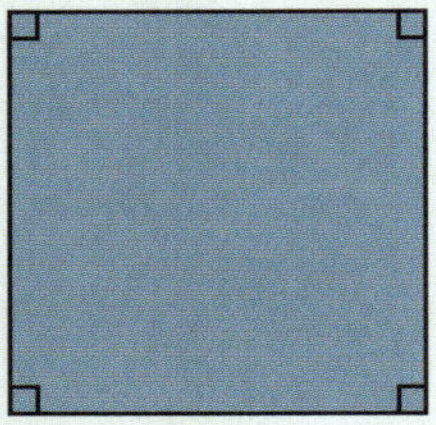

________ pair(s) of parallel sides

________ right angles

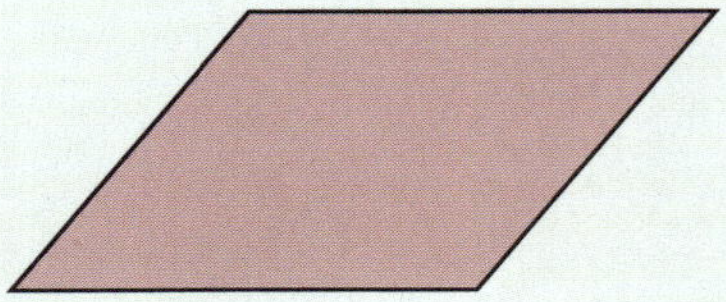

________ pair(s) of parallel sides

________ right angles

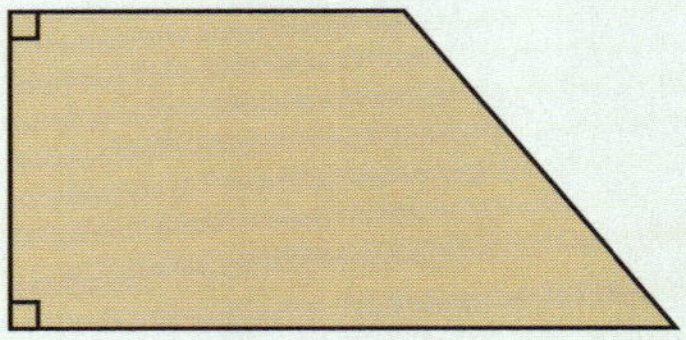

________ pair(s) of parallel sides

________ right angles

Complete.

560 ÷ 7 = ________

5,600 ÷ 7 = ________

56,000 ÷ 7 = ________

7,200 ÷ 8 = ________

720 ÷ 8 = ________

72,000 ÷ 8 = ________

300 ÷ 5 = ________

30,000 ÷ 5 = ________

3,000 ÷ 5 = ________

Solve. Write the equations you use.

Liza biked 4 miles.
Each mile equals 5,280 feet.
How many feet did she bike?

Mitch ran 1,650 meters.
John ran 3 times as far as Mitch.
How far did John run?

Lesson Activities

A

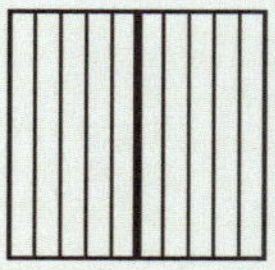
0.6

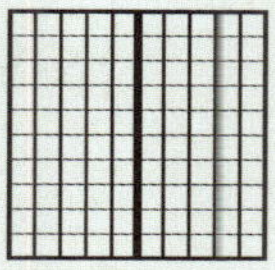
0.60

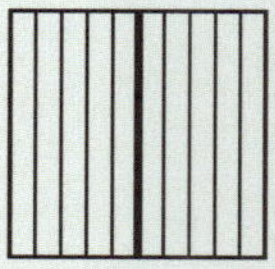
0.4

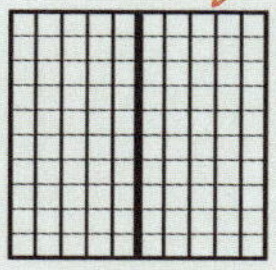
0.40

B

Mental Addition and Subtraction with Decimals

Ex. 0.5 + 0.4 = ?
5 tenths + 4 tenths = 9 tenths
0.5 + 0.4 = **0.9**

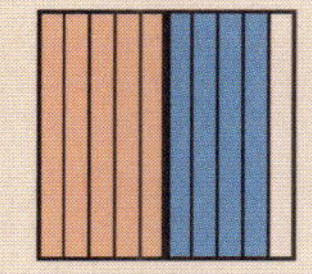

Ex. 0.07 − 0.03 = ?
7 hundredths − 3 hundredths = 4 hundredths
0.07 − 0.03 = **0.04**

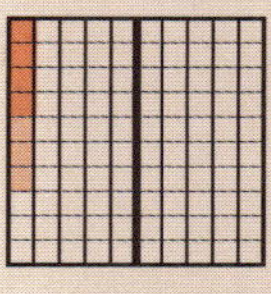

Ex. 0.3 + 0.07 = ?
3 tenths = 30 hundredths
0.30 + 0.07 = **0.37**

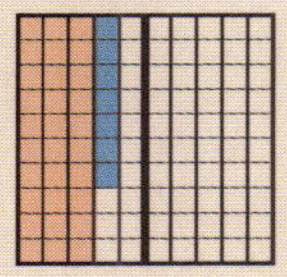

Ex. 0.5 − 0.02 = ?
5 tenths = 50 hundredths
0.50 − 0.02 = **0.48**

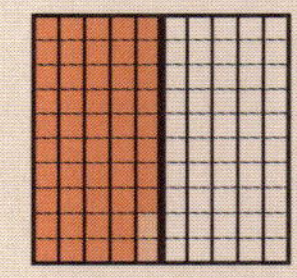

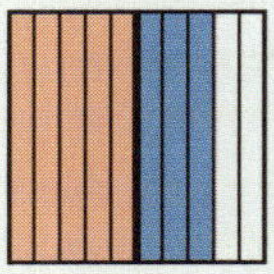
0.5 + 0.3 = ________

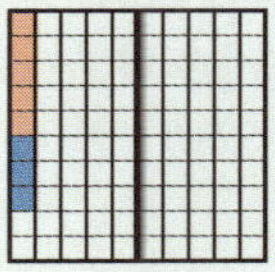
0.05 + 0.03 = ________

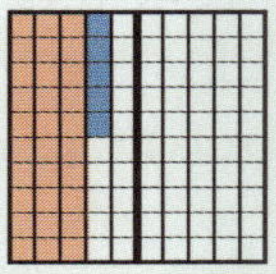
0.3 + 0.05 = ________

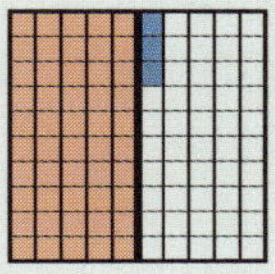
0.5 + 0.03 = ________

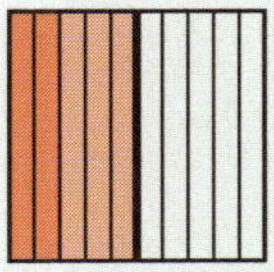
0.5 − 0.3 = ________

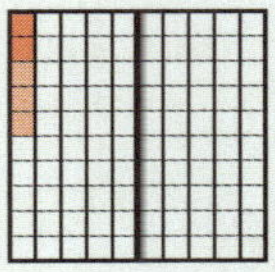
0.05 − 0.03 = ________

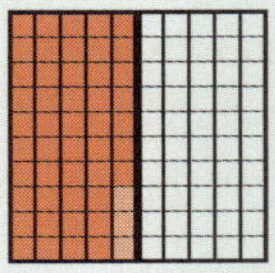
0.5 − 0.03 = ________

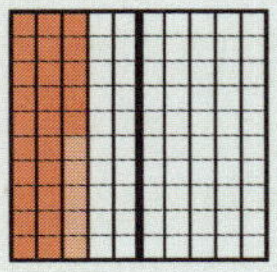
0.3 − 0.05 = ________

C

Four in a Row (2-Player Game)

0.4	0.03	0.30	0.95	0.09	0.97
0.94	0.01	0.50	0.07	0.20	0.9
0.10	0.5	0.06	0.8	0.05	0.99
0.08	0.60	0.91	0.7	0.93	0.92

Practice

Complete. Use the pictures to help.

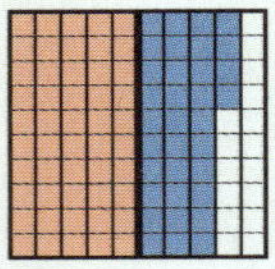

0.5 + 0.34 = ____________

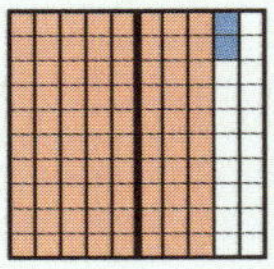

0.8 + 0.02 = ____________

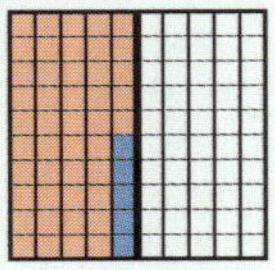

0.45 + 0.05 = ____________

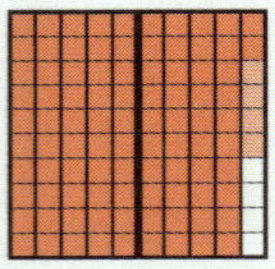

0.96 – 0.04 = ____________

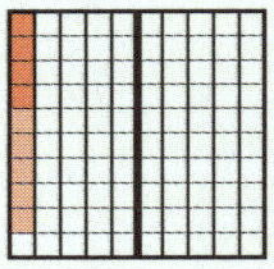

0.09 – 0.05 = ____________

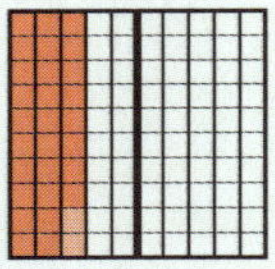

0.3 – 0.02 = ____________

Use mental math to solve. Write the equations you use.

Mateo ran 0.8 miles on Friday and 0.5 miles on Saturday. How much farther did he run on Friday than on Saturday?

Isabella has 0.9 kg of clay. She uses 0.7 kg to make a mug. How much clay does she have left?

Sutton fills two water bottles for the soccer game. One water bottle holds 0.43 L. The other water bottle holds 0.4 L. How much water do the bottles hold in all?

Ruby swims 0.3 km on Tuesday and 0.4 km on Thursday. How far does she swim in all?

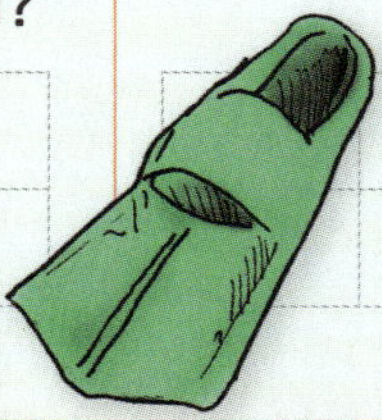

Review

Connect each number to its place on the number line.

$3\frac{3}{10}$ $3\frac{5}{10}$ $3\frac{9}{10}$ $4\frac{2}{10}$ $4\frac{8}{10}$

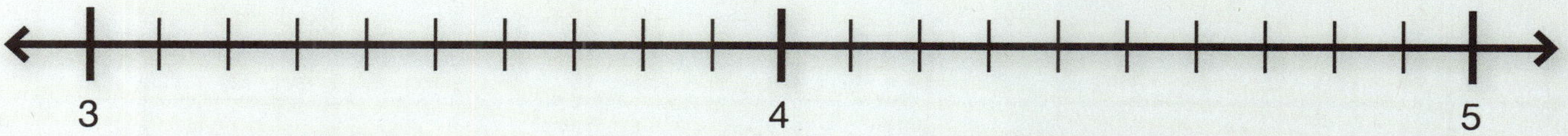

Evaluate.

$4 \times 2 + 8 \div 4$

$4 \times (2 + 8) \div 4$

Find the missing numbers. Write the equations you use.

42 + ________ = 81

________ − 27 = 35

7 × ________ = 140

54 ÷ ________ = 9

Round to the underlined digit.

$\underline{3}$,964,382 ≈ ____________

43$\underline{0}$,298 ≈ ____________

4$\underline{1}$,087,360 ≈ ____________

$\underline{9}$,874,621 ≈ ____________

2$\underline{9}$,999,999 ≈ ____________

Find the average of the ages. Write the equations you use.

Ages

14	9
6	16
9	8
8	10

Lesson Activities

A

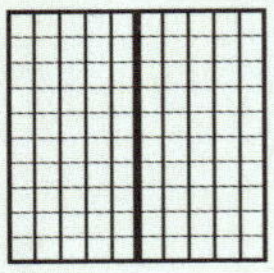

0.4 + 0.07 = ______

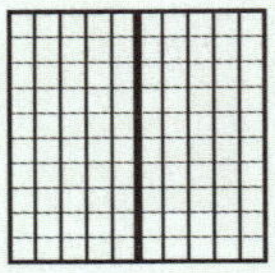

0.9 + 0.09 = ______

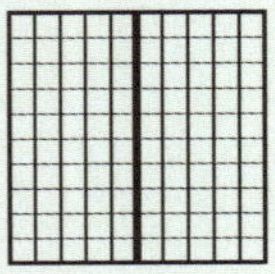

0.1 + 0.06 = ______

B

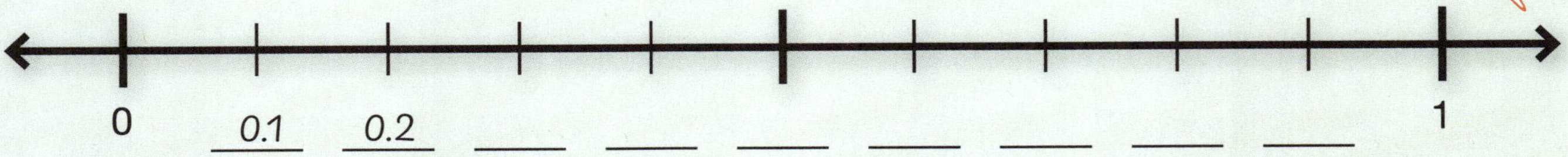

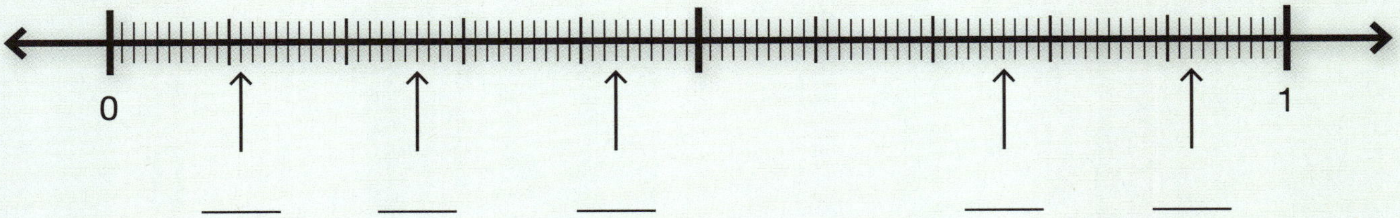

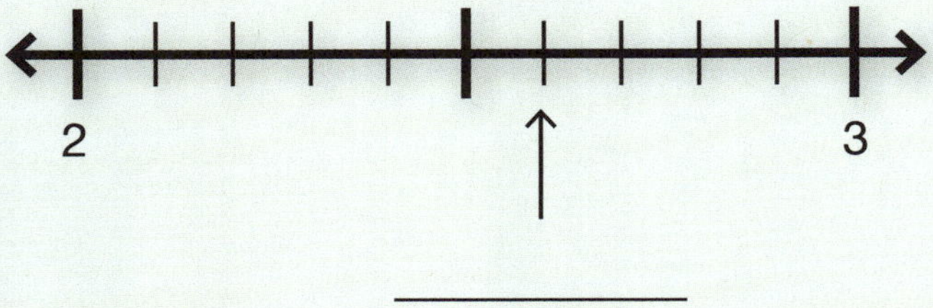

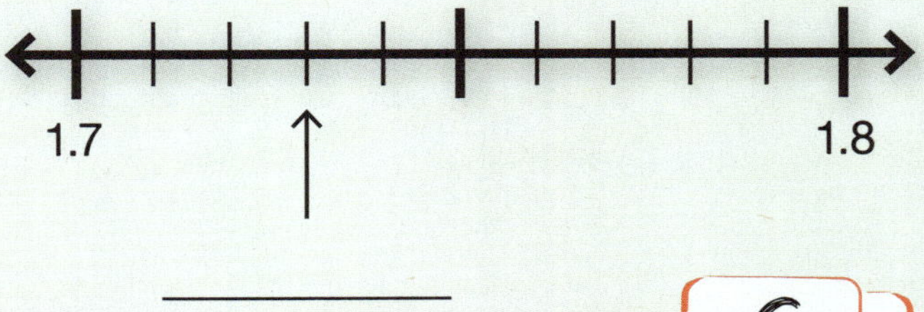

C

Round Decimals

Round decimals the same way you round whole numbers.

Ex. Round 1.28 to the nearest whole number.

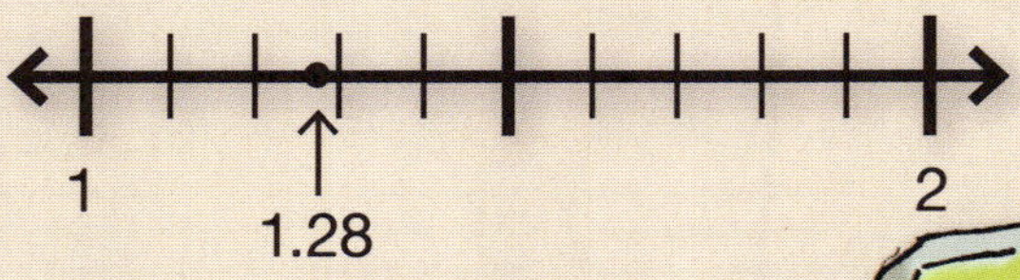

1.28 ≈ **1**

Ex. Round 1.28 to the nearest tenth.

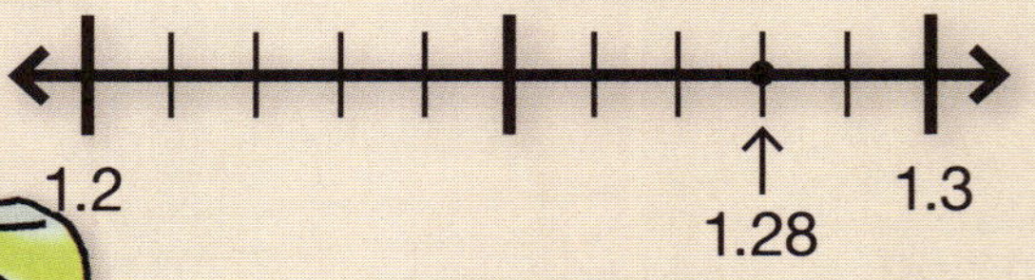

1.28 ≈ **1.3**

3.45 ≈ ______

3.45 ≈ ______

12.74 ≈ ______

12.74 ≈ ______

Practice

Connect each number to its place on the number line. Then, round each number to the underlined place.

3.4 | 4.6 | 4.1 | 3.9

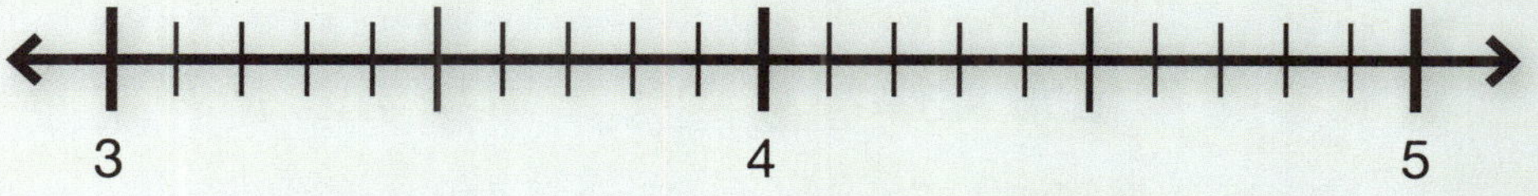

4.6 ≈ ______

3.4 ≈ ______

4.1 ≈ ______

3.9 ≈ ______

2.13 | 2.21 | 2.28 | 2.15

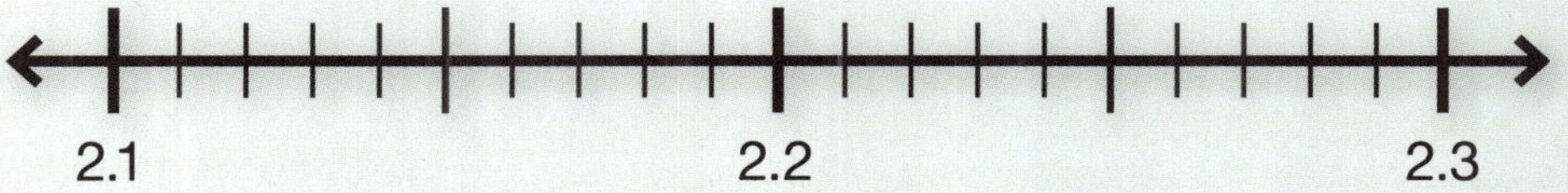

2.13 ≈ ______

2.21 ≈ ______

2.28 ≈ ______

2.15 ≈ ______

Label the number on the number line.

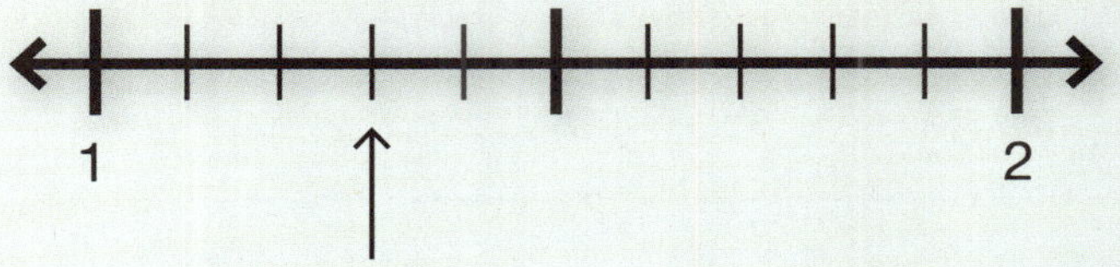

______

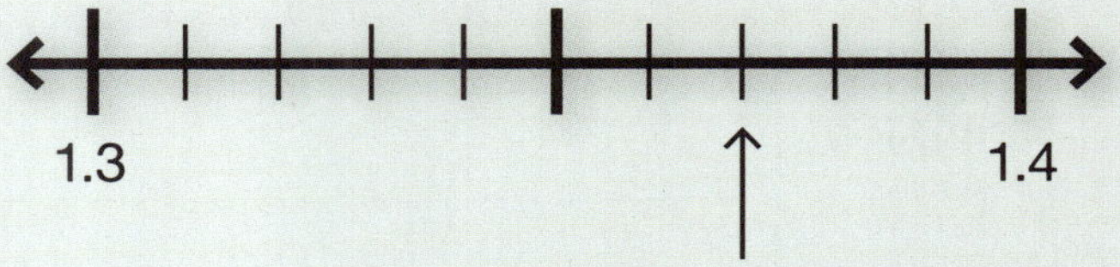

______

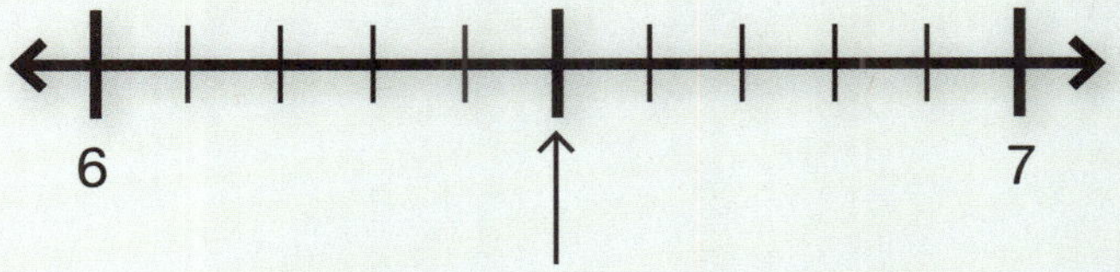

______

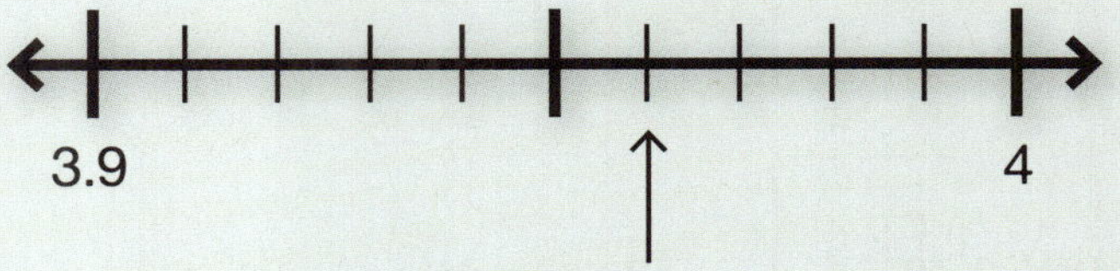

______

______

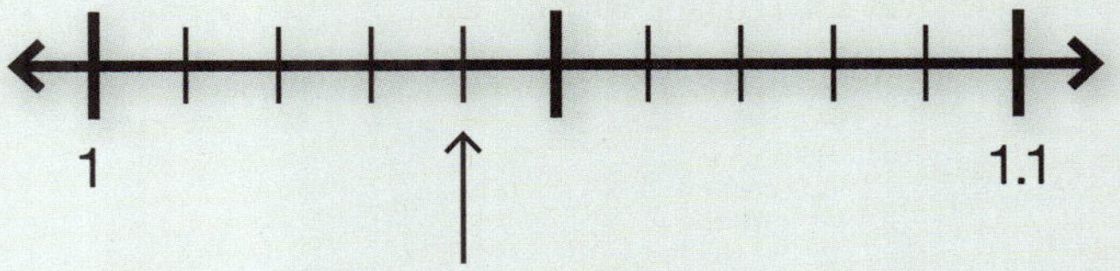

______

Review

Use long division to solve.

7 ⟌ 4 6 0

Use mental math to complete.

257 + 3 = ______	378 + 20 = ______
257 + 6 = ______	388 + 20 = ______
257 + 7 = ______	398 + 20 = ______
605 – 3 = ______	427 – 10 = ______
605 – 5 = ______	417 – 10 = ______
605 – 9 = ______	407 – 10 = ______

Find the sum or difference.

2,491 + 15,207

900 – 356

15,206 – 1,788

Write the multiples of each number in order. Then, answer the questions.

Multiples of 5: 5, 10, 15, ______, ______, ______, ______, ______, ______, ______

Multiples of 10: 10, 20, 30, ______, ______, ______, ______, ______, ______, ______

Multiples of 7: 7, 14, 21, ______, ______, ______, ______, ______, ______, ______

Which number(s) appear(s) on the list of multiples of 5 and the list of multiples of 10?

Which number(s) appear(s) on the list of multiples of 5 and the list of multiples of 7?

Which number(s) appear(s) on the list of multiples of 10 and the list of multiples of 7?

Lesson Activities

A

294 + 1,325

702 − 45

B

How to Add and Subtract Decimals

1. Line up the decimal points.
    - If one number is a whole number, write a decimal point after the whole number.
2. Tack on zeros until both numbers have the same number of decimal places.
3. Add or subtract like usual. Write a decimal point in the answer below the other decimal points.

Ex. 2.5 + 0.87 = ?

$$\begin{array}{r} 2.50 \\ +\,0.87 \\ \hline \end{array} \longrightarrow \begin{array}{r} {}^{1} \\ 2.50 \\ +\,0.87 \\ \hline \mathbf{3.37} \end{array}$$

Ex. 2 − 0.64 = ?

$$\begin{array}{r} 2.00 \\ -\,0.64 \\ \hline \end{array} \longrightarrow \begin{array}{r} {}^{1\;\not{10}\;10}_{\;\;\;9} \\ \not{2}.\not{0}\not{0} \\ -\,0.64 \\ \hline \mathbf{1.36} \end{array}$$

C

Leaf Fight (2-Player Game)

Player 1

\+ \+ − − −

Player 2

\+ \+ − − −

Practice

Find the sum or difference.

2.6 + 3.89

0.34 + 0.56

3 + 1.76

0.53 − 0.27

3.9 − 2.55

5 − 2.78

Solve. Write the equations you use.

David has $20.
He buys a picture frame for $16.47.
How much money does he have left?

Lynley was 0.49 m long when she was born. Now, she's 1.38 m tall. How much has she grown?

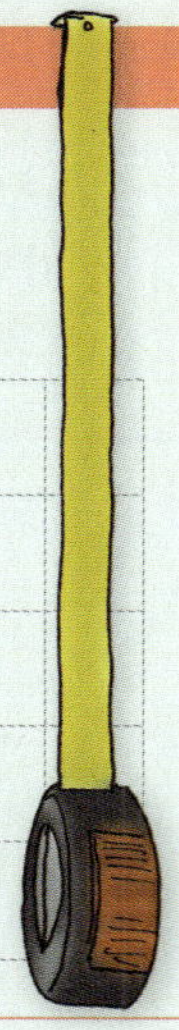

Elias uses 0.58 kg of white flour and 0.45 kg of wheat flour to make bread. How much flour does he use in all?

The fun run race course is 3.1 miles long. So far, Althea has run 1.65 miles. How much farther does she have to run to finish the race?

Review

Complete.

$\frac{5}{6} - \frac{2}{6} = \frac{3}{6}$

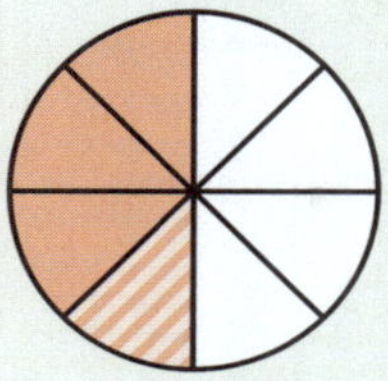

$\frac{4}{8} - \frac{1}{8} =$

$\frac{8}{10} - \frac{3}{10} =$

Round to the underlined place.

$\underline{2}.87 \approx$ ______________________

$2.\underline{8}7 \approx$ ______________________

$\underline{3}.09 \approx$ ______________________

$3.\underline{0}9 \approx$ ______________________

Complete.

	6	3	7
×			9

	8,	1	0	4
×				8

Complete the chart. Then, use the chart to answer the questions.

Gallons	1	2	3	4	5	6
Quarts	4					

James makes 1 gallon of tomato sauce. His mom uses 1 quart of sauce for spaghetti. How many quarts of tomato sauce are left?

Harper makes 3 gallons of lemonade. She pours the lemonade into 6 pitchers. How many quarts of lemonade are in each pitcher?

Lesson Activities

A

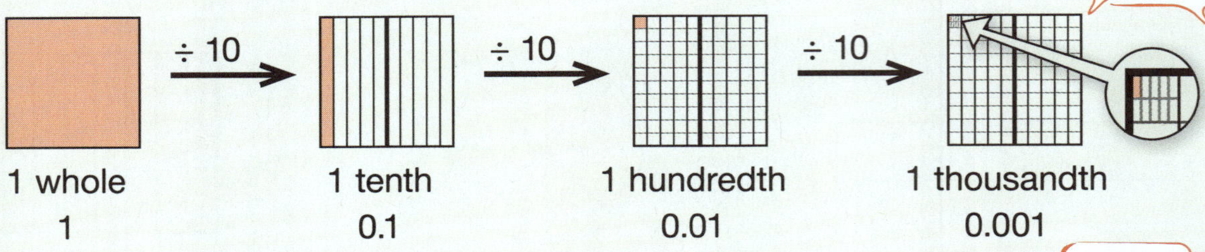

B

Decimals with Thousandths

Ex. A package of blueberries weighs 0.874 lb. What is the expanded form of 0.874?

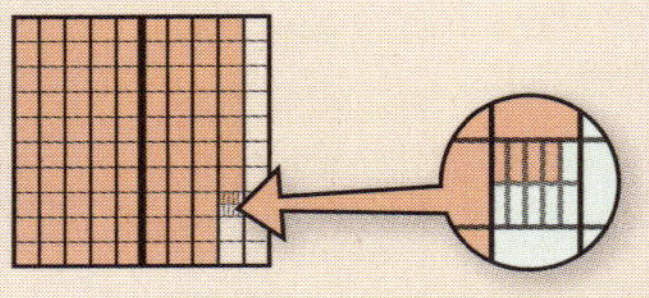

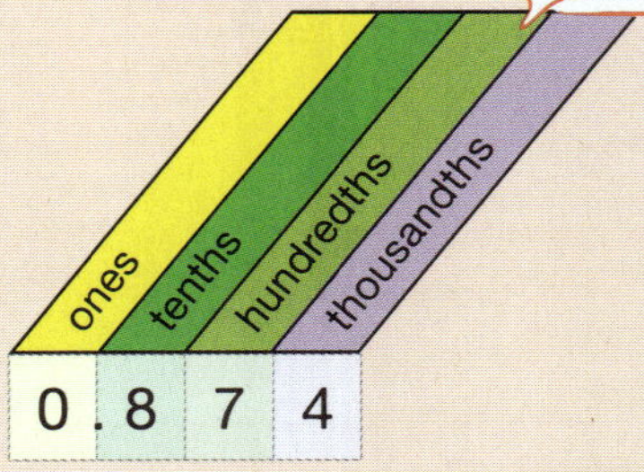

$$\frac{8}{10} + \frac{7}{100} + \frac{4}{1,000}$$

Weight (lb.)	Expanded Form
1.264	
0.916	
0.980	
1.307	

C

Decimal Compare

0.2 0.07 0.009 (2-Player Game)

	Round 1	Round 2	Round 3	Round 4
Player 1				
Player 2				

Practice

Color the decimal squares to match. Then, complete the circles with <, >, or =.

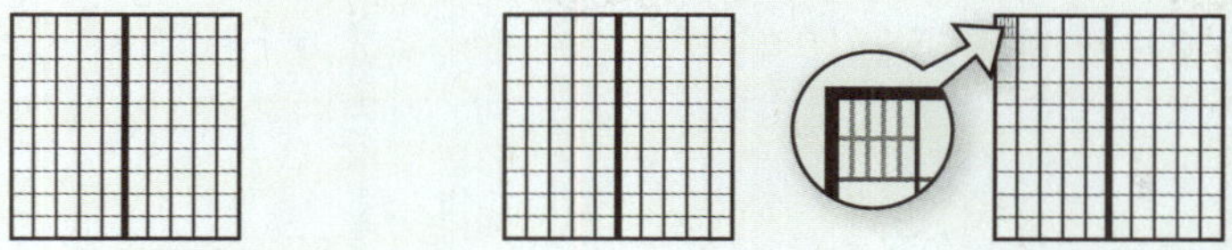

0.3 0.03 0.003

0.3 ◯ 0.003

0.003 ◯ 0.03

0.03 ◯ 0.3

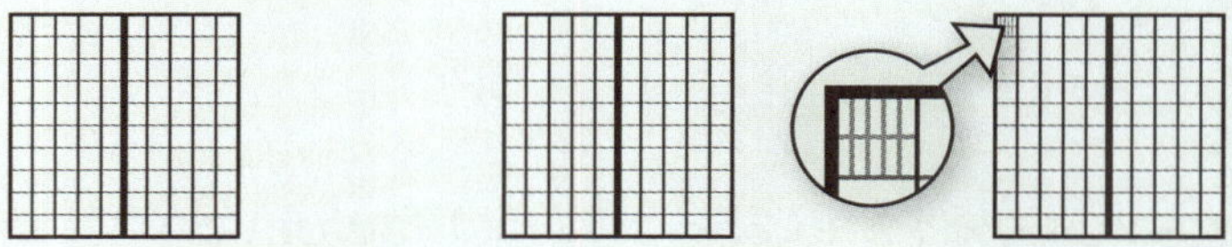

0.7 0.08 0.009

0.08 ◯ 0.7

0.7 ◯ 0.009

0.009 ◯ 0.08

Complete the chart.

Standard Form	Expanded Form
0.325	
0.76	
1.061	
	$\frac{8}{10} + \frac{1}{100} + \frac{5}{1{,}000}$
	$2 + \frac{4}{1{,}000}$

Match.

0.6	6 thousandths
0.07	6 tenths
0.006	7 hundredths
0.7	7 tenths

Review

Complete the missing factors in the factor pairs. Then, answer the questions.

Factor Pairs of 24	Factor Pairs of 28	Factor Pairs of 35
1 × 24	1 × ______	1 × ______
2 × ______	2 × ______	5 × ______
3 × ______	4 × ______	
4 × ______		
What factors do 24 and 28 have in common?	What factors do 28 and 35 have in common?	What factors do 24 and 35 have in common?

Match.

0.5 + 0.3	0.2
0.5 + 0.03	0.8
0.5 – 0.3	0.02
0.5 – 0.03	0.53
0.05 – 0.03	0.47

Label the numbers on the number line.

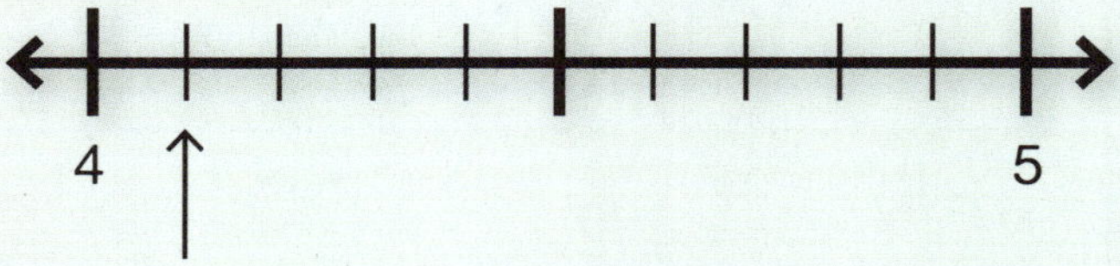

______

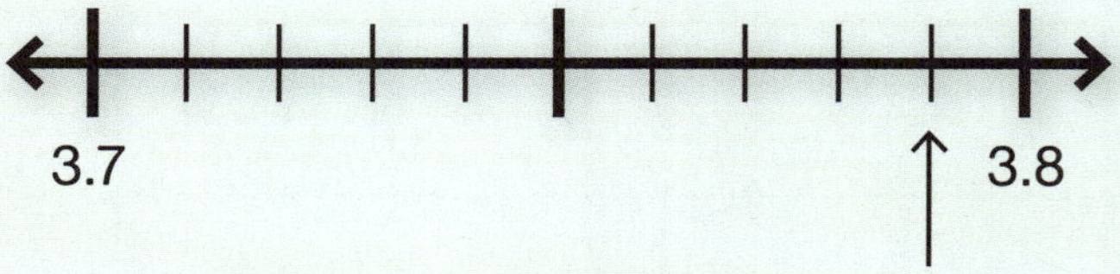

______

Solve. Write the equations you use.

Renting a bouncy house costs $279.99, plus $16.79 for sales tax. What is the total cost?

Renting a cotton candy machine costs $116.99, plus $7.02 for sales tax and $26.78 for supplies. What is the total cost?

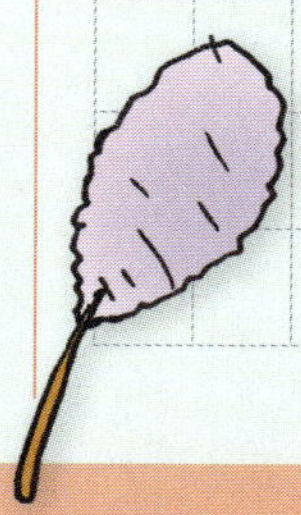

Lesson Activities

A

thousands	hundreds	tens	ones
2,	9	9	9
3,	2	0	9
	7	8	4

3,209 ◯ 2,999

784 ◯ 3,209

ones	tenths	hundredths
0.	8	
0.	2	9
1		

0.29 ◯ 0.8

1 ◯ 0.29

B

Compare Decimals

We can use place-value thinking or decimal squares to compare decimal numbers.

Ex. Max's reaction time is 0.219 seconds. Yuki's reaction time is 0.27 seconds. Who has the lower reaction time?

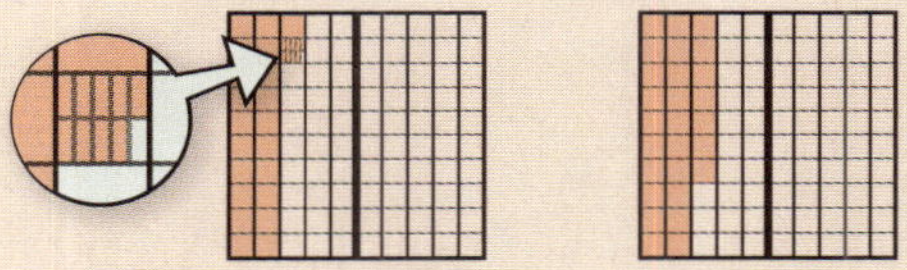

0.219 Max   0.27 Yuki

Max	0.	2	1	9
Yuki	0.	2	7	

0.219 < 0.27

Max has a lower reaction time than Yuki.

4 ◯ 3.999   0.67 ◯ 0.624   2.378 ◯ 3.374

0.040 ◯ 0.04   0.03 ◯ 0.003   6.0 ◯ 6

C

Decimal War

(2-Player Game)

	2: 0.400	3: 0.402	4: 0.420
5: 0.401	6: 0.4	7: 0.410	8: 0.042
9: 0.40	10: 0.412	11: 0.42	12: 0.41

Practice

Circle the greatest number in each group.

0.45	0.07	6.4	3.999
0.5	0.070	6.314	4.000
0.400	0.7	6.31	4.001

Circle the least number in each group.

0.39	0.082	3.20	76.104
0.325	0.07	2.7	76.7
0.378	0.4	1.999	76.32

Complete the circles with <, >, or =.

0.3 ◯ 0.03	0.50 ◯ 0.5	1.06 ◯ 1.060
2.8 ◯ 2.80	0.040 ◯ 0.004	3.000 ◯ 3.701
4 ◯ 4.0	0.60 ◯ 6	5.000 ◯ 5.00

Use the chart to answer the questions.

Which gymnast had the highest score and won the gold medal?

Which gymnast had the second-highest score and won the silver medal?

Which gymnast had the third-highest score and won the bronze medal?

2020 Olympics Women's All-Around Gymnastics Competition Top Scores

Name	Score
Angelina Melnikova	57.199
Mai Murakami	56.032
Sunisa Lee	57.433
Rebeca Andrade	57.298
Vladislava Urazova	56.996

Review

Write whether each angle is acute, right, obtuse, or straight.

Right angles measure 90°.

Straight angles measure 180°.

Acute angles measure less than 90°.

Obtuse angles measure more than 90° and less than 180°.

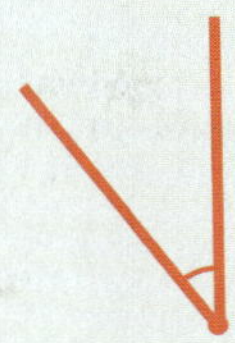

____

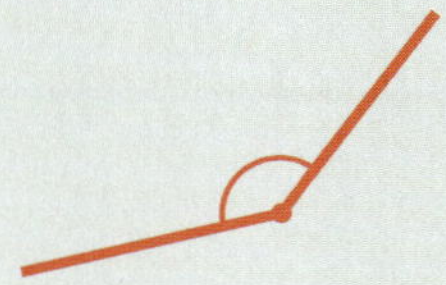

____

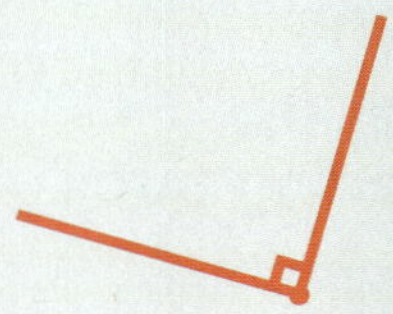

____

____

Round to the underlined place.

<u>3</u>.4 ≈ ______________

<u>4</u>.9 ≈ ______________

0.<u>6</u>8 ≈ ______________

0.<u>8</u>7 ≈ ______________

<u>0</u>.46 ≈ ______________

<u>0</u>.79 ≈ ______________

Use mental math to complete.

3,500 + 500 = ________

3,500 + 600 = ________

3,500 + 700 = ________

7,800 + 200 = ________

7,800 + 201 = ________

7,800 + 202 = ________

4,200 – 200 = ________

4,200 – 300 = ________

4,200 – 400 = ________

4,000 – 1 = ________

4,000 – 10 = ________

4,000 – 100 = ________

Write each length as a decimal.

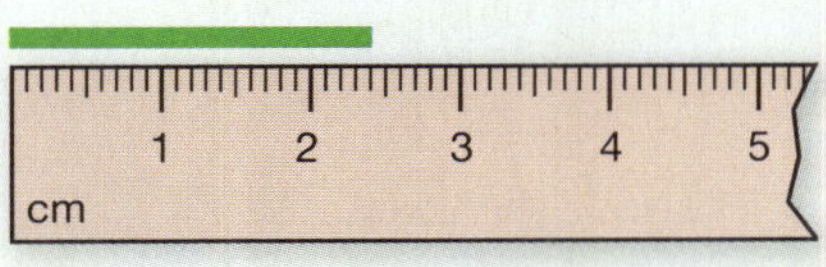

____2.4____ cm

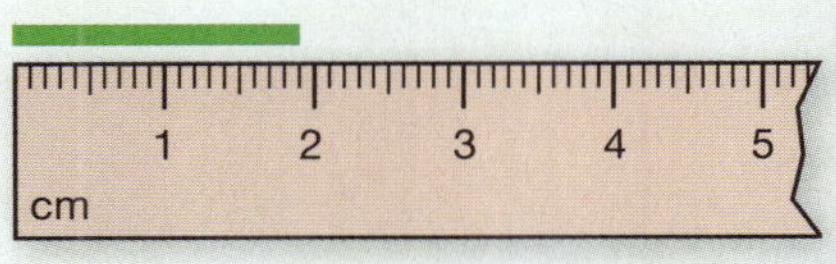

____________ cm

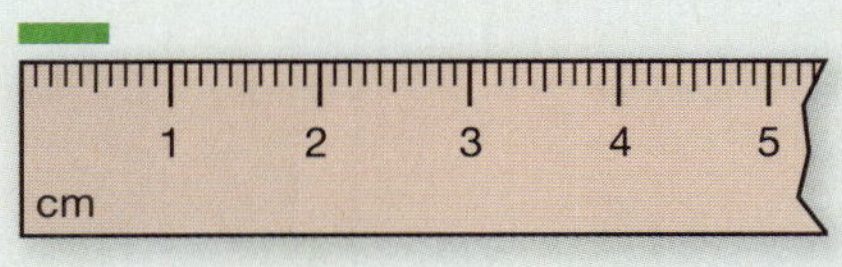

____________ cm

2.10

Lesson Activities

A

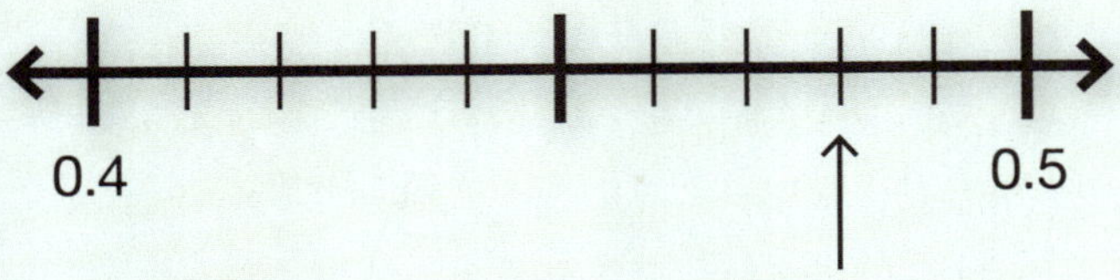

______

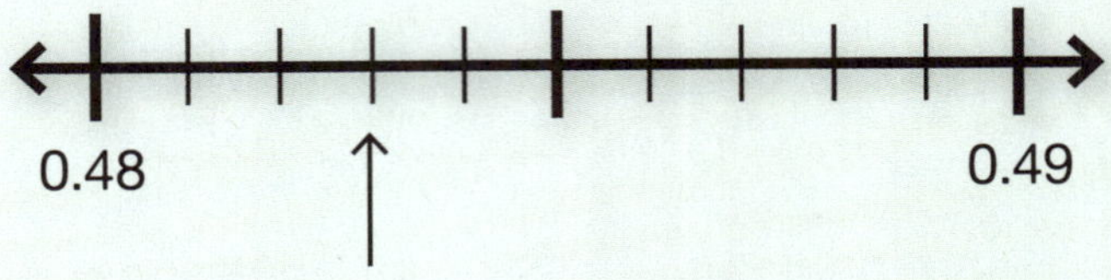

______

B

Write Decimals as Fractions

1. Write the decimal digits as the numerator. Ignore any leading zeros.
2. Write the decimal digits' smallest place value as the denominator.

Ex.

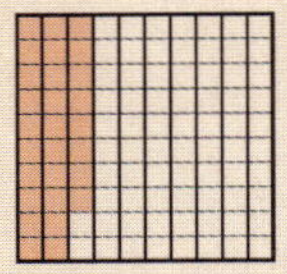

$0.28 = \frac{28}{100}$

Ex.

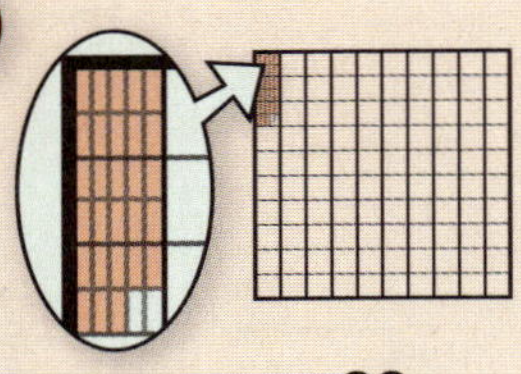

$0.028 = \frac{28}{1,000}$

Write Fractions as Decimals

1. Write the numerator as the decimal digits in the number.
2. If needed, add leading zeros to make the number's smallest place value match the denominator.

Ex.

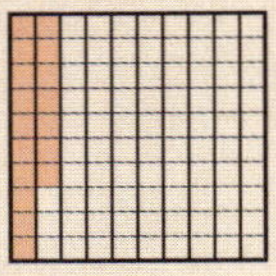

$\frac{17}{100} = 0.17$

Ex.

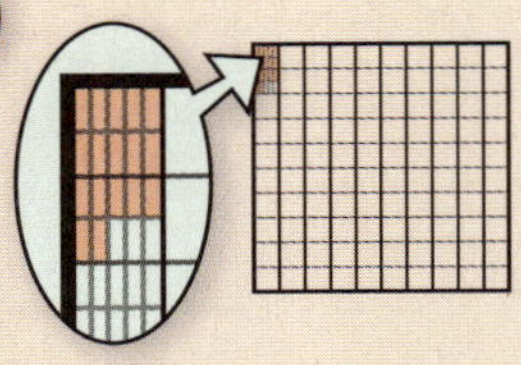

$\frac{17}{1,000} = 0.017$

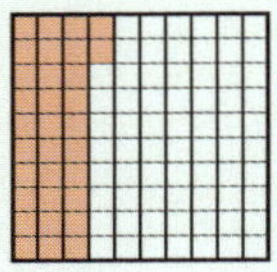

0.32 = ______

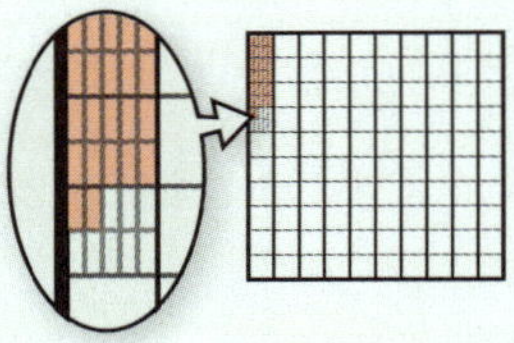

0.032 = ______

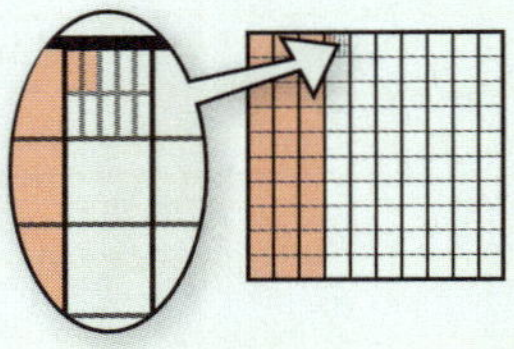

0.302 = ______

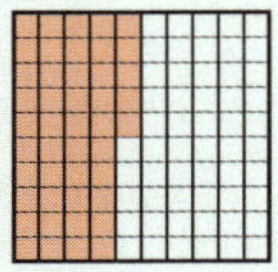

$\frac{45}{100}$ = ______

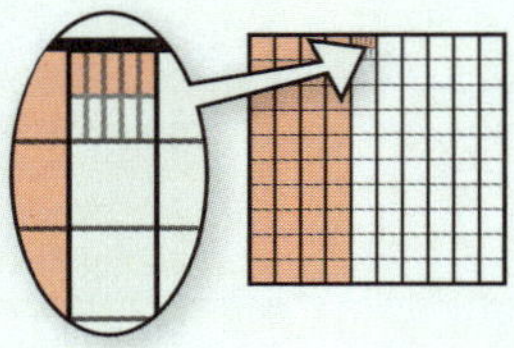

$\frac{405}{1,000}$ = ______

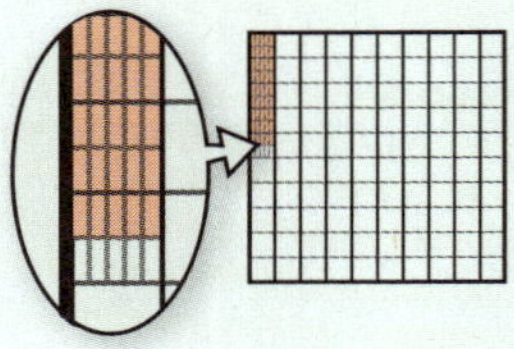

$\frac{45}{1,000}$ = ______

C

Four in a Row (2-Player Game)

2.80	$\frac{4}{10}$	0.004	$2\frac{804}{1,000}$	2.08
$1\frac{9}{10}$	0.7	$\frac{36}{1,000}$	2.840	$\frac{7}{100}$
0.036	$1\frac{918}{1,000}$	1.91	$\frac{4}{1,000}$	0.36
$2\frac{80}{100}$	2.804	$2\frac{8}{100}$	1.918	$1\frac{91}{100}$
0.07	$\frac{36}{100}$	1.9	$\frac{7}{10}$	0.4

Practice

Complete the charts.

Decimal	0.49	0.005	0.735	1.008	2.319	3.064
Fraction or Mixed Number						

Decimal						
Fraction or Mixed Number	$\frac{8}{100}$	$\frac{81}{1,000}$	$\frac{700}{1,000}$	$1\frac{375}{1,000}$	$4\frac{6}{1,000}$	$3\frac{25}{100}$

Label the numbers on the number line.

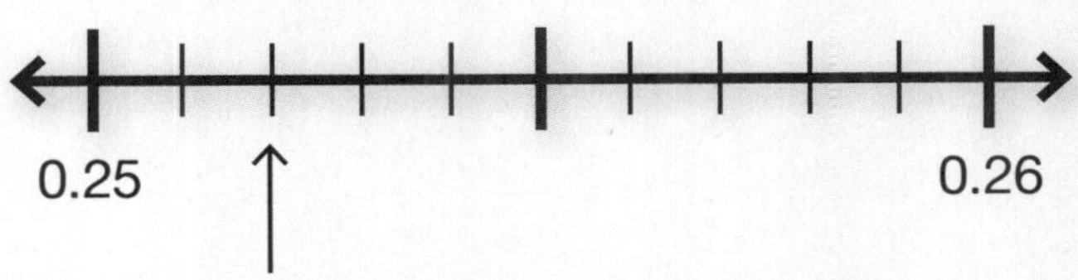

____

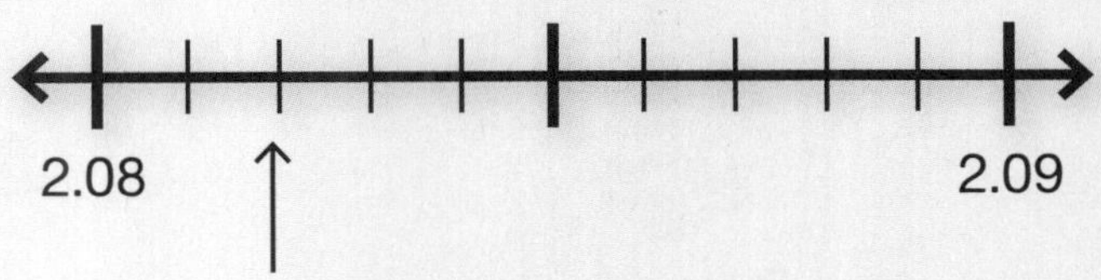

____

2.10

Review

Match each number to its dot on the number line.

0.9 | 0.09 | 0.6 | 1.5 | 1.34 | 1.75

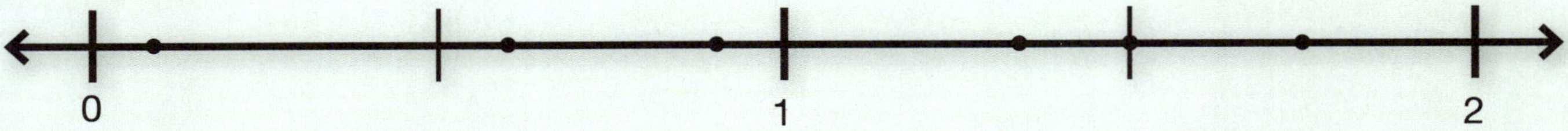

Use mental math to complete.

4 × 70 = ______________

50 × 60 = ______________

3,000 × 9 = ______________

240 ÷ 6 = ______________

4,800 ÷ 8 = ______________

21,000 ÷ 7 = ______________

300 ÷ 6 = ______________

2,000 ÷ 5 = ______________

1,400 ÷ 2 = ______________

Find the sum, product, or difference.

0.74 + 2.6

3,284 × 7

3.5 – 1.84

Solve. Write the equations you use.

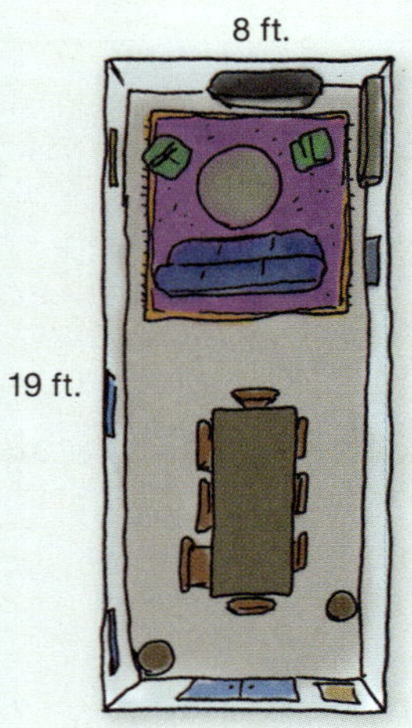

What is the perimeter of the room?

What is the area of the room?

Lesson Activities

A

Nate's Running Log

Day	Exact Distance (Miles)	Distance Rounded to the Nearest Mile
Monday	2.684	
Tuesday	1.37	
Wednesday	3.915	
Thursday	2.7	
Friday	1.826	

B

How to Add and Subtract Decimals

1. Line up the decimal points.
2. Tack on zeros until both numbers have the same number of decimal places.
3. Add or subtract like usual. Write a decimal point in the answer below the other decimal points.

Ex. How far did Nate run on Tuesday and Wednesday?

$$\begin{array}{r} 1.370 \\ +\,3.915 \\ \hline \end{array} \longrightarrow \begin{array}{r} \scriptstyle 1 \\ 1.370 \\ +\,3.915 \\ \hline \mathbf{5.285} \end{array} \textbf{ miles}$$

WORK SPACE

How much farther did Nate run on Thursday than Friday?

How far did Nate run in all?

Nate's goal is to run 15 miles this week. How many more miles does he need to run to meet his goal?

2.11

Practice

Use logical reasoning to circle the more reasonable answer for each problem.

1.999 + 0.999	0.005 + 2.381	0.68 + 1.14
2.998 / 2,998	2.386 / 23.86	0.182 / 1.82
1.623 – 0.582	3 – 0.741	5.657 – 1
10.41 / 1.041	2.259 / 0.259	4.657 / 5.557

Solve.

4.6 + 3.277

0.73 – 0.214

4 – 1.368

Use the map to answer the questions. Write the equations you use.

How much longer is the Rim Trail than the Rocky Flats Trail?

How much shorter is the Buffalo Creek Trail than the Rocky Flats Trail?

What is the total length of all three trails?

Review

Connect each number to its place on the number line. Then, round each number to the underlined place.

0.781 | 0.793 | 0.799 | 0.788

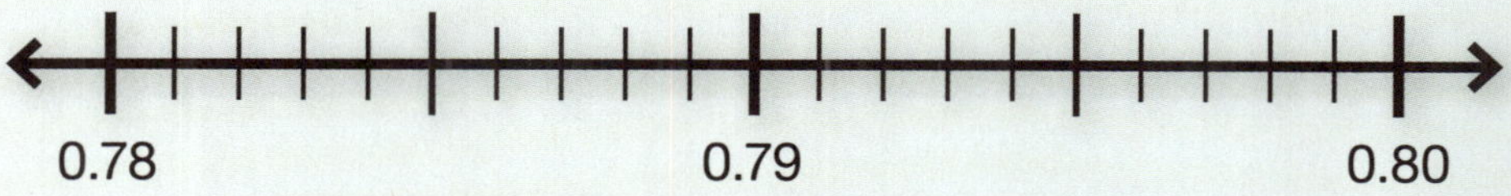

$0.7\underline{8}1 \approx$ ________

$0.7\underline{9}3 \approx$ ________

$0.7\underline{9}9 \approx$ ________

$0.7\underline{8}8 \approx$ ________

Complete. Write the equations you use.

410 cm = ____ m _____ cm

1 L 784 mL = ________ mL

3,250 g = ____ kg ______ g

Paisley asked her friends how many pets they have. Use her data to make a line plot and answer the questions.

Number of Pets

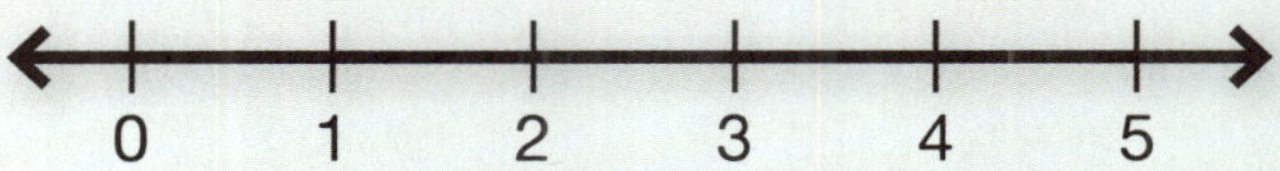

How many people have only one pet?

How many people do not have a pet?

What's the average number of pets Paisley's friends have?

2.12

Unit Wrap-Up

Write a decimal to match each decimal square.

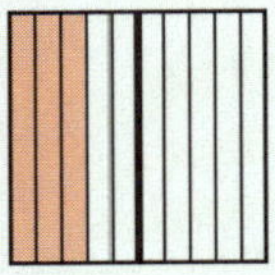 ______ 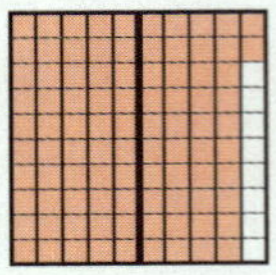 ______ 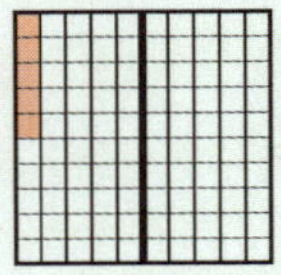 ______

Write each number in expanded form.

4,670,208 = ______________________

0.053 = ______________________

3.748 = ______________________

Round each number to the underlined place.

$\underline{2},964,708,310 \approx$ ______________ $\underline{1}.749 \approx$ ______________

$2,\underline{9}64,708,310 \approx$ ______________ $1.\underline{7}49 \approx$ ______________

$2,9\underline{6}4,708,310 \approx$ ______________ $1.7\underline{4}9 \approx$ ______________

Circle the greatest number in each group.

27,098,432	0.06	5.3	7.999
5,678,325	0.006	5.213	8
9,000,000,000	0.6	5.21	7.597

Circle the least number in each group.

5,000,000	0.075	4.50	6.103
5,000,001	0.09	3.7	6.102
50,000,000	0.3	2.977	6.13

Unit Wrap-Up

Write each decimal as a fraction or mixed number. Write each fraction or mixed number as a decimal.

4.7 = ________

0.31 = ________

6.093 = ________

$\frac{315}{1,000}$ = ________

$6\frac{74}{100}$ = ________

$2\frac{5}{100}$ = ________

Label the numbers on the number line.

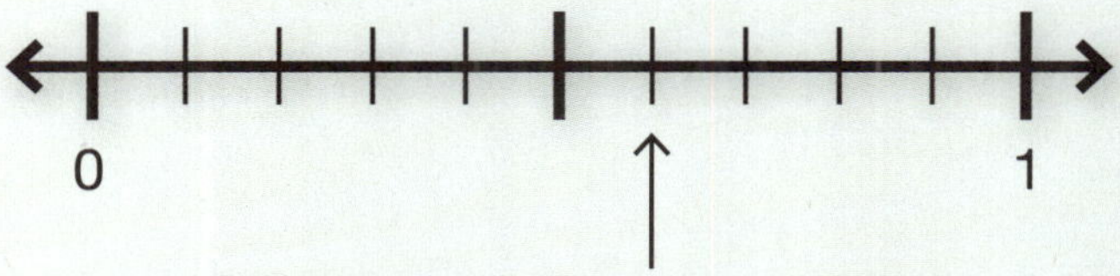

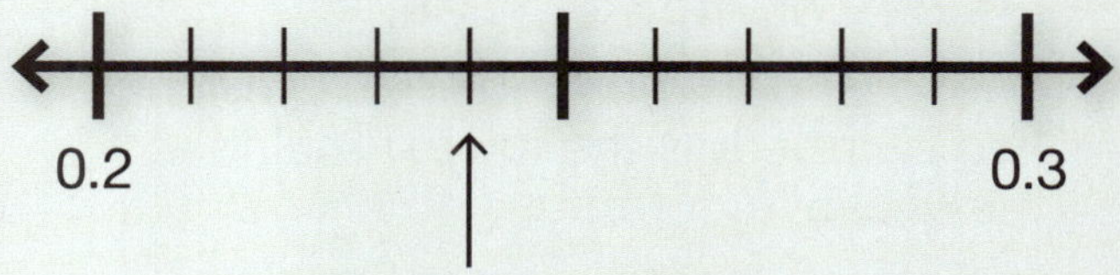

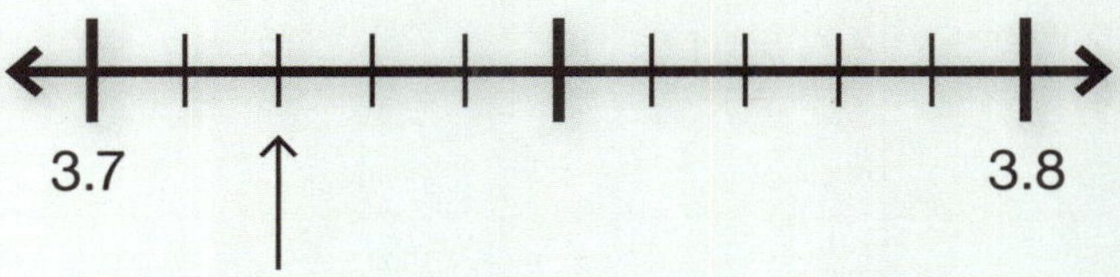

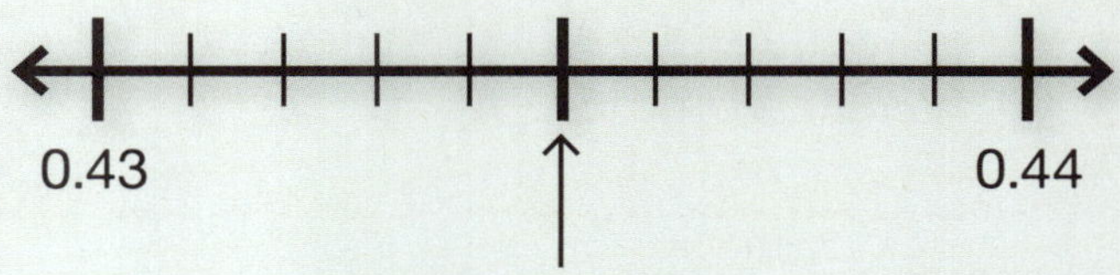

Use the scorecard from the robotics competition to answer the questions. Write the equations you use.

Team Name	Round 1 Score	Round 2 Score
Mega Bot	17.604	20.3
Nuts and Bolts	15.93	23.417

How many points did the Mega Bot team score in all?

How many points did the Nuts and Bolts team score in all?

Which team scored more points? How many more points did they score than the other team?

Lesson Activities

A

Multiples of 8: ______, ______, ______, ______, ______

Multiples of 6: ______, ______, ______, ______, ______

B

Least Common Multiple

The least common multiple (LCM) of two numbers is the lowest multiple they have in common.

To find the least common multiple:

1. Make a list of the first few multiples of each number.
2. Look for the lowest multiple they have in common.

Ex. Find the least common multiple of 5 and 6.

Multiples of 5: 5, 10, 15, 20, 25, 30, 35...

Multiples of 6: 6, 12, 18, 24, 30, 36, 42...

LCM of 5 and 6: **30**

LCM of 2 and 4: ______________

LCM of 9 and 6: ______________

C

Least Common Multiple War

(2-Player Game)

Player 1								
Numbers							Total
LCM							

Player 2								
Numbers							Total
LCM							

Practice

Use the lists of multiples to find the least common multiple for each pair of numbers.

LCM of 3 and 4: ______________

3, 6, 9, 12, 15

4, 8, 12, 16, 20

LCM of 9 and 3: ______________

9, 18, 27, 36, 45

3, 6, 9, 12, 15

LCM of 6 and 10: ______________

6, 12, 18, 24, 30

10, 20, 30, 40, 50

LCM of 6 and 15: ______________

6, 12, 18, 24, 30

15, 30, 45, 60, 75

LCM of 100 and 20: ______________

100, 200, 300, 400, 500, 600

20, 40, 60, 80, 100, 120

LCM of 25 and 30: ______________

25, 50, 75, 100, 125, 150

30, 60, 90, 120, 150, 180

Find the least common multiple for each pair of numbers. Make your own lists of multiples.

LCM of 2 and 5: ______________

LCM of 6 and 12: ______________

LCM of 8 and 10: ______________

LCM of 5 and 7: ______________

Review

Find the product.

$$\begin{array}{r} 38 \\ \times \quad 9 \\ \hline \end{array} \qquad \begin{array}{r} 87 \\ \times \quad 5 \\ \hline \end{array} \qquad \begin{array}{r} 999 \\ \times \quad 6 \\ \hline \end{array} \qquad \begin{array}{r} 4,036 \\ \times \quad 3 \\ \hline \end{array}$$

Complete the chart.

	Double
20	
50	
100	
500	
5,000	

Match each number to its dot on the number line.

1.03 1.1 1.426

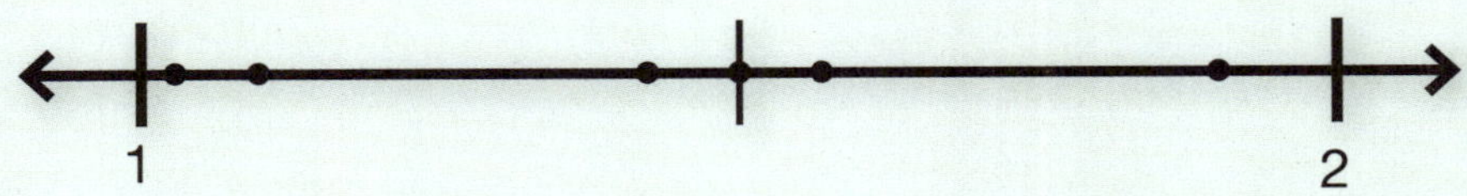

1.57 1.5 1.90

Color the diagrams to match the mixed numbers.
Then, write <, >, or = to compare the mixed numbers.

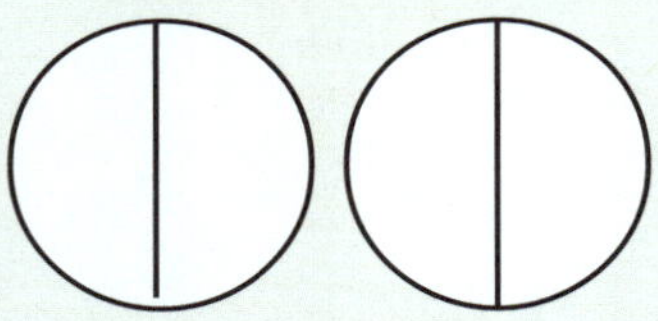

$1\frac{1}{2}$

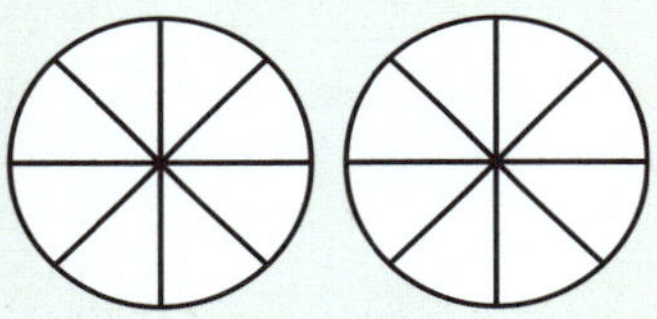

$1\frac{3}{8}$

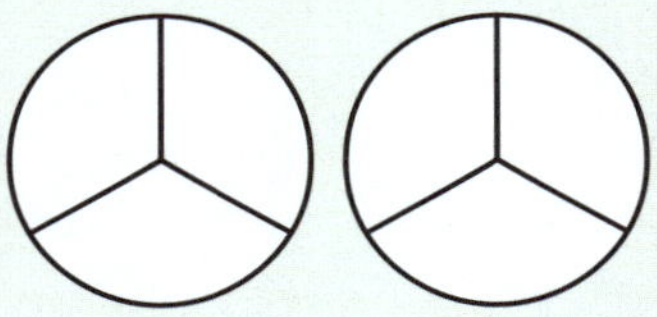

$1\frac{2}{3}$

$1\frac{1}{2} \bigcirc 1\frac{3}{8}$

$1\frac{1}{2} \bigcirc 1\frac{2}{3}$

$1\frac{2}{3} \bigcirc 1\frac{3}{8}$

Solve. Write the equations you use.

What is the perimeter of the room?

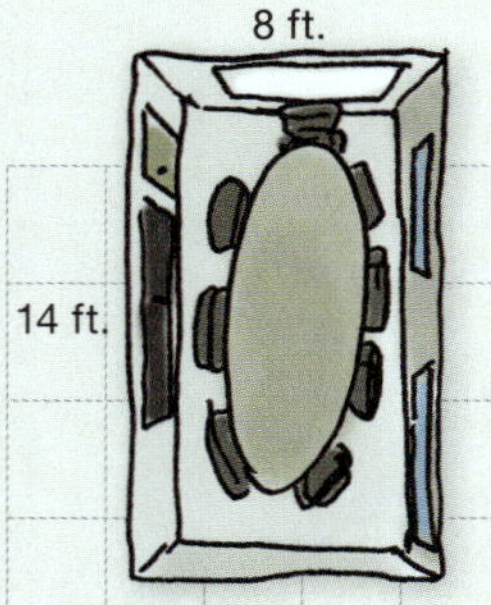

The perimeter of the field is 800 m.
All sides of the field are equal.
What is the length of each side?

Lesson Activities

A

Packs	18	19	20	21	22
Buns			120		

B

Two Ways to Mentally Multiply

Box Method

Ex. There are 6 buns in each pack. How many buns are in 43 packs?

	40	3
6	240	18

240 + 18 = 258

43 × 6 = **258 buns**

Multiply and Adjust

Ex. There are 6 buns in each pack. How many buns are in 43 packs?

40 packs: 40 × 6 = 240
+6
41 packs: 41 × 6 = 246
+6
42 packs: 42 × 6 = 252
+6
43 packs: 43 × 6 = 258

43 × 6 = **258 buns**

70 × 4 = ______

71 × 4 = ______

90 × 3 = ______

89 × 3 = ______

80 × 5 = ______

82 × 5 = ______

C

Climb the Ladder (2-Player Game)

34 × 8 = ______
33 × 8 = ______
32 × 8 = ______
31 × 8 = ______
30 × 8 = 240

16 × 9 = ______
17 × 9 = ______
18 × 9 = ______
19 × 9 = ______
20 × 9 = 180

68 × 3 = ______
66 × 3 = ______
64 × 3 = ______
62 × 3 = ______
60 × 3 = 180

3.2

Practice

Complete the charts. Use the completed boxes to help.

Packs	28	29	30	31	32
Hot Dogs			240		

Packs	98	99	100	101	102
Hot Dogs			800		

Find the products. Use the completed product to help.

$40 \times 3 =$ 120

$41 \times 3 =$ ______

$42 \times 3 =$ ______

$30 \times 5 =$ 150

$29 \times 5 =$ ______

$28 \times 5 =$ ______

$50 \times 6 =$ 300

$51 \times 6 =$ ______

★ $57 \times 6 =$ ______

Use the box method to find the product.

	70	3
4		

$73 \times 4 =$ ______

	90	9
7		

$99 \times 7 =$ ______

Use any method to solve. Write the equations you use.

Yazmin is planning a party. She buys 24 packs of balloons. Each pack holds 8 balloons. How many balloons does she buy?

Yazmin also buys 72 cupcakes. Each cupcake costs $3. What is the total cost of the cupcakes?

Yazmin decides to buy 1 more pack of balloons. How many balloons does she have now?

Yazmin decides to buy 2 more cupcakes. What is the total cost of all the cupcakes now?

Review

Write each decimal as a fraction or mixed number. Write each fraction or mixed number as a decimal.

4.109 = ________	0.87 = ________	3.061 = ________
$1\frac{28}{100}$ = ________	$6\frac{3}{10}$ = ________	$2\frac{4}{1{,}000}$ = ________

Color the diagrams to match the fractions. Then, write <, >, or = to compare the fractions.

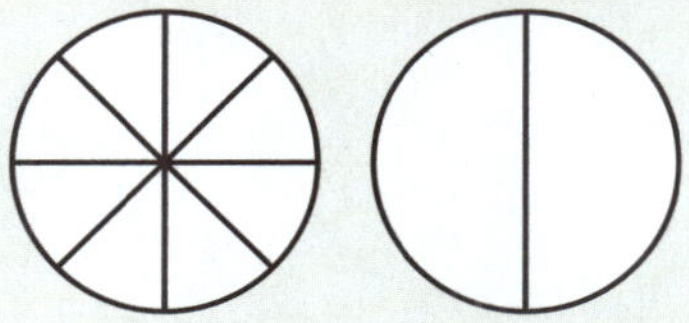

$\frac{5}{8}$ ◯ $\frac{1}{2}$

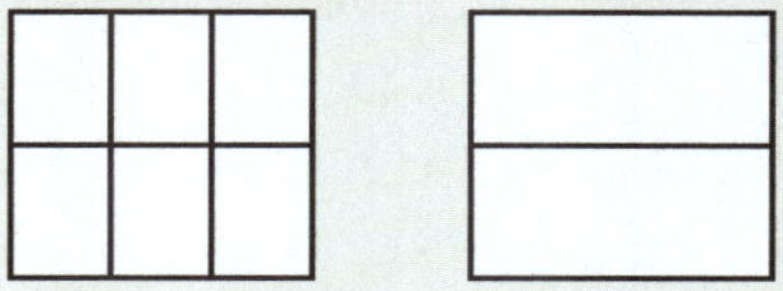

$\frac{3}{6}$ ◯ $\frac{1}{2}$

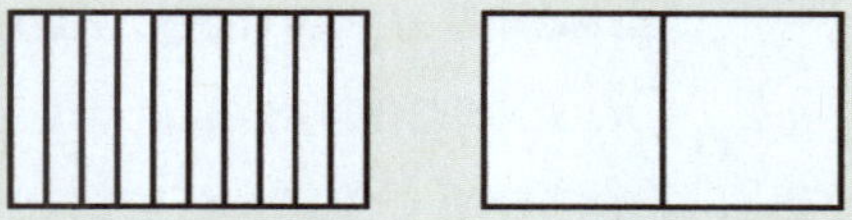

$\frac{7}{10}$ ◯ $\frac{1}{2}$

Write whether each angle is acute, right, obtuse, or straight.

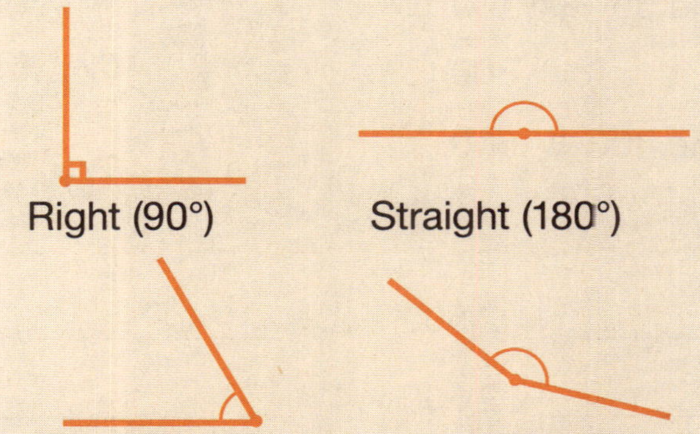

Right (90°)

Straight (180°)

Acute (less than 90°)

Obtuse (more than 90° and less than 180°)

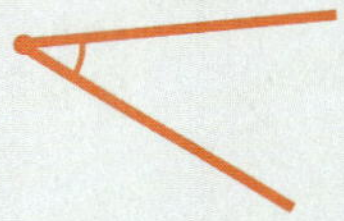

____

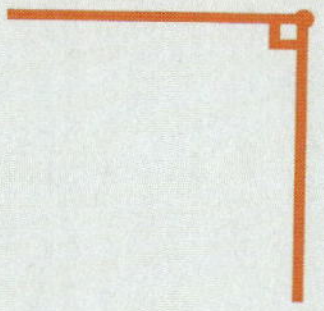

____

____

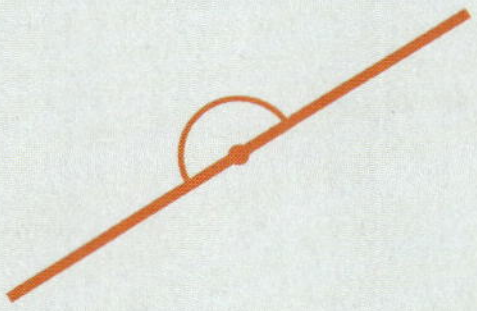

____

Solve. Write the equations you use.

Joan ran 3.39 miles on Monday. She ran 2.84 miles on Tuesday. How much farther did she run on Monday than Tuesday?

Otis' family drove 6.7 miles to swim practice. Then, they drove 4.54 miles to his grandparents' house. How far did they drive in all?

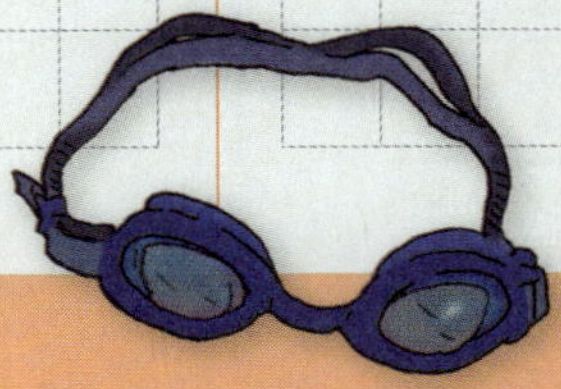

3.3

Lesson Activities

A

Double 25 → ________

Double 50 → ________

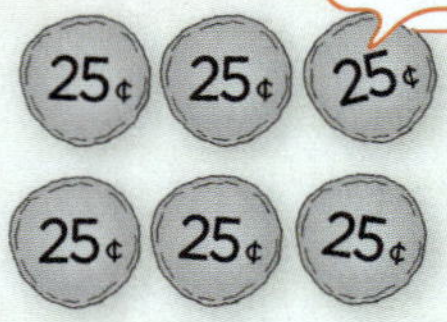

Double 75 → ________

B

Mentally Multiply by 2 or 4

Multiplying a number by 2 is the same as doubling the number.

1. Break the number into parts.
2. Double each part.
3. Add the doubled parts together.

Ex. 45 × 2 = ?

Double 40 → 80
Double 5 → 10
90

45 × 2 = **90**

Multiplying a number by 4 is the same as doubling the number twice.

Ex. 150 × 4 = ?

Double 100 → 200
Double 50 → 100
300

Double 300 → 600
150 × 4 = **600**

35 × 2 = ________
35 × 4 = ________

125 × 2 = ________
125 × 4 = ________

2,500 × 2 = ________
2,500 × 4 = ________

C

Flip and Multiply (2-Player Game)

Player 1	Player 2
55 × ______ = ________	55 × ______ = ________
85 × ______ = ________	85 × ______ = ________
325 × ______ = ________	325 × ______ = ________
450 × ______ = ________	450 × ______ = ________
3,500 × ______ = ________	3,500 × ______ = ________
Player 1 Total ______	Player 2 Total ______

Practice

Complete.

25 → × 2 → 50 → × 2 → ______ → × 2 → ______ → × 2 → ______

105 → × 2 → ______ → × 2 → ______ → × 2 → ______ → × 2 → ______

300 → × 2 → ______ → × 2 → ______ → × 2 → ______ → × 2 → ______

1,250 → × 2 → ______ → × 2 → ______ → × 2 → ______ → × 2 → ______

Find the products.

$15 \times 2 =$ ______	$55 \times 2 =$ ______	$75 \times 2 =$ ______
$15 \times 4 =$ ______	$55 \times 4 =$ ______	$75 \times 4 =$ ______
$225 \times 2 =$ ______	$4{,}500 \times 2 =$ ______	★ $4{,}501 \times 2 =$ ______
$225 \times 4 =$ ______	$4{,}500 \times 4 =$ ______	★ $4{,}501 \times 4 =$ ______

Solve. Write the equations you use.

Angelina's parents bought 4 kitchen chairs. Each chair cost $85. How much did the chairs cost in all?

Garrett's backyard is shaped like a square. Each side of the yard is 135 feet long. What is the perimeter of his backyard?

135 ft.

3.3

Review

Find the least common multiple for each pair of numbers.

LCM of 5 and 3: ____________________

LCM of 5 and 20: ____________________

Color the diagram to match the fraction. Then, convert to a mixed number.

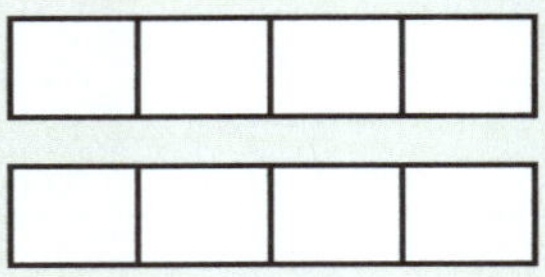

$\frac{7}{4}$ = ____________

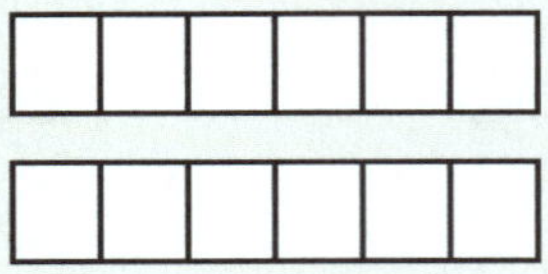

$\frac{7}{6}$ = ____________

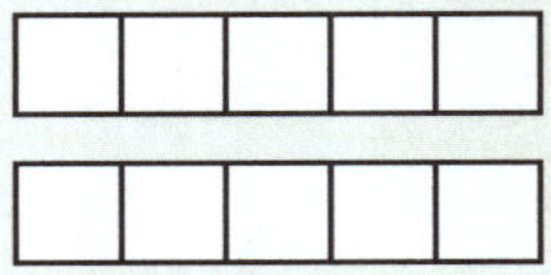

$\frac{7}{5}$ = ____________

Match each shape to the name and definition that most specifically describe it.

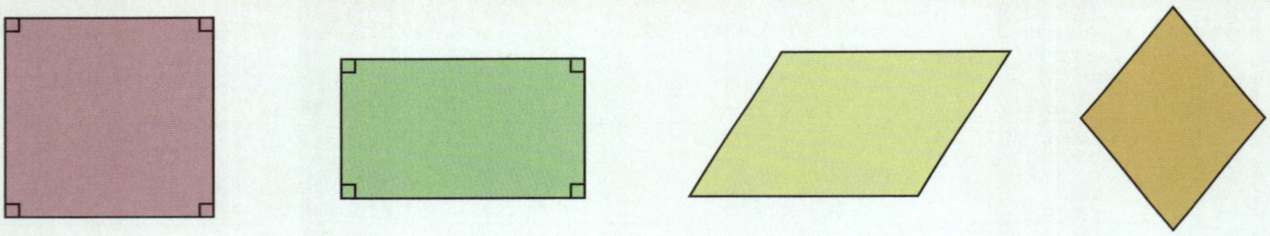

Rectangle (4 right angles)	Parallelogram (2 pairs of parallel sides)	Rhombus (2 pairs of parallel sides and 4 equal sides)	Square (4 equal sides and 4 right angles)

Solve. Write the equations you use.

Marcus had $5,682 in his savings account. Then, he used $4,599 to buy a used car. How much money did he have left?

Lesson Activities

A

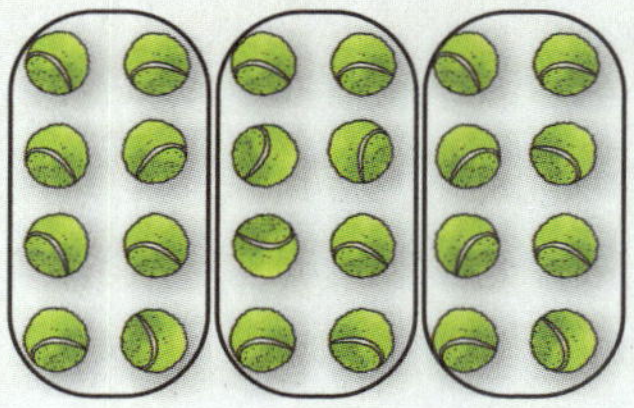

$3 \times (4 \times 2) =$ ______

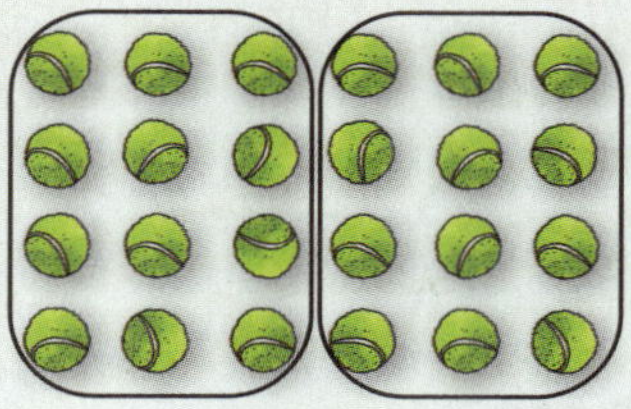

$2 \times (4 \times 3) =$ ______

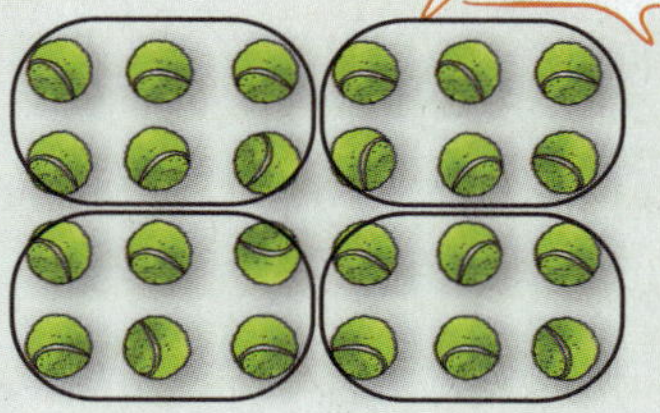

$4 \times (2 \times 3) =$ ______

B

Associative Property

When you multiply 3 or more numbers, the product remains the same no matter how you group them.

If the only operation in an expression is multiplication, you can multiply the numbers in any order.

Ex. $9 \times 4 \times 5$ → 9×20 → **180**

Multiplying 9×20 is easier than 36×5, so multiply 4×5 first.

Ex. $8 \times 2 \times 9$ → 72×2 → **144**

Multiplying by 2 is the same as doubling, so multiply 8×9 first. Then, double the result.

C

Dice Tic-Tac-Toe 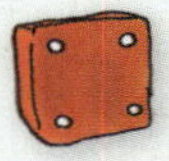 (2-Player Game)

4 × 5 × 8	4 × 45 × 2	2 × 7 × 6	7 × 250 × 2	45 × 3 × 2
9 × 2 × 15	2 × 7 × 5	8 × 35 × 2	2 × 4 × 15	8 × 2 × 7
2 × 7 × 7	25 × 2 × 4	5 × 6 × 9	35 × 2 × 2	150 × 9 × 2
7 × 35 × 2	8 × 429 × 0	7 × 25 × 2	8 × 5 × 6	9 × 4 × 2
8 × 4 × 2	25 × 3 × 2	6 × 2 × 6	6 × 15 × 2	297 × 7 × 0

Practice

Draw a line from Start to End so that each problem is followed by the correct answer. You do not have to solve every problem.

Solve. Write the equations you use.

Avery goes to 2 gymnastics lessons each week. Each lesson costs $15. How much do 8 weeks of lessons cost?

Each box of graham crackers has 3 packs in it. Each pack holds 10 crackers. How many crackers are in 7 boxes?

Review

Complete the missing addends. Use the pictures to help.

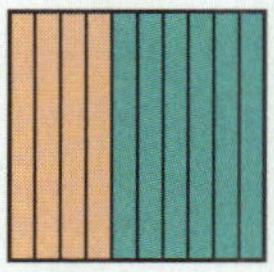

0.4 + _______ = 1

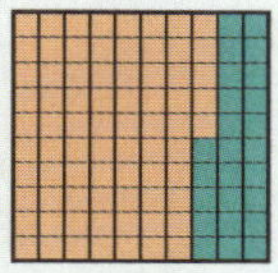

0.75 + _______ = 1

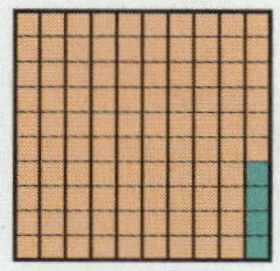

0.96 + _______ = 1

Use the pictures to complete the equivalent fractions.

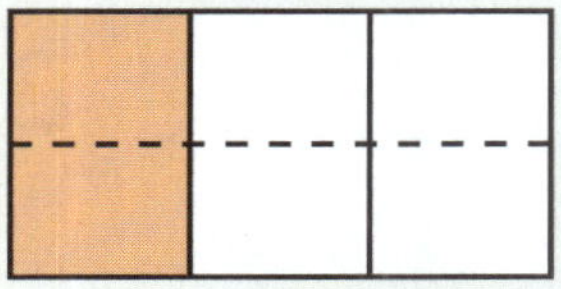

$\frac{1}{3} = \frac{}{6}$

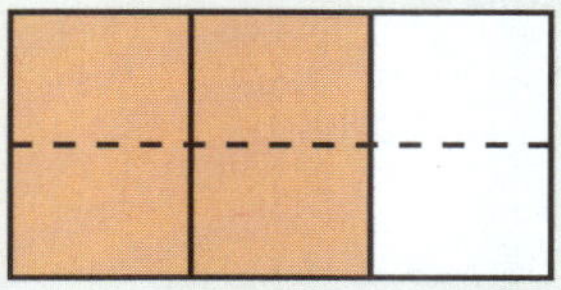

$\frac{2}{3} = \frac{}{6}$

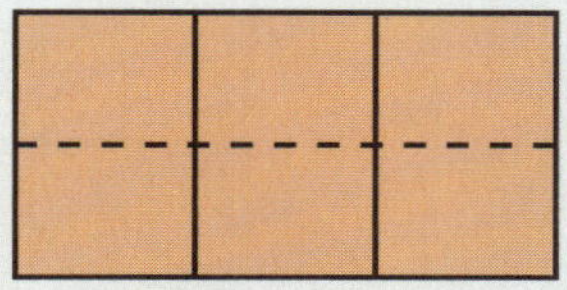

$\frac{3}{3} = \frac{}{6}$

Match.

70 × 7	4,000	49 × 10
600 × 5	2,700	4 × 1,000
50 × 80	490	3 × 1,000
300 × 9	3,000	27 × 100

Solve. Write the equations you use.

The ice cream stand earned $1,578 in May. It earned 3 times as much in June as it did in May. How much did it earn in June?

How much did the ice cream stand earn in all in May and June?

3.5

Lesson Activities

A

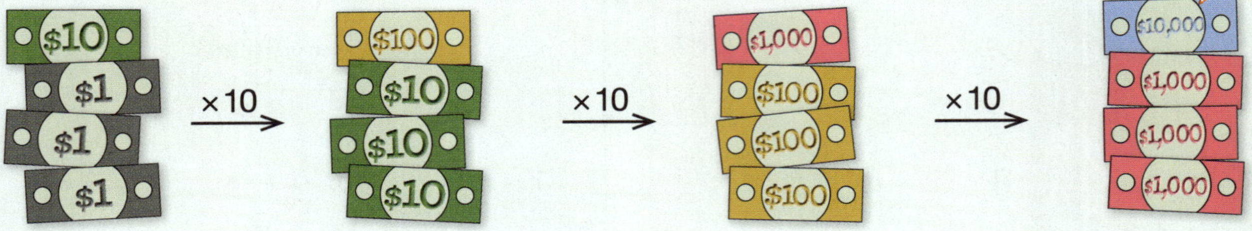

$13 ____________ ____________ ____________

B

hundred thousands	ten thousands	thousands	hundreds	tens	ones	
				1	3	13 × 1
						13 × 10
						13 × 100
						13 × 1,000

hundred thousands	ten thousands	thousands	hundreds	tens	ones	
			3	1	4	314 × 1
						314 × 10
						314 × 100
						314 × 1,000

C

Mental Multiplication

1. Underline the trailing zeros.
2. Multiply the non-zero digits.
3. Tack on the trailing zeros.

Ex. 300 × 20 = ?

3 hundreds × 2 tens = 6 thousands

3<u>00</u> × 2<u>0</u> = **6,000**

The associative property allows us to break numbers apart in this way to make multiplication easier.

Ex. 300 × 20 = ?

3 × 100 × 2 × 10

6 × 1,000

6,000

128 × 10 = ____________________

128 × 100 = ____________________

128 × 1,000 = ____________________

40 × 20 = ____________________

400 × 20 = ____________________

4,000 × 20 = ____________________

D

Multiplication Master (1-Player Game)

90 2,000 50 80 600

	Product
30 × ______	
70 × ______	
200 × ______	
500 × ______	
4,000 × ______	
Total	

The highest possible total is 8,325,100. How close can you get?

Practice

Complete.

367 × 10 = ______

367 × 100 = ______

367 × 1,000 = ______

60 × 70 = ______

600 × 70 = ______

6,000 × 70 = ______

10 × 508 = ______

100 × 508 = ______

1,000 × 508 = ______

50 × 40 = ______

50 × 400 = ______

50 × 4,000 = ______

Solve. Write the equations you use.

A party planner bought 40 rolls of streamers. Each roll was 100 feet long. How many feet of streamers did she buy?

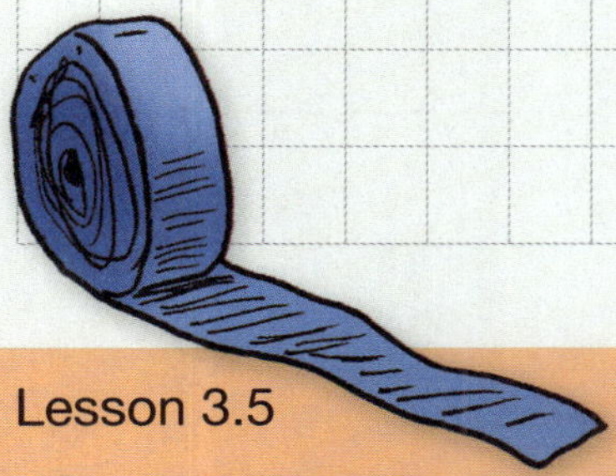

A food pantry received 80 crates of apples to give away. Each crate contained 200 apples. How many apples did the food pantry receive?

3.5

Review

Color the diagram to match the mixed number. Then, complete the missing numerator in the fraction.

$2\frac{1}{5} = \frac{\quad}{5}$

$2\frac{3}{4} = \frac{\quad}{4}$

$2\frac{3}{6} = \frac{\quad}{6}$

Find the product.

$$\begin{array}{r} 146 \\ \times \quad 9 \\ \hline \end{array} \qquad \begin{array}{r} 378 \\ \times \quad 6 \\ \hline \end{array}$$

Evaluate.

P

M or D →

A or S →

$10 - 3 \times 2 \div 2$

Complete the chart. Use the completed box to help.

Pages	28	29	30	31	32
Trading Cards			270		

Round each weight to the underlined place.

$0.6\underline{1}5 \approx$ ____________

$0.\underline{6}15 \approx$ ____________

$0.0\underline{1}7 \approx$ ____________

$0.\underline{0}17 \approx$ ____________

$0.3\underline{9}7 \approx$ ____________

$0.\underline{3}97 \approx$ ____________

Lesson Activities

A

				2	8	28 × 1
						28 × 10
						28 × 100
						28 × 1,000

				8	4	28 × 3
						28 × 30
						28 × 300
						28 × 3,000

			1	2	9	129 × 1
						129 × 10
						129 × 100
						129 × 1,000

			9	0	3	129 × 7
						129 × 70
						129 × 700
						129 × 7,000

B

How to Multiply Numbers with Trailing Zeros

1. Stack the numbers vertically. Write the number with trailing zeros on the bottom.
2. Count the number of trailing zeros. Write this number of zeros in the answer.
3. Multiply the non-zero digits like usual.

Ex.

$$\begin{array}{r} 28 \\ \times\ 30 \\ \hline \end{array} \longrightarrow \begin{array}{r} 28 \\ \times\ 30 \\ \hline 0 \end{array} \longrightarrow \begin{array}{r} {}^{2}\ \ \\ 28 \\ \times\ 30 \\ \hline 840 \end{array}$$

	1	2		6	1		4	3	7		1,	2	8	9
×	4	0	×	3	0	×	5	0	0	×	3,	0	0	0

3.6

Practice

Complete each multiplication problem. Then, find the blanks that match the letter for each problem. Write the letter in the matching blanks to solve the riddle.

V) 82×30

M) 73×50

O) 541×600

H) $3{,}196 \times 2{,}000$

R) 97×40

E) 55×90

T) 208×700

S) $1{,}739 \times 4{,}000$

How do you make seven an even number?

___	___	___	___	___	___		___	___	___		___
3,880	4,950	3,650	324,600	2,460	4,950		145,600	6,392,000	4,950		6,956,000

Solve. Write the equations you use.

The animal shelter buys 32 bags of dog food. Each bag weighs 40 lb. How many pounds of dog food do they buy?

The animal shelter buys 20 bags of guinea pig pellets. Each bag weighs 14 kg. How many kilograms of guinea pig pellets do they buy?

The animal shelter buys 30 cases of cat food. Each case contains 24 cans. How many cans of cat food do they buy?

The animal shelter buys 20 dog collars. Each collar costs $18. How much do they spend?

Review

Circle yes or no to answer the questions.

12 ÷ 4 = 3
12 is divisible by 4.

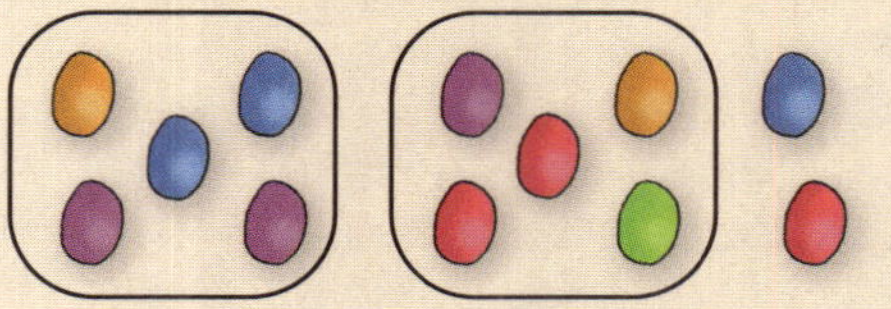

12 ÷ 5 = 2 R2
12 is not divisible by 5.

Is 12 divisible by 3? **Yes | No**	Is 24 divisible by 3? **Yes | No**
Is 12 divisible by 6? **Yes | No**	Is 24 divisible by 6? **Yes | No**
Is 12 divisible by 8? **Yes | No**	Is 24 divisible by 8? **Yes | No**

Use the number lines to compare the fractions. Write <, >, or =.

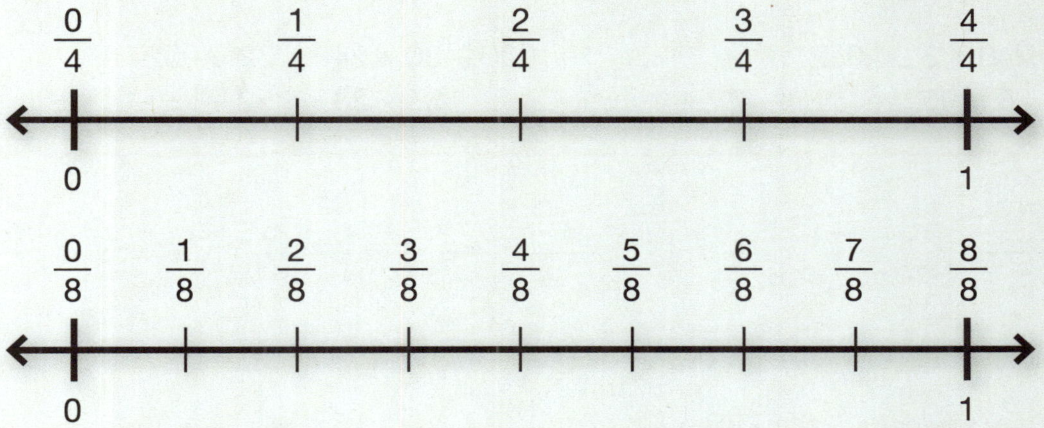

$\frac{1}{4}$ ◯ $\frac{1}{8}$

$\frac{2}{4}$ ◯ $\frac{4}{8}$

$\frac{3}{4}$ ◯ $\frac{7}{8}$

$\frac{4}{4}$ ◯ $\frac{8}{8}$

Use the box method to solve.

	60	8
5		

68 × 5 = ______________________

	30	7
9		

37 × 9 = ______________________

Find the area.

5 ft.

3 ft.

Area: ______________________

15 cm

10 cm

Area: ______________________

Lesson Activities

A

90 × 40 = ________ 300 × 20 = ________ 900 × 200 = ________

B

Area Model

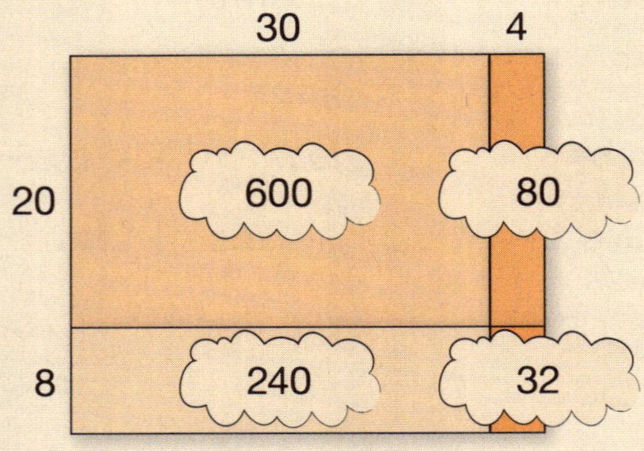

600 + 80 + 240 + 32 = 952

34 × 28 = **952**

Box Method

	30	4
20	**600**	**80**
8	**240**	**32**

600 + 80 + 240 + 32 = 952

34 × 28 = **952**

	60	5
40		
9		

65 × 49 = ________

73 × 54 = ________

C

	100	20	5
80			
4			

125 × 84 = ________

Practice

Use the box method to find the products.

	20	6
90		
5		

26 × 95 = ______________________

	40	3

43 × 62 = ______________________

100		

153 × 64 = ______________________

Use the box method to find the area. Make sure to include the correct units.

The Olympic swimming pool is 164 ft. by 82 ft. What is its area?

164 ft.

82 ft.

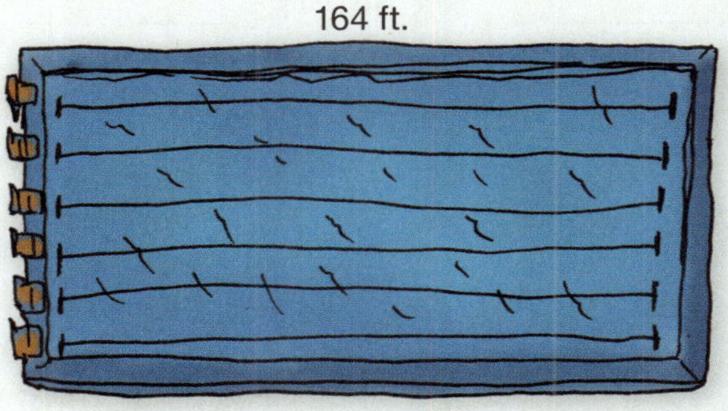

164 × 82 = ______________________

Review

Complete the missing fractions on the number line. Then, write <, >, or = to compare the numbers.

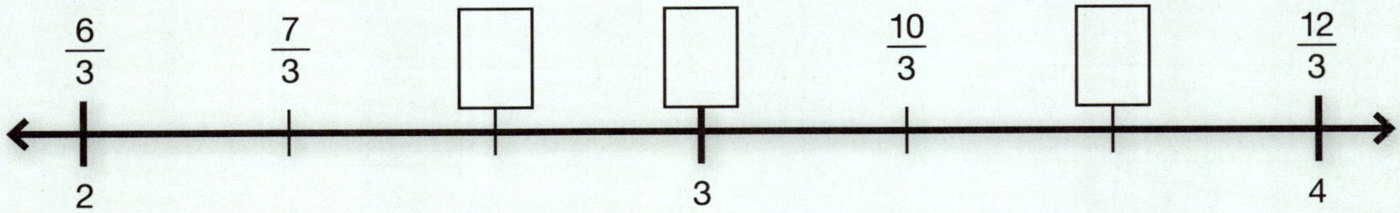

$\frac{7}{3}$ ◯ 2	$\frac{8}{3}$ ◯ 3	$\frac{9}{3}$ ◯ 3
$\frac{10}{3}$ ◯ 3	$\frac{11}{3}$ ◯ 4	$\frac{12}{3}$ ◯ 4

Use mental math to complete.

35 × 2 = ______	80 × 9 = ______	7 × 25 × 2 = ______
35 × 4 = ______	81 × 9 = ______	8 × 2 × 15 = ______
300 × 20 = ______	50 × 6 = ______	17 × 6 × 0 = ______
300 × 200 = ______	49 × 6 = ______	1 × 54 × 1 = ______

Use the printed protractors to measure the angles.

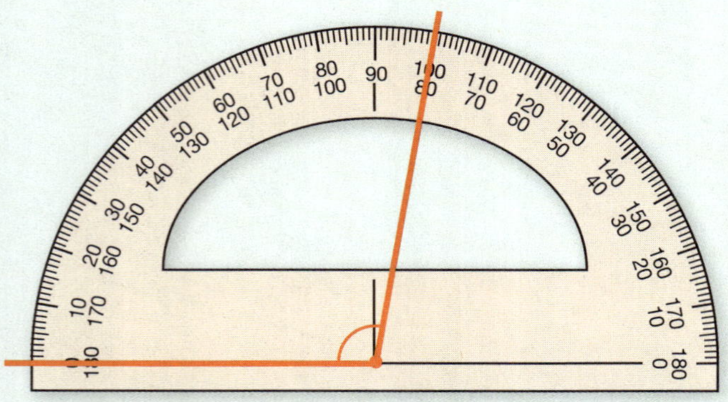

______°

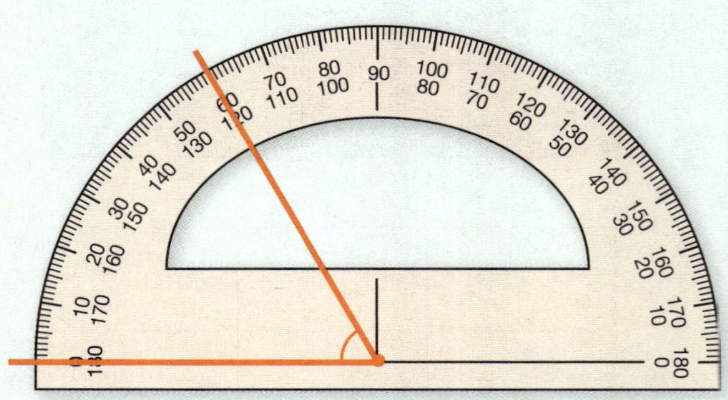

______°

Lesson Activities

A

What is the area of the driveway?

What is the area of the lawn?

What is the total area of the driveway and lawn?

B

The Multiplication Algorithm

The multiplication algorithm breaks multiplication problems into parts. You multiply each part separately. Then, you add the parts to find the final product.

Ex.

$$\begin{array}{r} 42 \\ \times\ 38 \\ \hline 336 \\ +\ 1{,}260 \\ \hline 1{,}596 \end{array}$$

336 ← 42 × 8
1,260 ← 42 × 30
1,596 ← 42 × 38

1. Multiply the top number by the bottom number's ones-place.
2. Write a place-holder zero.
3. Multiply the top number by the bottom number's tens-place.
4. Add.

Ex.

$$\begin{array}{r} {}^{1}\\ 42 \\ \times\ 38 \\ \hline \mathbf{336} \end{array} \rightarrow \begin{array}{r} {}^{1}\\ 42 \\ \times\ 38 \\ \hline 336 \\ \mathbf{0} \end{array} \rightarrow \begin{array}{r} {}^{1}\\ 42 \\ \times\ 38 \\ \hline 336 \\ \mathbf{1{,}26}0 \end{array} \rightarrow \begin{array}{r} {}^{1}\\ 42 \\ \times\ 38 \\ \hline 336 \\ +\ 1{,}260 \\ \hline \mathbf{1{,}596} \end{array}$$

$$\begin{array}{r} 61 \\ \times\ 43 \\ \hline \end{array} \qquad \begin{array}{r} 32 \\ \times\ 74 \\ \hline \end{array} \qquad \begin{array}{r} 45 \\ \times\ 37 \\ \hline \end{array}$$

C

Product Power 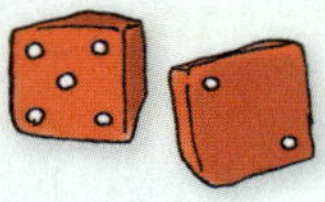 (2-Player Game)

Player 1	×	×	×	+
Player 2	×	×	×	+

Practice

Solve. Write the equations you use in the work space.

It takes 45 apples to make one gallon of apple cider. How many apples does it take to make 36 gallons of cider?

One medium pumpkin weighs about 18 pounds. How much do 75 pumpkins weigh?

One day, the farm stand sells 18 trays of donuts. Each tray holds 32 donuts. How many donuts do they sell?

WORK SPACE

Review

Use the pictures to complete the equivalent fractions.

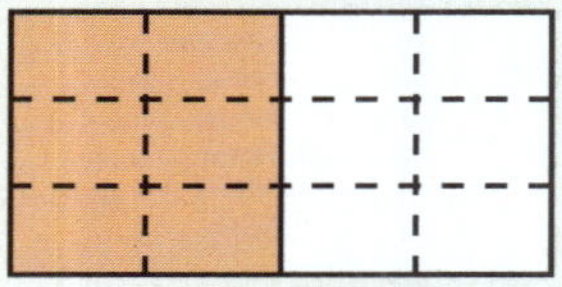

$\frac{1}{2} = \frac{\quad}{12}$

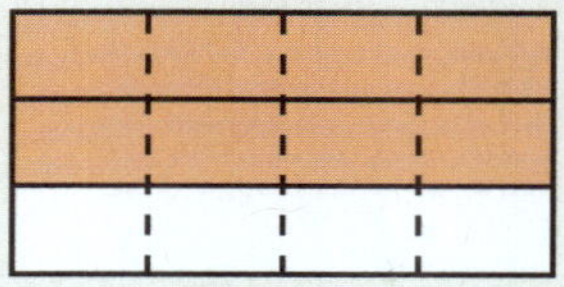

$\frac{2}{3} = \frac{\quad}{12}$

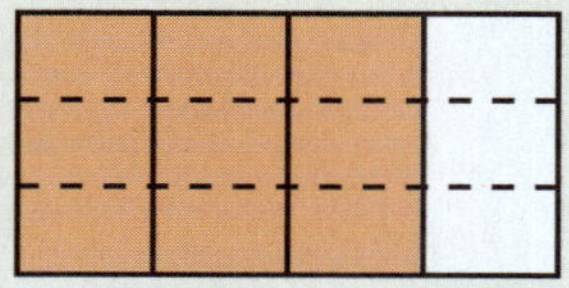

$\frac{3}{4} = \frac{\quad}{12}$

Complete the circles with <, >, or =.

0.325 ◯ 0.76

0.513 ◯ 0.205

1.061 ◯ 2.4

1.061 ◯ 1.036

1.061 ◯ 0.897

0.897 ◯ 2.4

Use long division to solve.

$4\overline{)97}$

$5\overline{)387}$

Use the line plot to answer the questions.

Weight of Apples

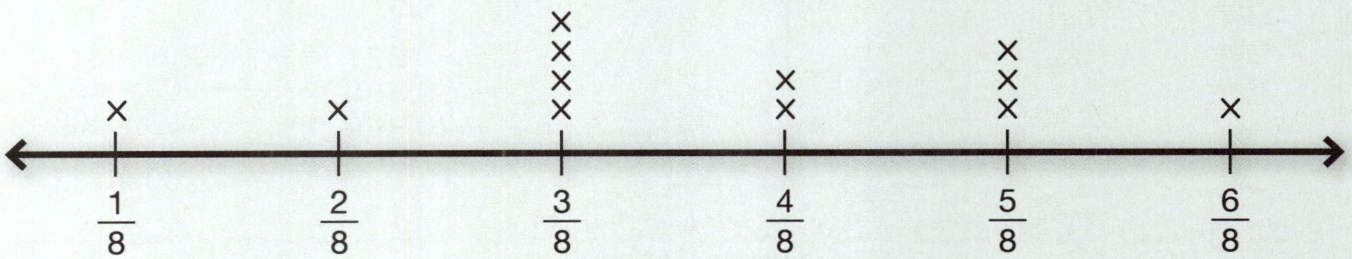

Weight (lb.)

How much does the heaviest apple weigh?

How much does the lightest apple weigh?

How many apples weigh less than $\frac{4}{8}$ lb.?

How many apples weigh more than $\frac{4}{8}$ lb.?

Lesson Activities

A

	10	4
30		
6		

14 × 36 = ____________

```
    1 4
×   3 6
```

B

Extending the Multiplication Algorithm

You can use the multiplication algorithm to multiply numbers with any number of digits.

Write the number with more digits on top. Then, multiply the top number by each digit in the bottom number.

Write as many place-holder zeros as you need to put the digits in the correct place.

Ex.

```
       2
     1 41
    4,172
  ×    36
  -------
   25,032  <---- 4,172 × 6
+ 125,160  <---- 4,172 × 30
  -------
  150,192  <---- 4,172 × 36
```

Ex.

```
       3
       2
      209
    × 143
   ------
      627  <---- 209 × 3
    8,360  <---- 209 × 40
 + 20,900  <---- 209 × 100
   ------
   29,887  <---- 209 × 143
```

```
  8,9 2 6
×     1 4
```

```
  6 1 2
× 5 4 3
```

Pick the Product (2-Player Game)

$$\begin{array}{r} 518 \\ \times\ 386 \\ \hline \end{array}$$

$$\begin{array}{r} 467 \\ \times\ 428 \\ \hline \end{array}$$

$$\begin{array}{r} 1{,}149 \\ \times\ 174 \\ \hline \end{array}$$

$$\begin{array}{r} 739 \\ \times\ 271 \\ \hline \end{array}$$

$$\begin{array}{r} 631 \\ \times\ 316 \\ \hline \end{array}$$

$$\begin{array}{r} 3{,}078 \\ \times\ 65 \\ \hline \end{array}$$

Practice

Solve. Write the equations you use.

The food pantry gives away 3,475 kg of food each day. It is open 16 days per month. How much food does it give away each month?

The recycling center processes 116 tons of recyclables each day. It is open 345 days per year. How many tons of recyclables does it process each year?

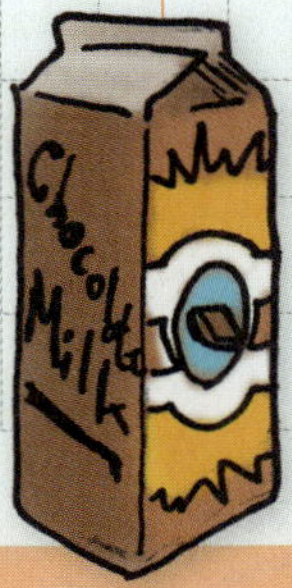

Review

Round each number to the underlined place.

0.549 ≈ ____________________

0.814 ≈ ____________________

1.493 ≈ ____________________

3.275 ≈ ____________________

Circle the greatest number in each group.

0.04	0.62
0.009	0.2
0.1	0.602

2.5	4.47
3.71	4.474
1.894	4.7

Find the least common multiple for each pair of numbers.

LCM of 4 and 3: ____________________

LCM of 4 and 6: ____________________

Use the printed rulers to measure the lines. Write each length as a decimal.

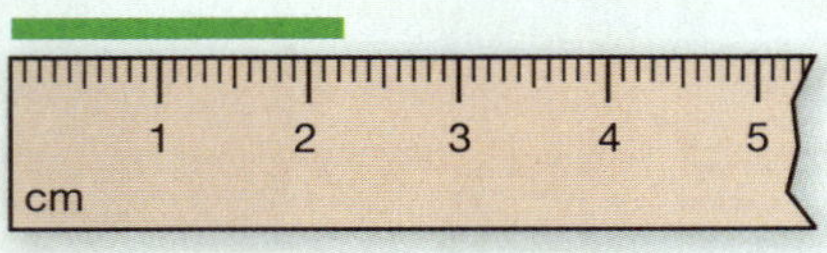

____________ cm

____________ cm

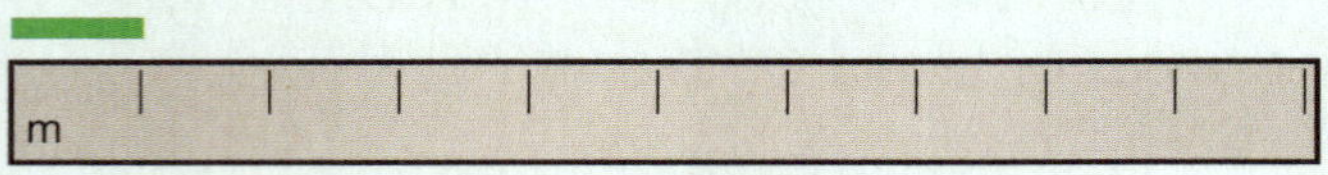

0.1 m

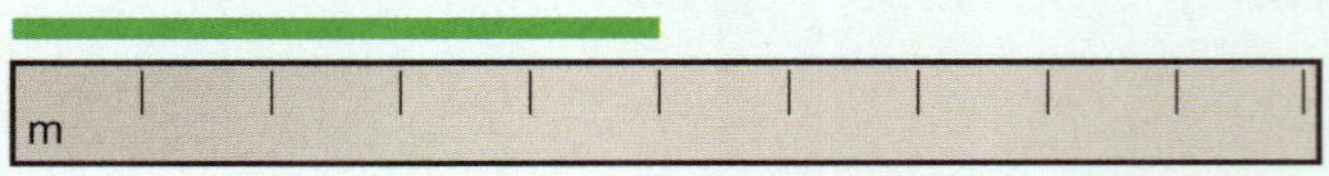

____________ m

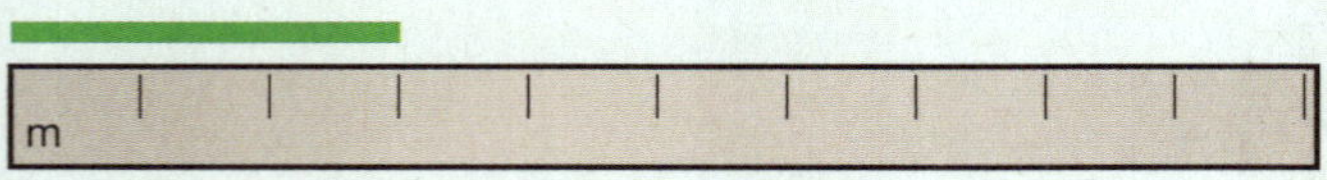

____________ m

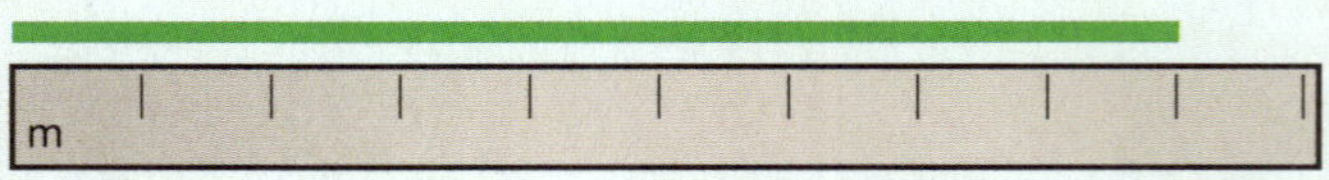

____________ m

Unit Wrap-Up

Find the least common multiple for each pair of numbers.

LCM of 9 and 12: ____________

LCM of 5 and 8: ____________

Use mental math to complete.

9 × 6 × 2 = ____________

8 × 25 × 2 = ____________

45 × 2 = ____________

45 × 4 = ____________

80 × 6 = ____________

81 × 6 = ____________

200 × 70 = ____________

8,000 × 30 = ____________

9,185 × 10 = ____________

1,000 × 486 = ____________

17 × 6 × 0 = ____________

1 × 14 × 1 = ____________

Complete.

$$\begin{array}{r} 36 \\ \times\ 20 \\ \hline \end{array} \qquad \begin{array}{r} 519 \\ \times\ 400 \\ \hline \end{array} \qquad \begin{array}{r} 2,871 \\ \times\ 3,000 \\ \hline \end{array}$$

Use both the box method and the multiplication algorithm to find the product of 137 and 42.

137 × 42 = ____________

$$\begin{array}{r} 137 \\ \times\ 42 \\ \hline \end{array}$$

Unit Wrap-Up

Use the brochure to answer the questions. Write your equations in the work space.

WORK SPACE

What is the area of each stall?

There are 32 horses on the farm. How many pounds of hay do they eat each day?

How much hay does each horse eat in 1 year? (There are 365 days in 1 year.)

What is the area of the outdoor exercise arena?

How much does it cost to board a horse at Meadowlark Farm for 1 year?

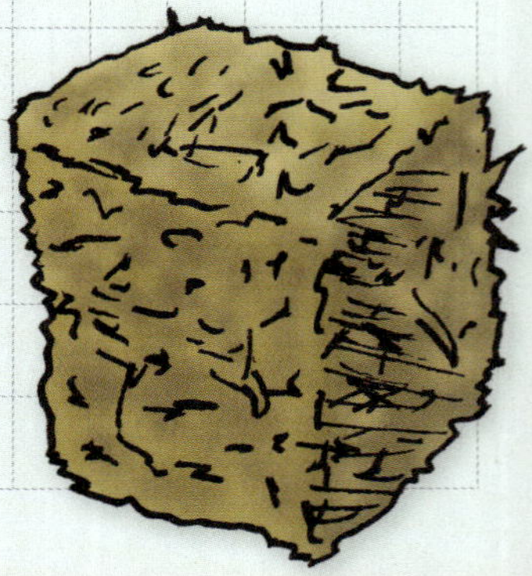

Lesson Activities

A

Volume

The volume of a three-dimensional solid is the amount of space the solid takes up.

We measure volume with cubic units. A cube that is 1 centimeter on each side has a volume of 1 cubic centimeter.

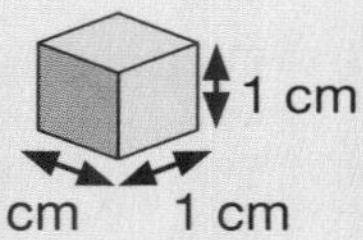

Ex. What is the volume of this solid?

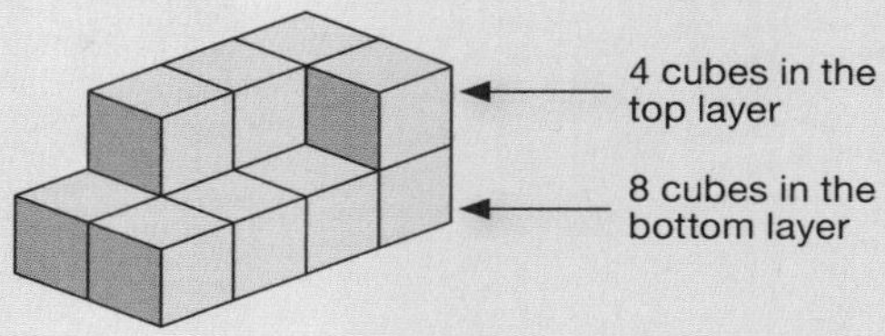

This solid is made from 12 cubes, so it has a volume of 12 cubic cm.

Volume: ________ cubic cm

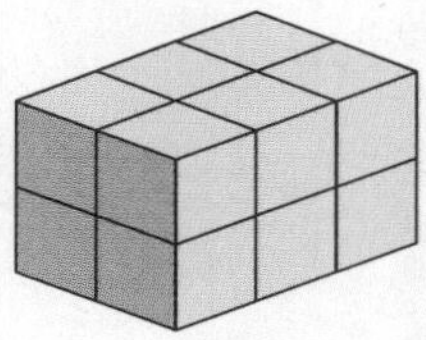

Volume: ________ cubic cm

Volume: ________ cubic cm

B

Rectangular Prisms

A rectangular prism is a three-dimensional shape with 6 rectangular faces.

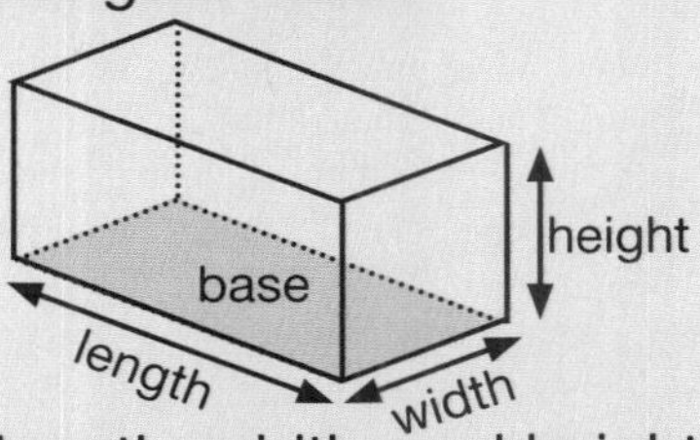

The length, width, and height of the prism are called its dimensions. The bottom face is called the base of the prism.

Ex. What is the volume of this solid?

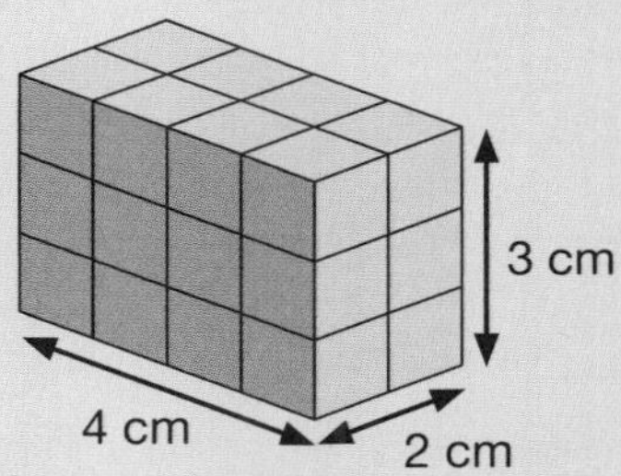

Each layer has 8 cubes. There are 3 layers, so we multiply 8 times 3 to find the total number of cubes.

$8 \times 3 =$ **24 cubic cm**

Volume: ________ cubic cm

Volume: ________ cubic cm

Volume: ________ cubic cm

Practice

**Find the volume of each solid.
(Each cube has a volume of 1 cubic cm.)**

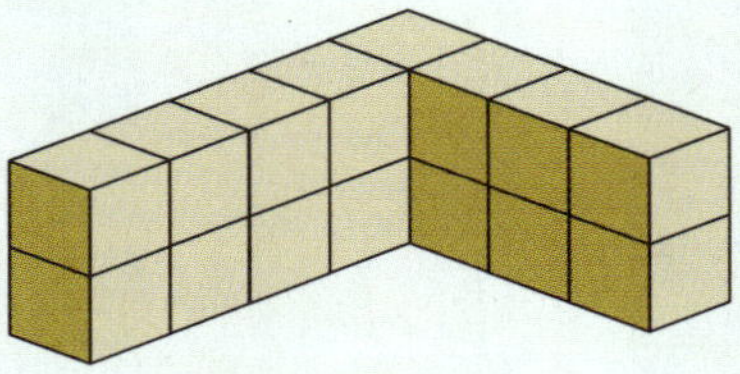

Volume: ________ cubic cm

Volume: ________ cubic cm

Volume: ________ cubic cm

Label the dimensions of each rectangular prism. Then, find the volume.

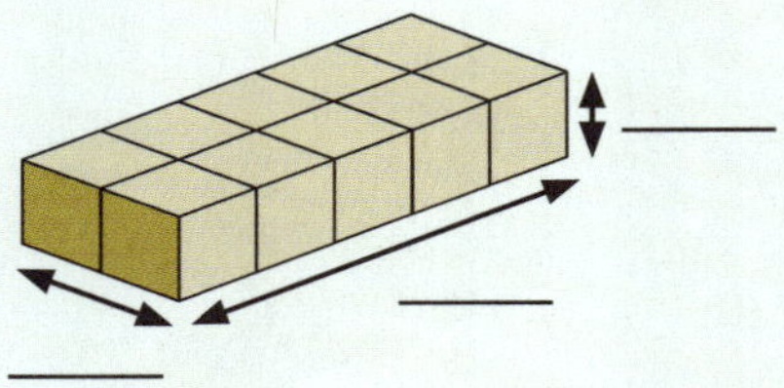

Volume: ________ cubic cm

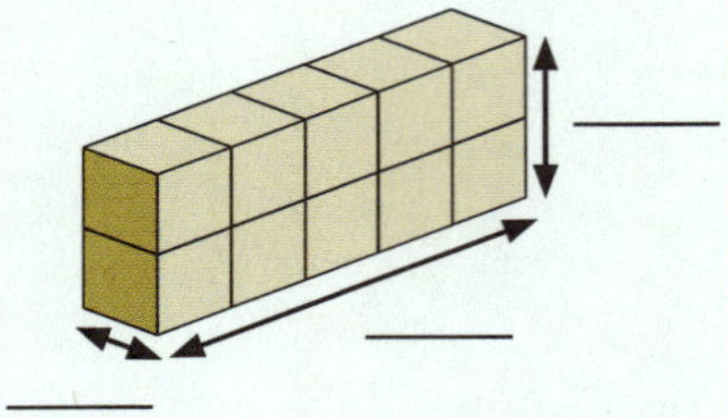

Volume: ________ cubic cm

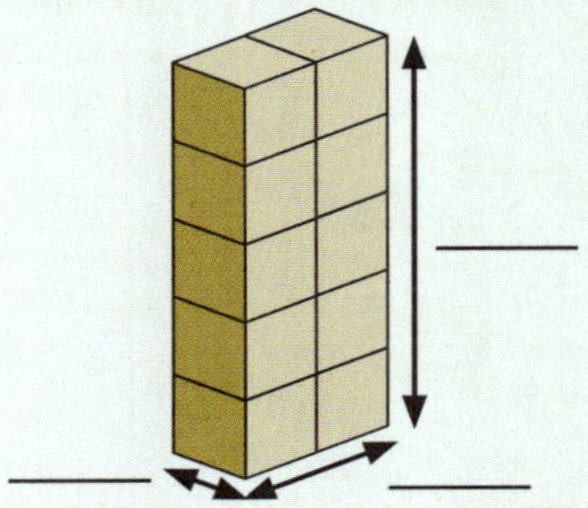

Volume: ________ cubic cm

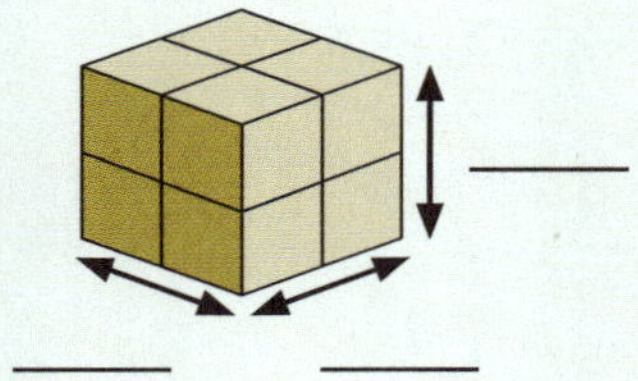

Volume: ________ cubic cm

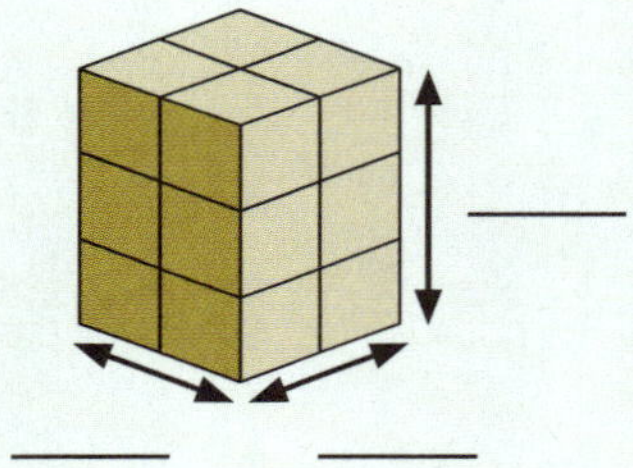

Volume: ________ cubic cm

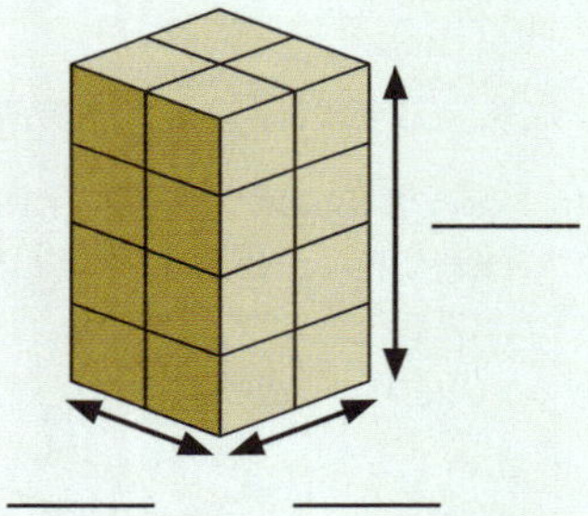

Volume: ________ cubic cm

Solve. Write the equations you use.

Chloe builds a rectangular prism.
She uses 6 cubes for each layer, and she builds 10 layers. How many cubes are in the rectangular prism?

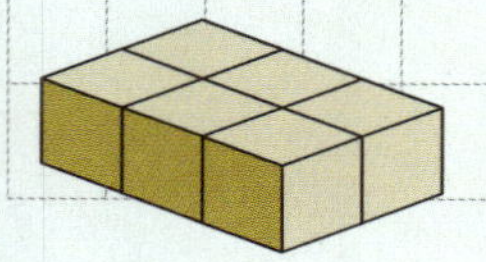

Dmitri builds a rectangular prism.
He uses 9 cubes for each layer, and he uses 45 cubes in all.
How many layers does he build?

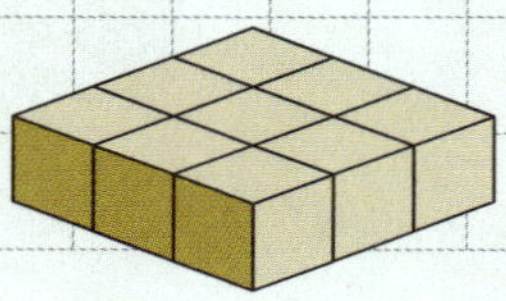

Review

Write each decimal as a fraction or mixed number.

2.88 = ______________

2.8 = ______________

2.088 = ______________

Find the area of each shape.

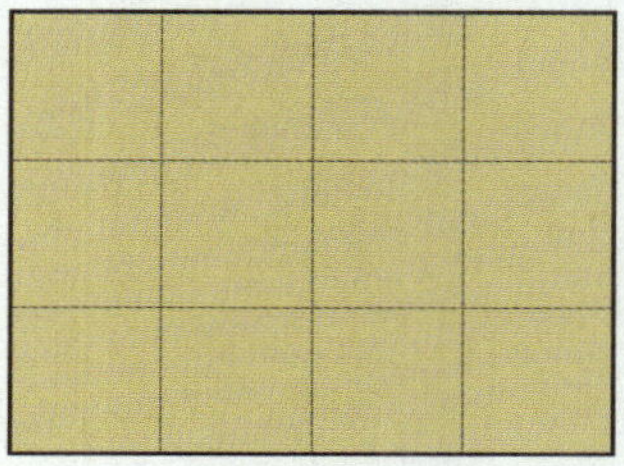

Area: ______________ sq. cm

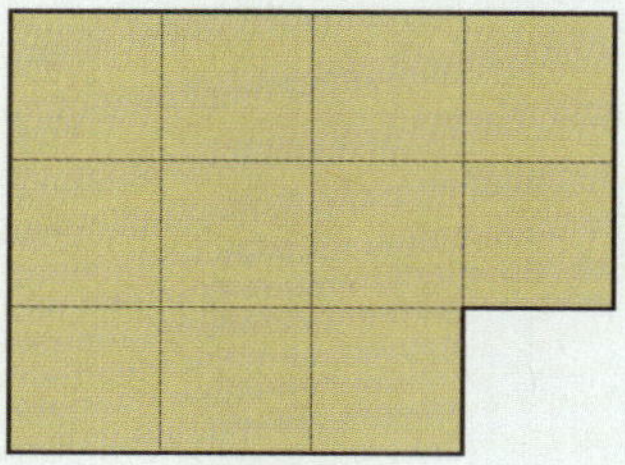

Area: ______________ sq. cm

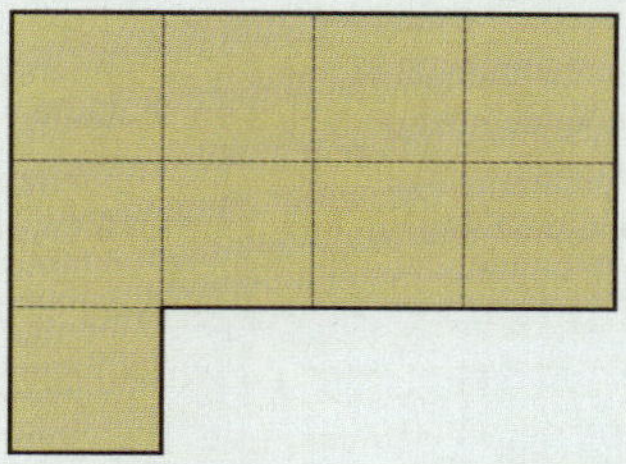

Area: ______________ sq. cm

Complete. Write the equations you use.

4 days = ______________ hr.

6 c. 4 fl. oz. = ________ fl. oz.

20 in. = ______ ft. ______ in.

Find the product.

$$\begin{array}{r} 821 \\ \times\ 345 \\ \hline \end{array}$$

Solve. Write the equations you use.

Teams of volunteers helped plant trees at the nature center. Find the average number of trees each team planted.

Lesson Activities

A

Volume: ________ cubic cm

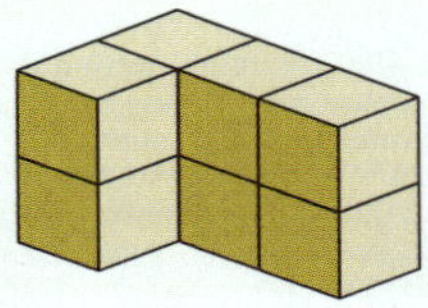

Volume: ________ cubic cm

Volume: ________ cubic cm

B

Volume of a Rectangular Prism

To find the volume of a rectangular prism, we multiply its length times its width times its height.

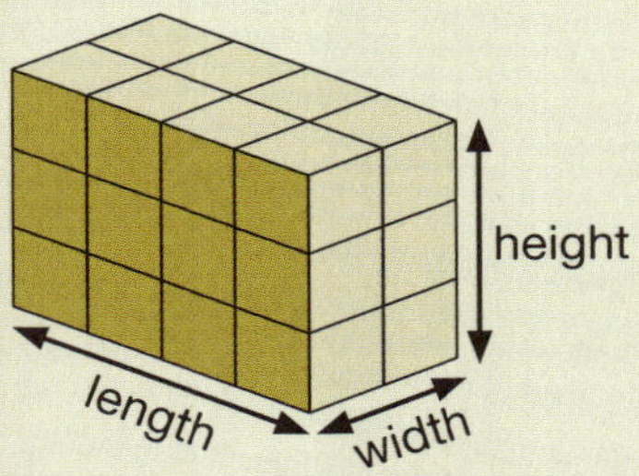

length × width × height = volume

Ex. What is the volume of a 4 cm by 2 cm by 3 cm rectangular prism?

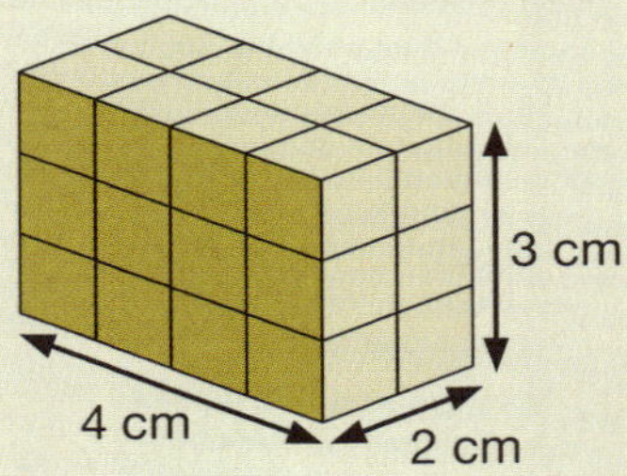

$4 \times 2 \times 3 =$ **24 cubic cm**

Volume: ________ cubic cm

Volume: ________ cubic cm

Volume: ________ cubic cm

C

Build the Box (2-Player Game)

Dimensions (cm)	Volume (cubic cm)
_____ × _____ × _____	
_____ × _____ × _____	
_____ × _____ × _____	
Player 1 Total:	

Dimensions (cm)	Volume (cubic cm)
_____ × _____ × _____	
_____ × _____ × _____	
_____ × _____ × _____	
Player 2 Total:	

Practice

Find the volume of each solid. (All dimensions are in cm.)

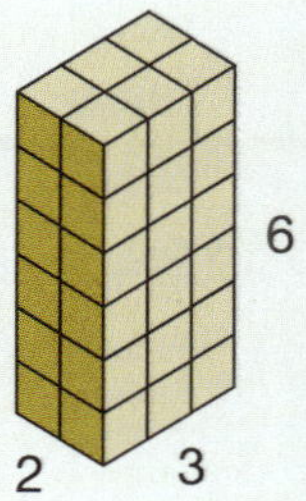

Volume: ________ cubic cm

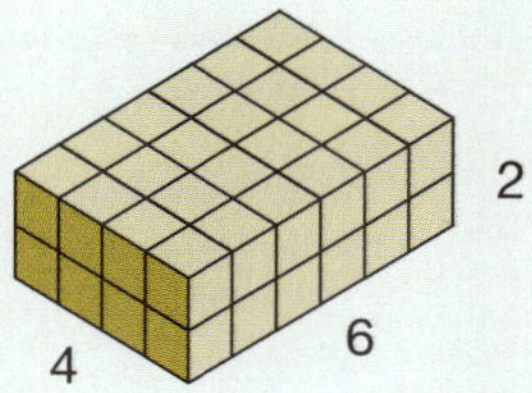

Volume: ________ cubic cm

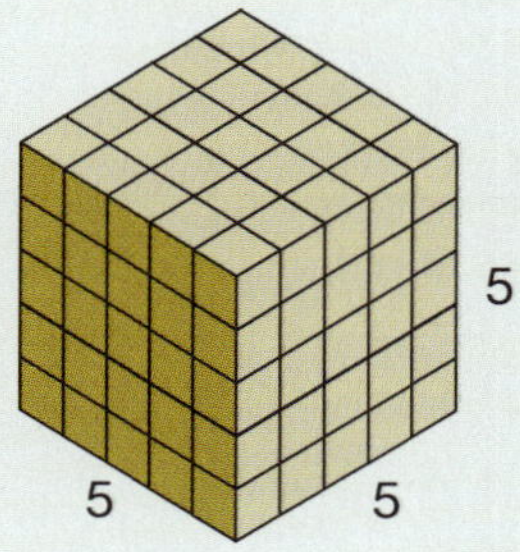

Volume: ________ cubic cm

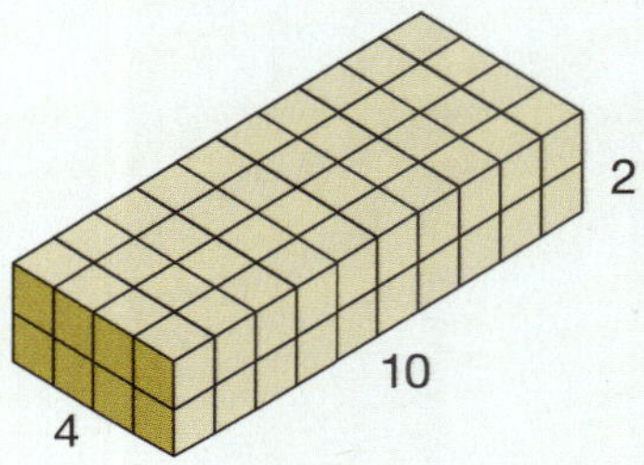

Volume: ________ cubic cm

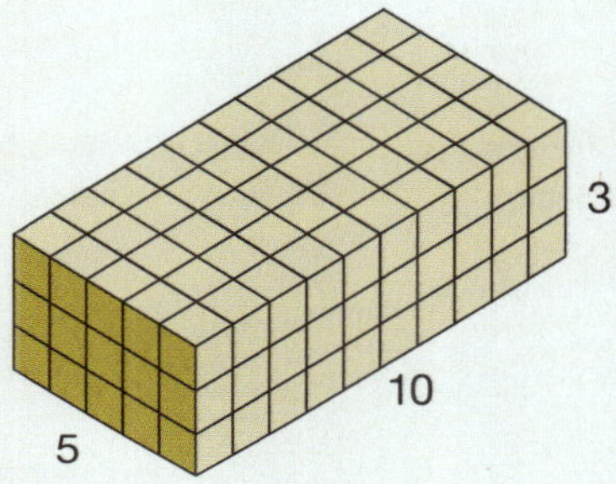

Volume: ________ cubic cm

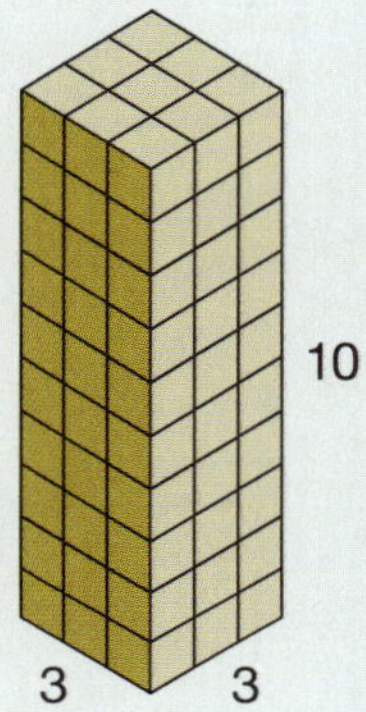

Volume: ________ cubic cm

Solve. Write the equations you use.

Etta uses cubes to build 4 rectangular prisms. Each rectangular prism is 2 × 5 × 3. How many cubes does she use in all?

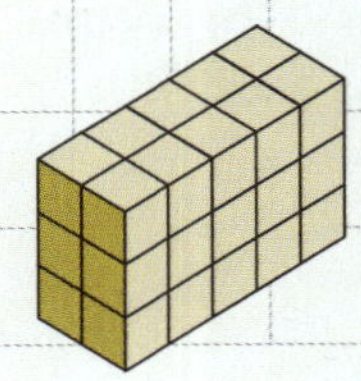

Holden uses cubes to build a 3 × 5 × 4 rectangular prism. Then, he removes 4 cubes from the top layer. How many cubes remain in his construction?

Review

Complete the missing numerator in each fraction. Use the number line to help.

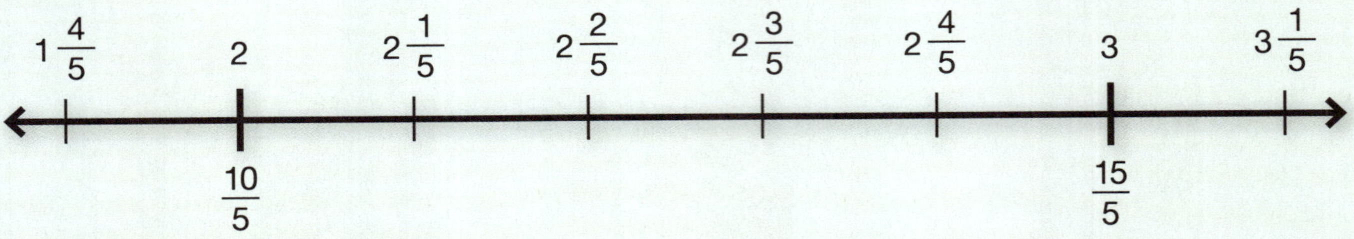

Example: $2\frac{4}{5} = \frac{14}{5}$ (+, ×)

$2\frac{2}{5} = \frac{\_\_}{5}$

$2\frac{3}{5} = \frac{\_\_}{5}$

$3 = \frac{\_\_}{5}$

$3\frac{1}{5} = \frac{\_\_}{5}$

$1\frac{4}{5} = \frac{\_\_}{5}$

Find the quotient.

9) 6 4 2

Find the missing side lengths.

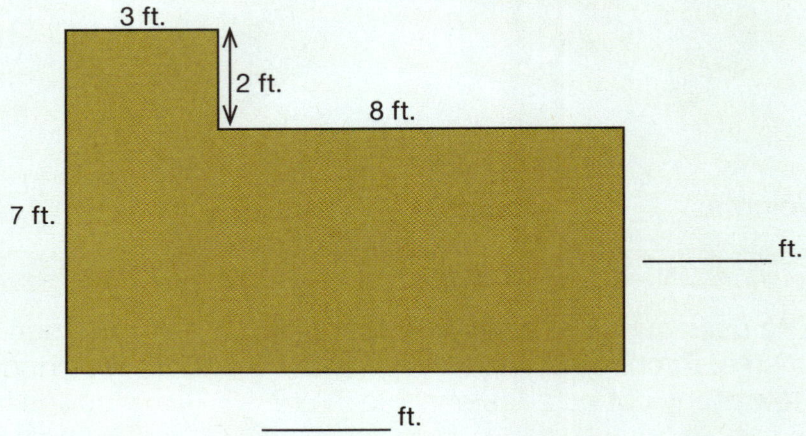

Circle the equation that you could use to find the answer to the word problem. (You do not have to solve.)

Mihika has $34. Then, she works for 3 hours and earns $15 per hour. How much money does she have now?

- 34 + (3 × 15)
- (34 + 3) × 15

Asher has $30. He buys 2 sandwiches for $12 each. How much money does he have now?

- (30 – 2) × 12
- 30 – (2 × 12)

Silas buys 3 drinks for $4 each and 2 tubs of popcorn for $6 each. How much does he spend in all?

- (3 × 4) + (2 × 6)
- 3 × (4 + 2) × 6

Phoebe buys 4 packs of candy. There are 6 pieces of candy in each pack. She eats 2 pieces. How many pieces are left?

- 4 × (6 – 2)
- (4 × 6) – 2

Lesson Activities

A

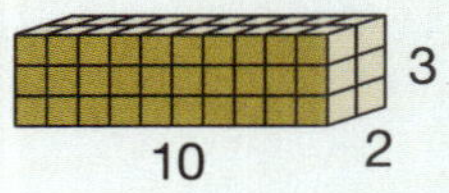

Volume: ________ cubic cm

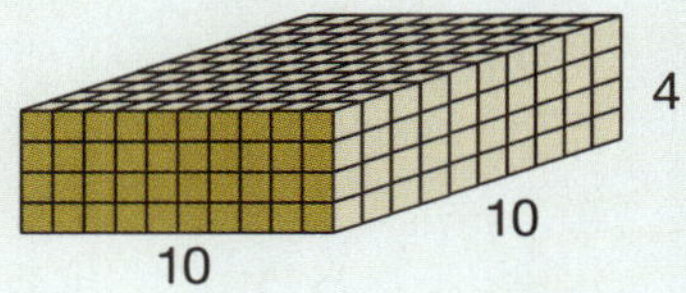

Volume: ________ cubic cm

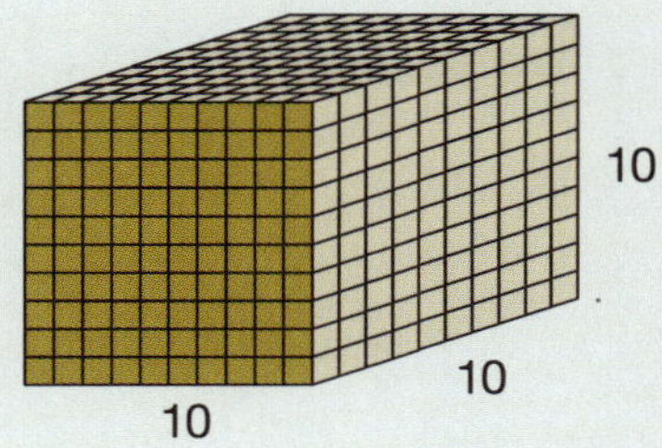

Volume: ________ cubic cm

B

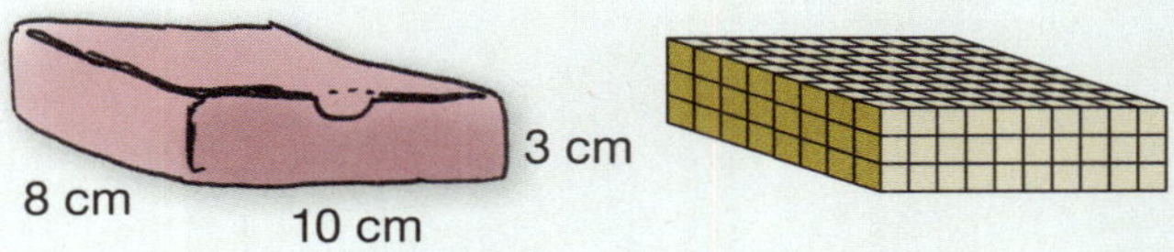

Volume: ____________________ cubic cm

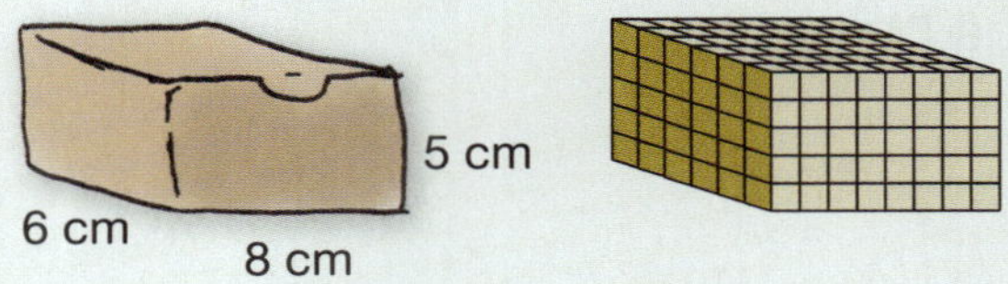

Volume: ____________________ cubic cm

C

Box	Dimensions (cm)	Volume (cubic cm)

WORK SPACE

Practice

Find the volume of each solid. (All dimensions are in cm.)

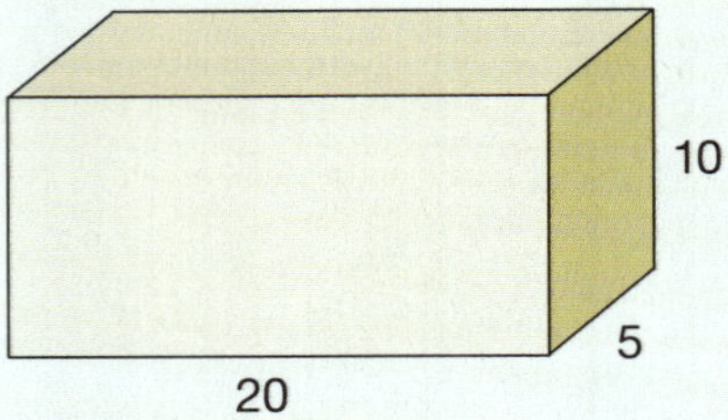

Volume: ________ cubic cm

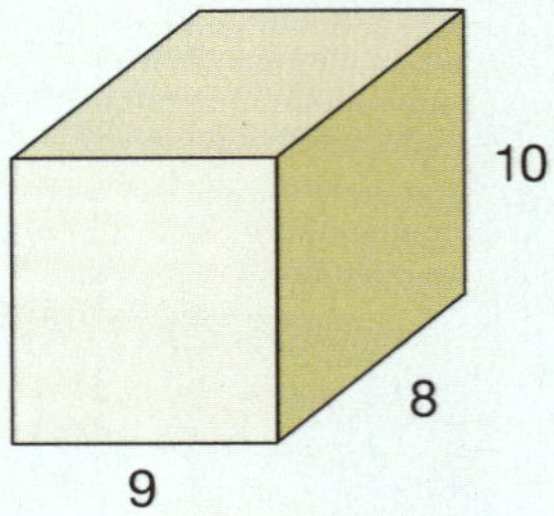

Volume: ________ cubic cm

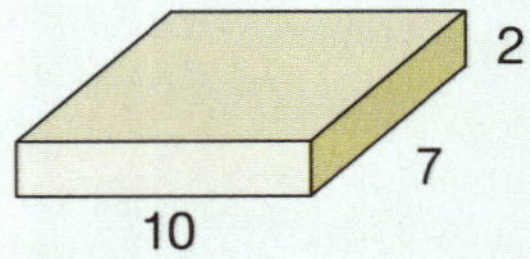

Volume: ________ cubic cm

Solve. Write the equations you use.

Willow buys a rectangular storage basket that is 25 cm long, 10 cm wide, and 20 cm high. What is the volume of the storage basket?

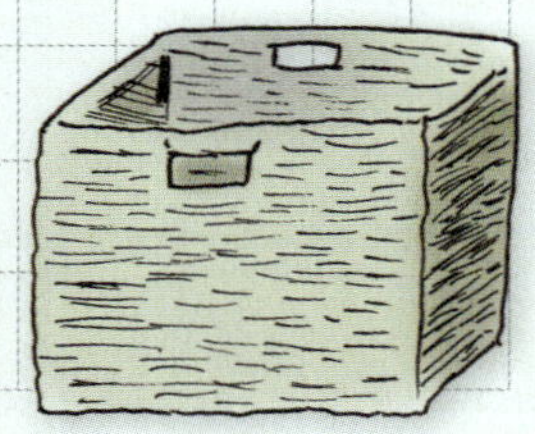

The cereal box is 20 cm long, 4 cm wide, and 30 cm high. What is its volume?

Aven wants to fill this planter with dirt. How many cubic centimeters of dirt does he need?

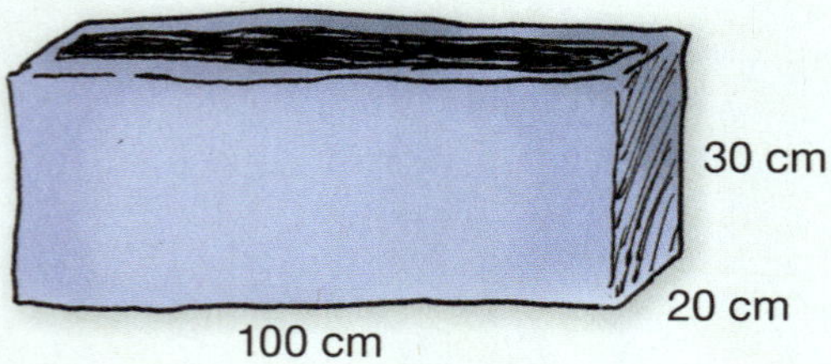

★ This planter is 10 cm wide and 10 cm long. It has a volume of 800 cubic cm. What is its height?

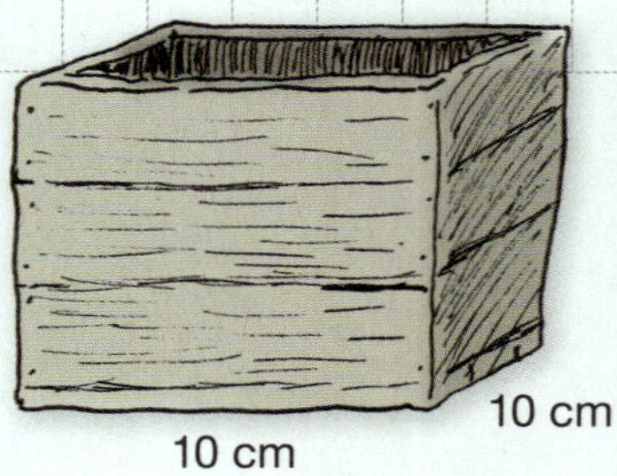

Review

Use mental math to complete.

4 × 8 × 2 = ______	205 × 2 = ______	70 × 7 = ______
6 × 8 × 5 = ______	205 × 4 = ______	71 × 7 = ______
900 × 60 = ______	420 ÷ 7 = ______	200 ÷ 4 = ______
9,000 × 60 = ______	4,200 ÷ 7 = ______	2,000 ÷ 4 = ______

Find the product.

$$\begin{array}{r} 804 \\ \times\ 136 \\ \hline \end{array}$$

Find the least common multiple for each pair of numbers.

LCM of 5 and 6: ______

LCM of 5 and 15: ______

Solve. Write the equations you use.

The bucket holds 20 liters of water. It holds 4 times as many liters of water as the watering can. How many liters of water does the watering can hold?

How many milliliters of water does the watering can hold? (1 liter equals 1,000 milliliters.)

Lesson Activities

A

How to Find a Missing Dimension

If you know the volume of a rectangular prism and two of its dimensions, you can use the volume formula to find the missing dimension.

1. Use the volume formula to write an equation. Write a blank for the missing dimension.
2. Multiply the two dimensions you know.
3. Divide the volume by the product of the two dimensions you know.

Ex. The box's volume is 30 cubic cm. What is its height?

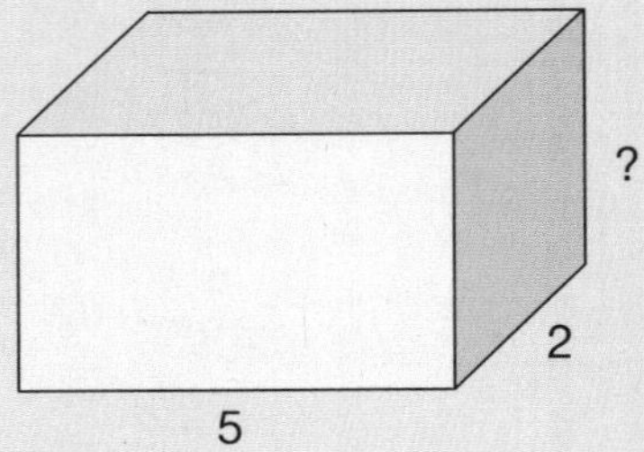

length × width × height = volume

5 × 2 × ____ = 30

10 × ____ = 30

30 ÷ 10 = **3 cm**

The box's volume is 70 cubic cm. What is its length?

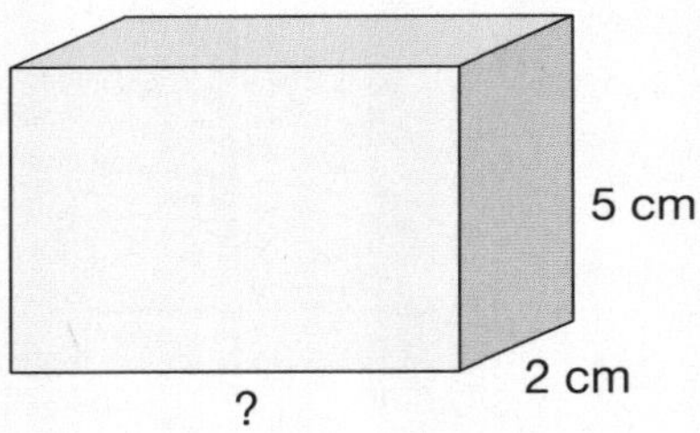

The box's volume is 56 cubic cm. What is its width?

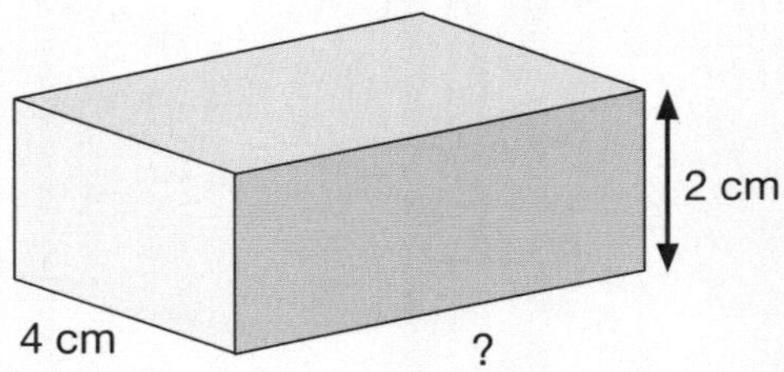

B

Disappearing Dimensions (2-Player Game)

length: ____ cm width: 3 cm height: 2 cm vol.: 36 cu. cm	length: 3 cm width: 2 cm height: ____ cm vol.: 54 cu. cm	length: ____ cm width: 5 cm height: 4 cm vol.: 100 cu. cm	length: 2 cm width: ____ cm height: 6 cm vol.: 24 cu. cm
length: 2 cm width: 2 cm height: ____ cm vol.: 40 cu. cm	length: ____ cm width: 4 cm height: 3 cm vol.: 48 cu. cm	length: 8 cm width: ____ cm height: 1 cm vol.: 72 cu. cm	length: 6 cm width: 5 cm height: ____ cm vol.: 60 cu. cm

Practice

Find the missing dimension for each solid. All measurements are in centimeters.

Volume: 30 cu. cm

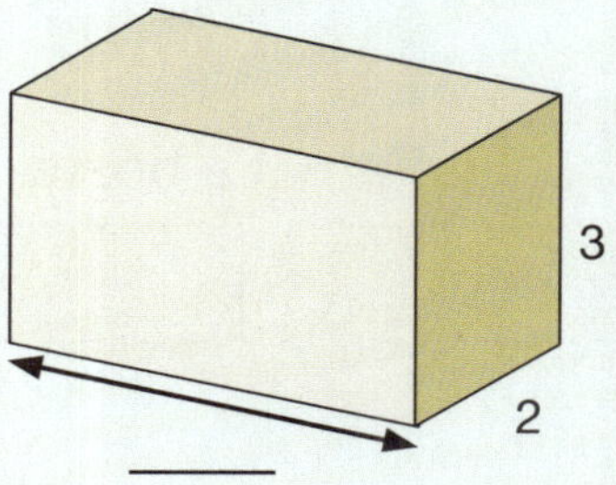

Volume: 30 cu. cm

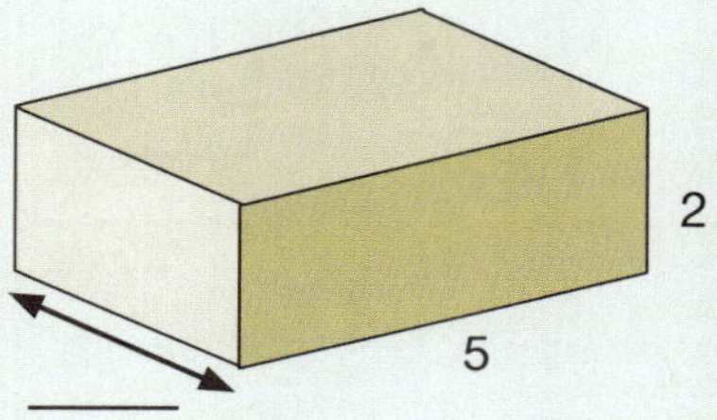

Volume: 30 cu. cm

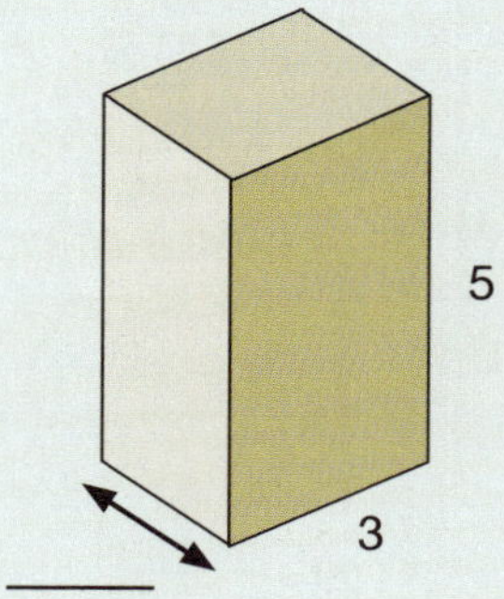

Volume: 48 cu. cm

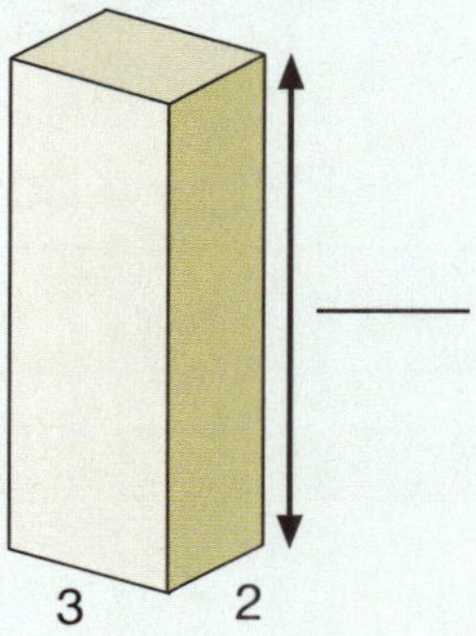

Volume: 48 cu. cm

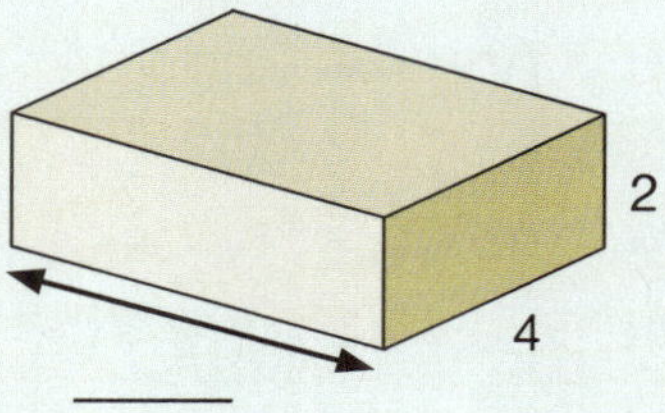

Volume: 48 cu. cm

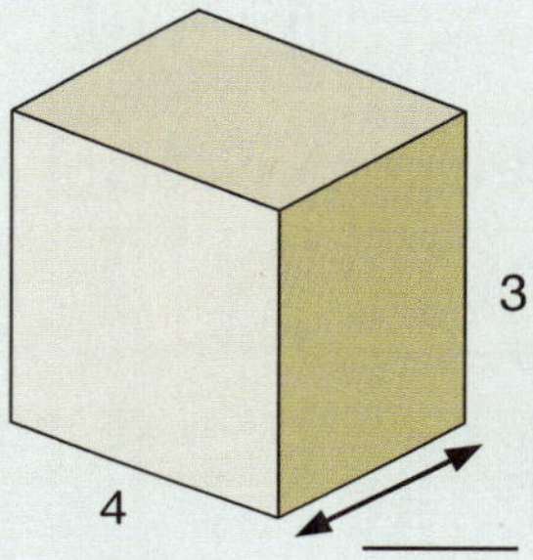

Volume: 60 cu. cm

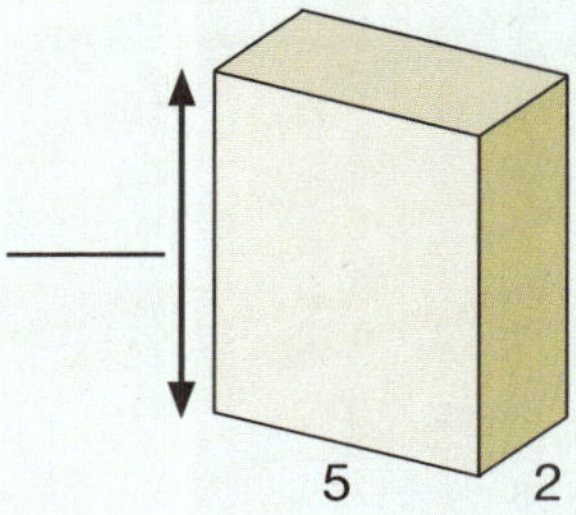

Volume: 70 cu. cm

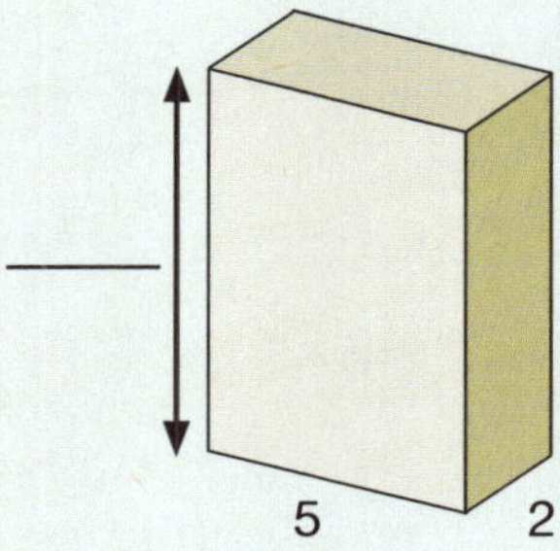

Volume: 80 cu. cm

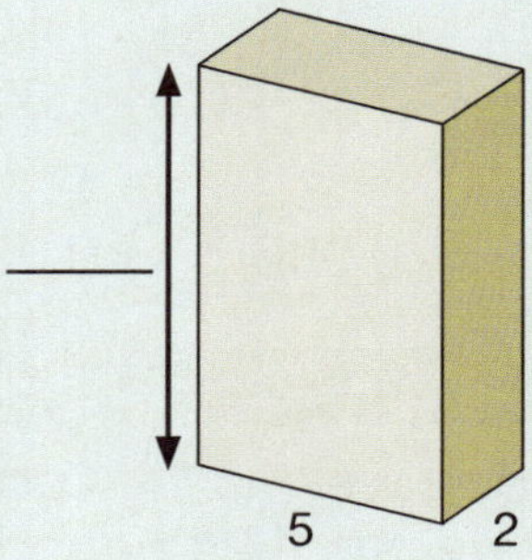

Use the clues to find the dimensions for each solid.

I have a volume of 36 cu. cm.
My length is 3 cm.
My length and width are the same.

Length: ______________________ cm

Width: ______________________ cm

Height: ______________________ cm

★ I have a volume of 40 cu. cm.
My length is 5 cm.
My height is twice my width.

Length: ______________________ cm

Width: ______________________ cm

Height: ______________________ cm

Review

Circle the more sensible measurement for each item.

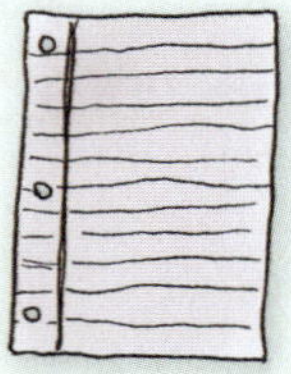

Width of a piece of paper

8 in. | 8 sq. in.

Height of a poster

3 ft. | 3 sq. ft.

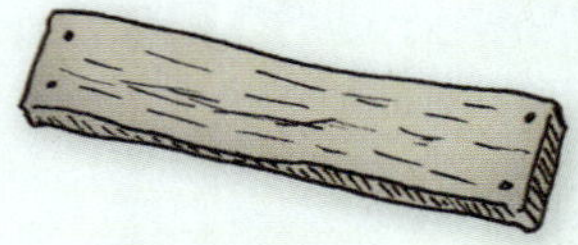

Length of a board

4 ft. | 4 sq. ft.

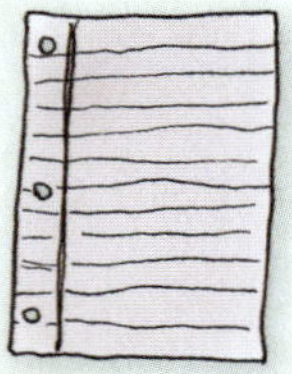

Area of a piece of paper

88 in. | 88 sq. in.

Area of a poster

6 ft. | 6 sq. ft.

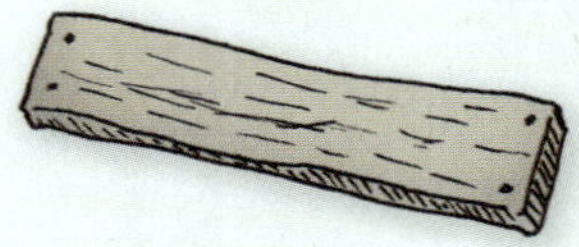

Area of a board

8 ft. | 8 sq. ft.

Complete the circles with <, >, or =.

4.89 ◯ 4.90

1.62 ◯ 1.621

2.4 ◯ 2.39

0.006 ◯ 0.03

Find the product.

$$\begin{array}{r} 781 \\ \times\ 60 \\ \hline \end{array} \qquad \begin{array}{r} 429 \\ \times\ 800 \\ \hline \end{array}$$

Solve. Write the equations you use.

Lilian's dog weighs 14.4 pounds.
Her cat weighs 5.94 pounds.
How much more does her dog weigh than her cat?

Lilian buys 2 cases of cat food.
Each case holds 12 cans.
Each can holds 3 oz. of cat food.
What is the total weight of the cat food?

Lesson Activities

A

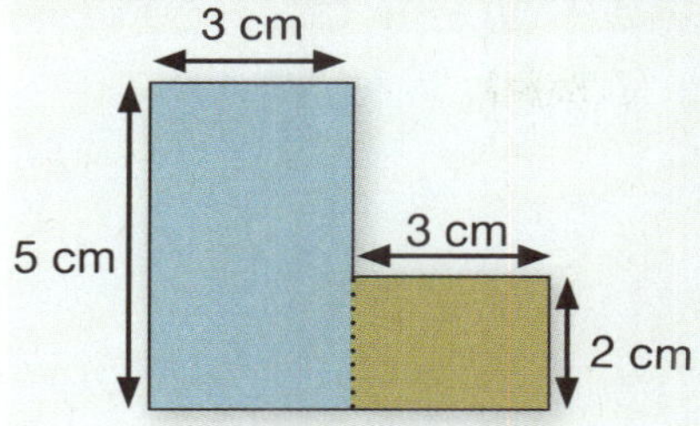

Area: ____________________

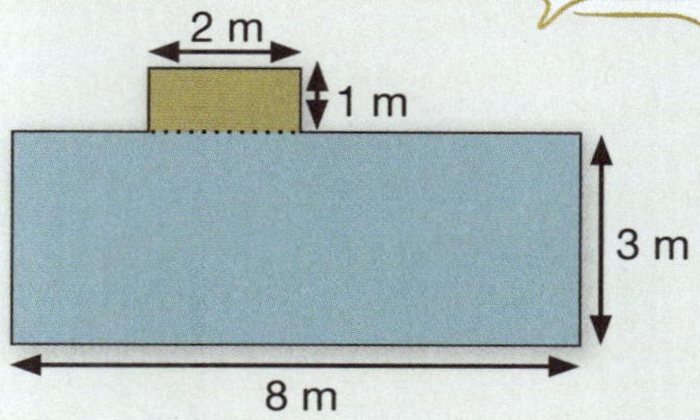

Area: ____________________

B

Cubic Meters

A cube that is 1 meter on each side has a volume of 1 cubic meter.

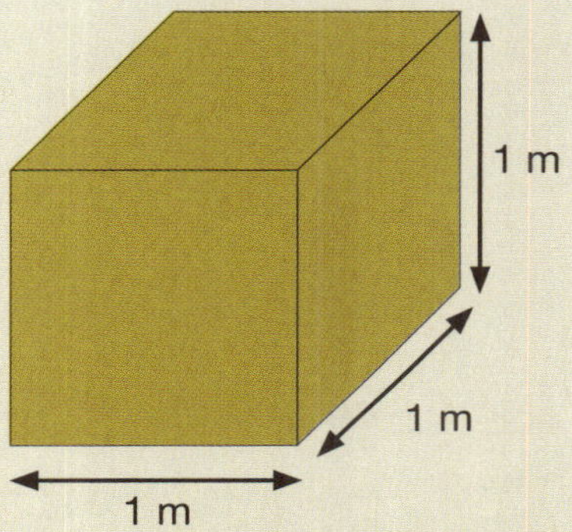

1 million cubic centimeters can fit inside 1 cubic meter!

Ex. What is the total volume of the pool?

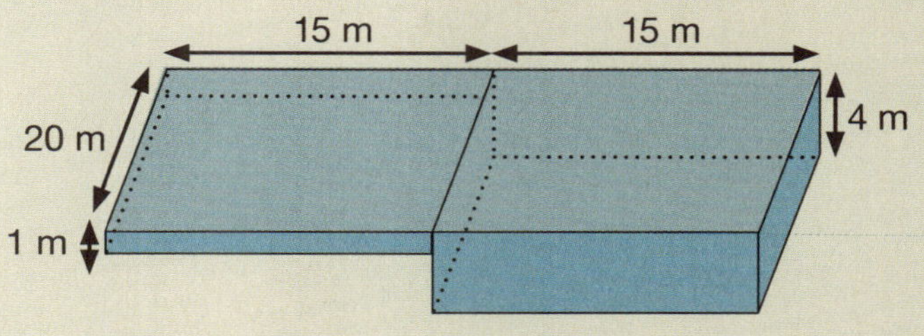

Volume of the shallow end:
$20 \times 15 \times 1 =$ **300 cu. m**

Volume of the deep end:
$20 \times 15 \times 4 =$ **1,200 cu. m**

Volume of the whole pool:
$300 + 1{,}200 =$ **1,500 cu. m**

The pool is 2 m deep. What is its volume?

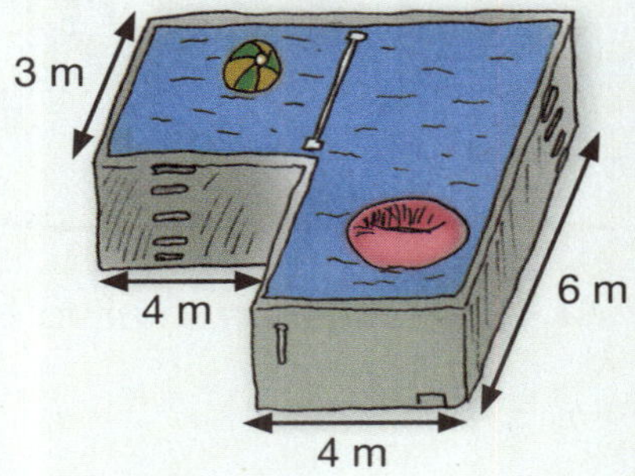

Mallory glued two pieces of wood together to make a step stool.
What is the volume of the step stool?

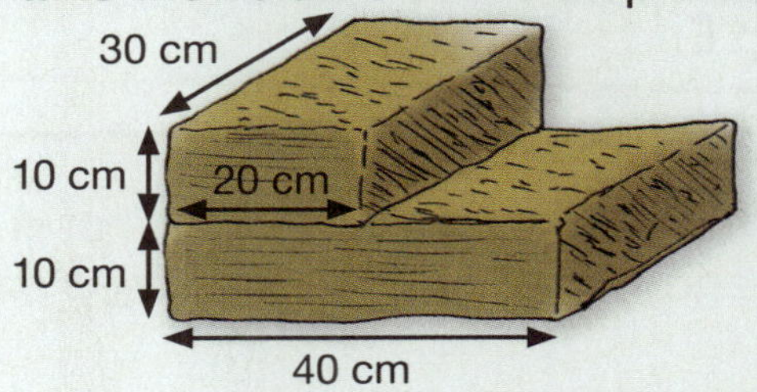

Practice

Find the total volume of each solid. Write the equations you use. All measurements are in meters.

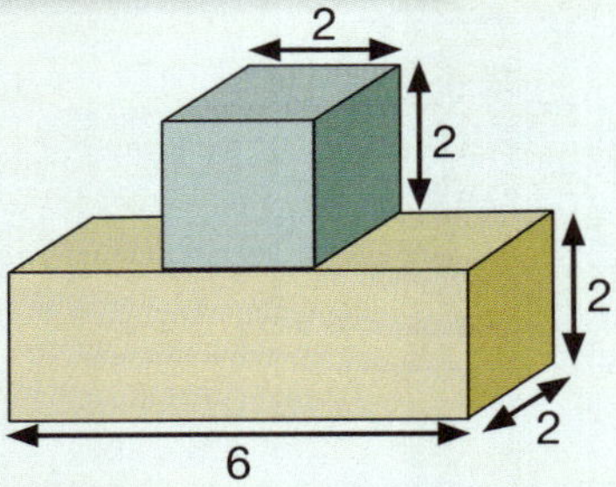

Volume: ________________ cu. m

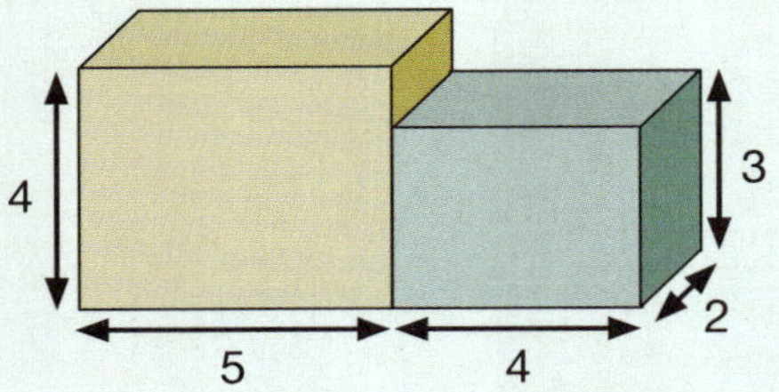

Volume: ________________ cu. m

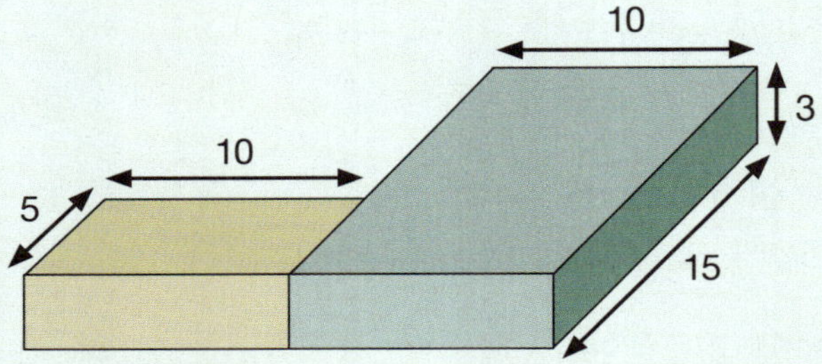

Volume: ________________ cu. m

Choose dimensions for the shallow end and deep end of a pool. Then, use your dimensions to answer the questions.

	Length (m)	Width (m)	Depth (m)
Shallow End			
Deep End			

What is the volume of the shallow end?

What is the volume of the deep end?

What is the total volume of the pool?

Review

Find the sum or difference.

$\frac{3}{10} + \frac{4}{10} = \frac{7}{10}$

$\frac{2}{6} + \frac{3}{6} =$ ______

$\frac{1}{4} + \frac{2}{4} =$ ______

$\frac{3}{5} - \frac{1}{5} = \frac{2}{5}$

$\frac{7}{8} - \frac{2}{8} =$ ______

$\frac{3}{3} - \frac{1}{3} =$ ______

Use the box method to find the product.

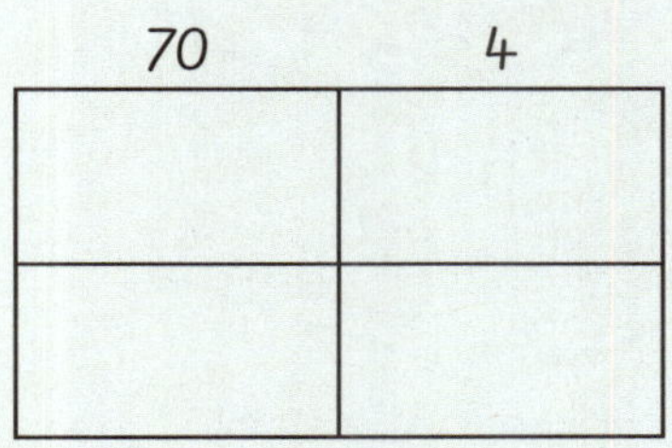

74 × 31 = ______

Round to the underlined digit.

$\underline{2}54{,}018 \approx$ ______

$2\underline{5}4{,}018 \approx$ ______

$25\underline{4}{,}018 \approx$ ______

$\underline{3}.705 \approx$ ______

$3.\underline{7}05 \approx$ ______

$3.7\underline{0}5 \approx$ ______

Colton counted how many candies were in each pack.
Use his data to create a line plot.

Number of Candies

16	15
17	16
15	14
16	18
14	13
15	16
18	15

Number of Candies in Each Pack

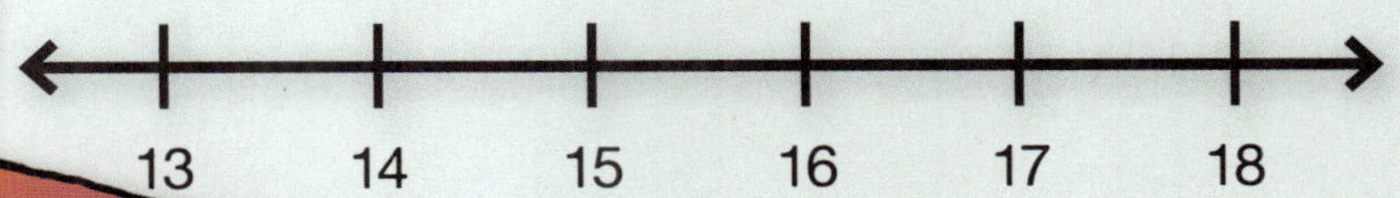

Lesson Activities

A

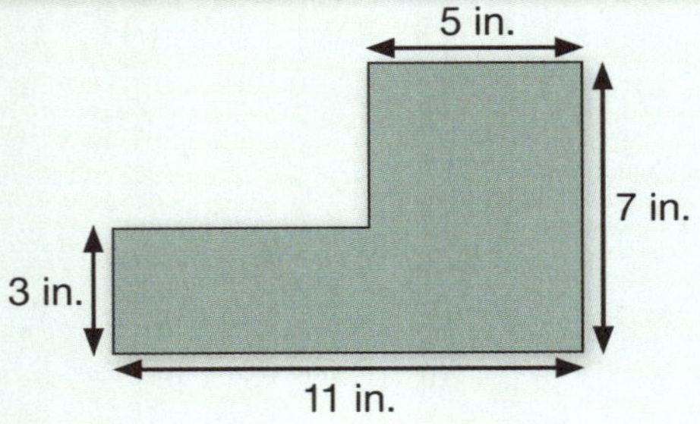

Area: ______________________

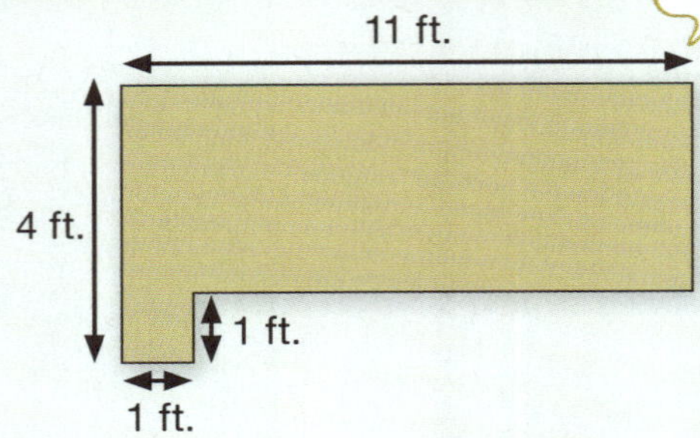

Area: ______________________

B

Cubic Inches, Feet and Yards

A cube that is 1 inch on each side has a volume of 1 cubic inch.

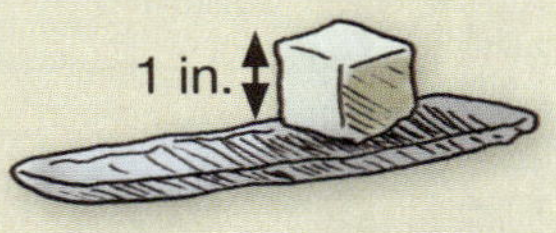

A cube that is 1 foot on each side has a volume of 1 cubic foot.

A cube that is 1 yard on each side has a volume of 1 cubic yard.

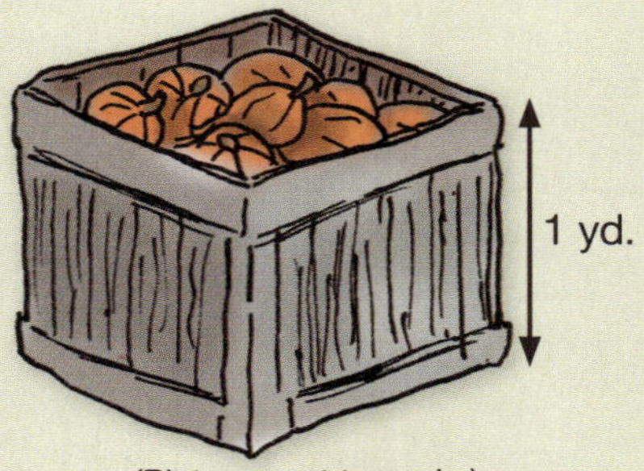

(Pictures not to scale.)

C

Peter made a fort from cardboard boxes. What is the volume of the fort?

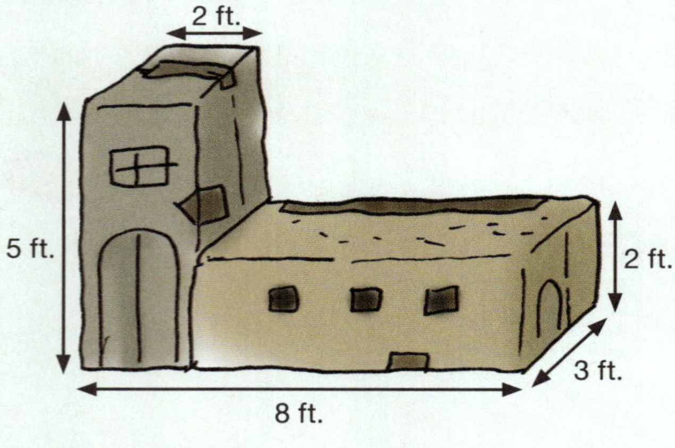

The foam pit at the trampoline park is filled 3 ft. deep with foam blocks. What is the volume of the foam blocks?

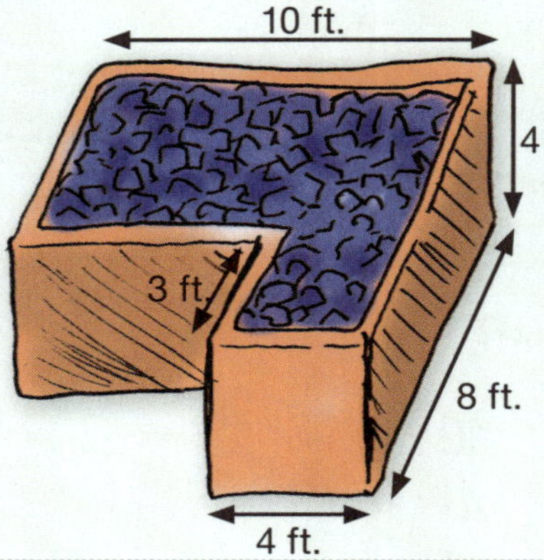

Practice

Find the volume of each solid.
Make sure to include the correct units.

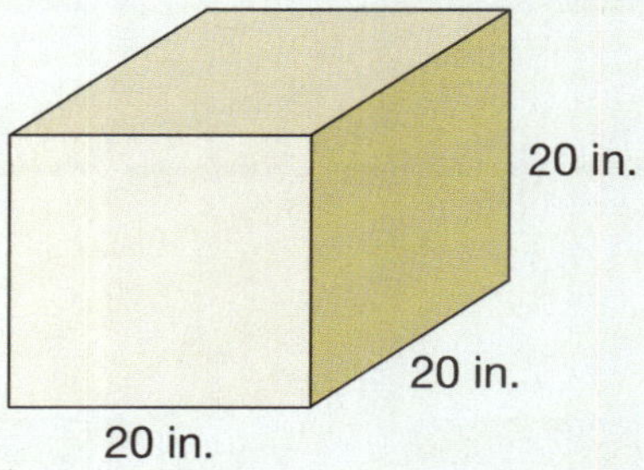

Volume: ________________

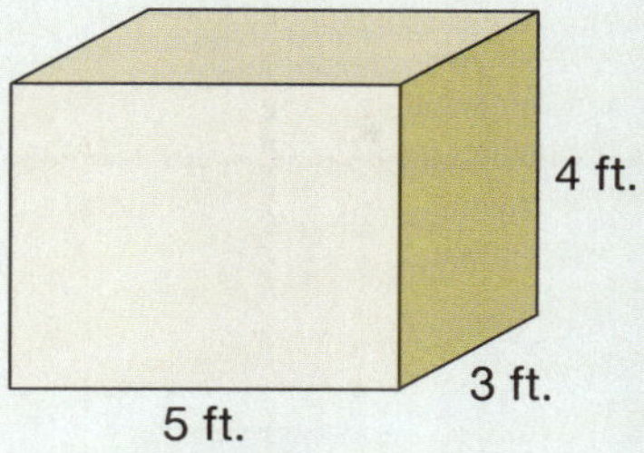

Volume: ________________

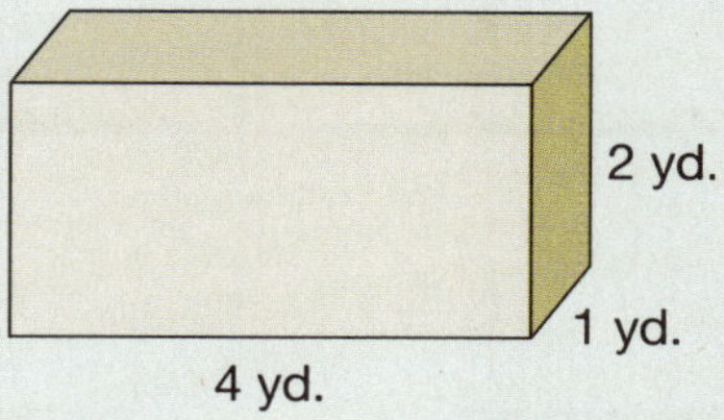

Volume: ________________

Solve. Write the equations you use.

Ahren fills the planter 6 inches high with dirt.
What is the volume of the dirt?

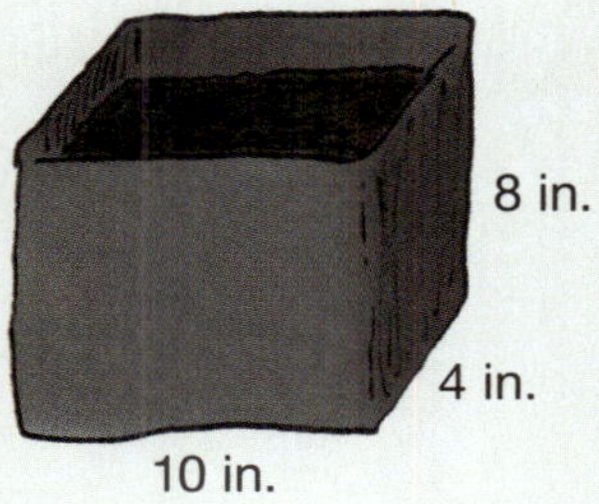

Poppy makes a robot sculpture from clay.
She makes a 3-inch cube for the head.
She makes a 5-inch cube for the body.
How many cubic inches of clay does she use?

Reagan makes a fort out of cardboard.
What is the volume of the fort?

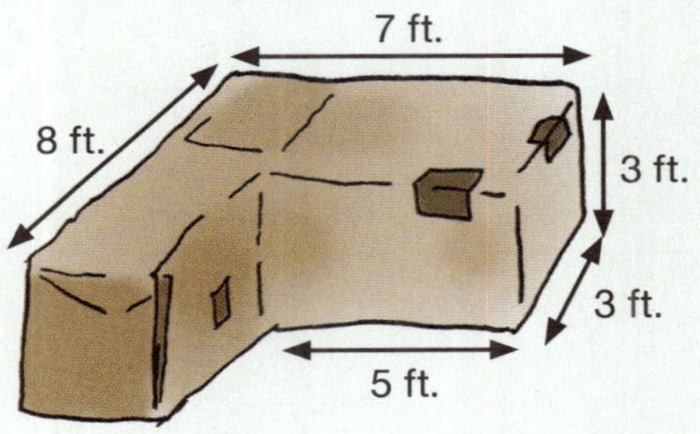

4.6

Review

Connect each number to its place on the number line.

1.245 | 1.249 | 1.248 | 1.255 | 1.256

2.06 | 2.04 | 2.11 | 2.17 | 2.15

Complete the list of factors.

Factors of 30

1 × ______

2 × __15__

3 × ______

5 × ______

Use mental math to complete the missing numbers.

5 + ______ = 9 + 4	______ × 8 = 4 × 4
15 − 7 = 10 − ______	5 × 4 × ______ = 60
★ 25 × ______ = 200	★ 300 × ______ = 6,000

Use the printed protractors to measure the angles.

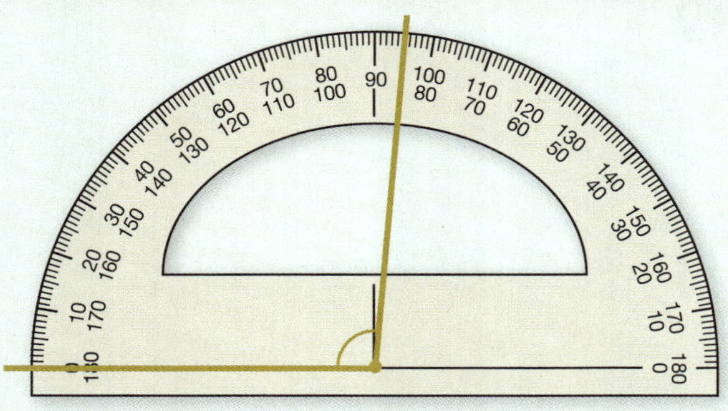

______°

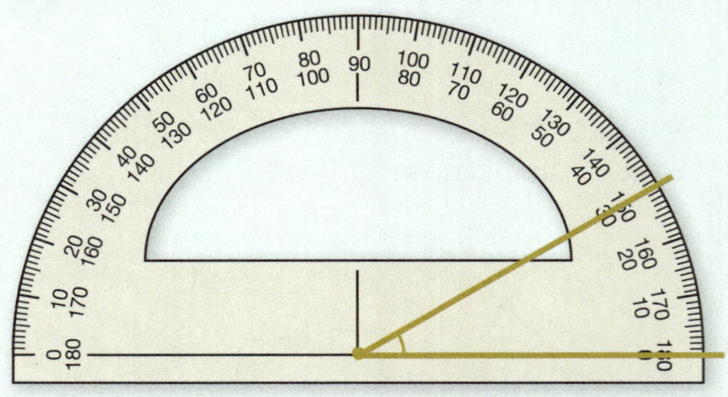

______°

Lesson Activities

A

length × width = area

Room	Area
Living Room	
Dining Room	
Kitchen	

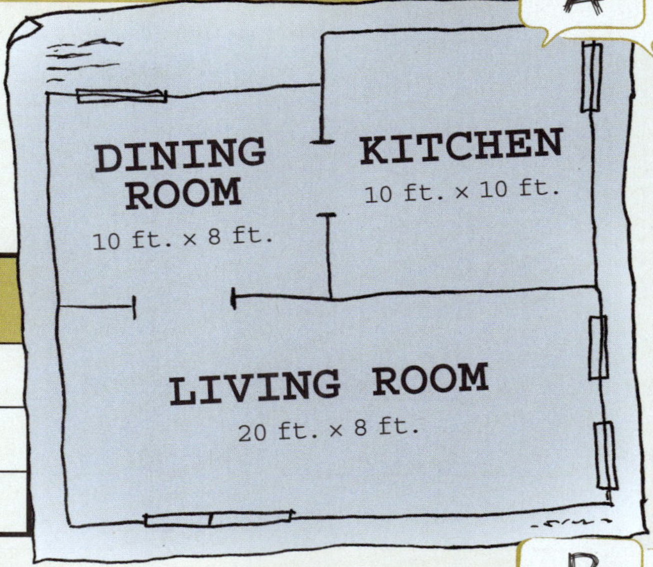

B

Area and Volume

If you know the area of the base of a rectangular prism, you've already found its length times its width.

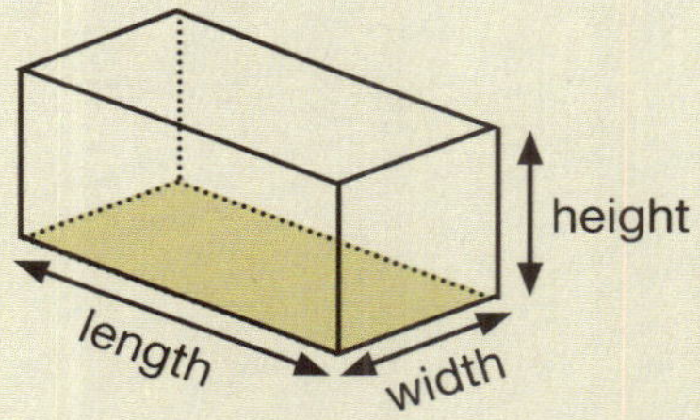

So, you can multiply the base area times its height to find its volume.

length × width × height = volume

base area × height = volume

Ex. The bathroom floor has an area of 54 sq. ft. The ceilings in the bathroom are 8 ft. high. What is the volume of the bathroom?

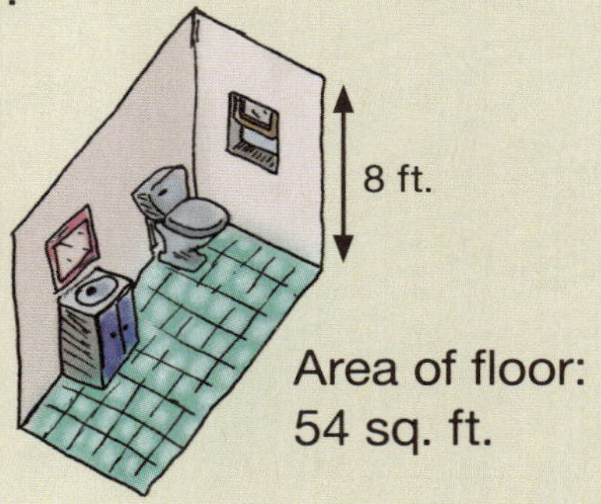

base area × height = volume

54 × 8 = **432 cu. feet**

Room	Area	Ceiling Height	Volume
Living Room		20 ft.	
Dining Room		10 ft.	
Kitchen		8 ft.	

4.7

Practice

Find the base area, height, and volume of each rectangular prism. All measurements are in feet.

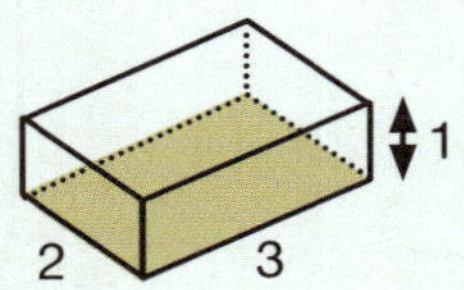

Base area: ________ sq. ft.

Height: ______________ ft.

Volume: __________ cu. ft.

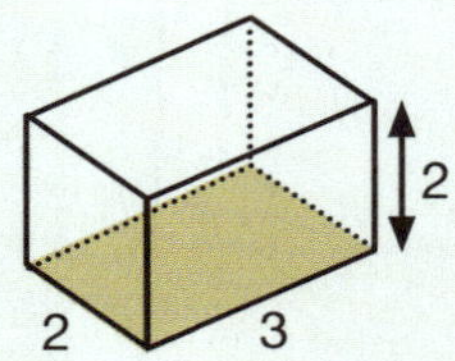

Base area: ________ sq. ft.

Height: ______________ ft.

Volume: __________ cu. ft.

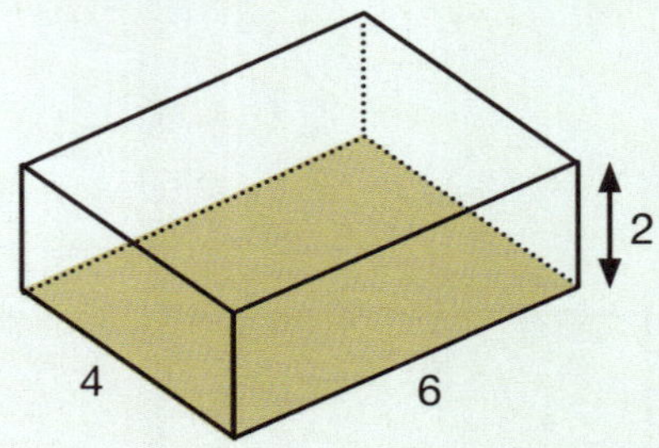

Base area: ________ sq. ft.

Height: ______________ ft.

Volume: __________ cu. ft.

Find the base area and volume of each solid. All measurements are in inches.

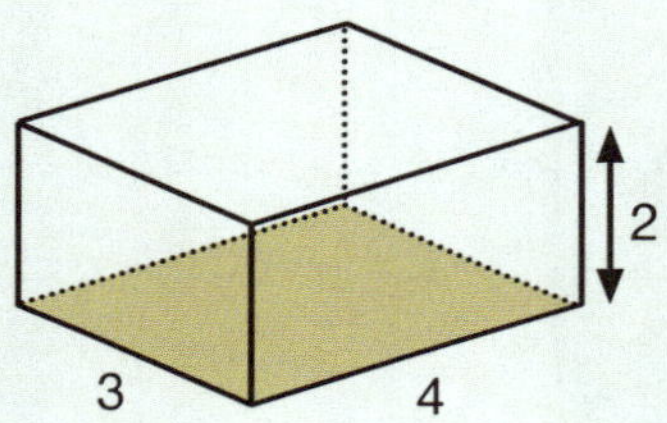

Base area: ________ sq. in.

Volume: __________ cu. in.

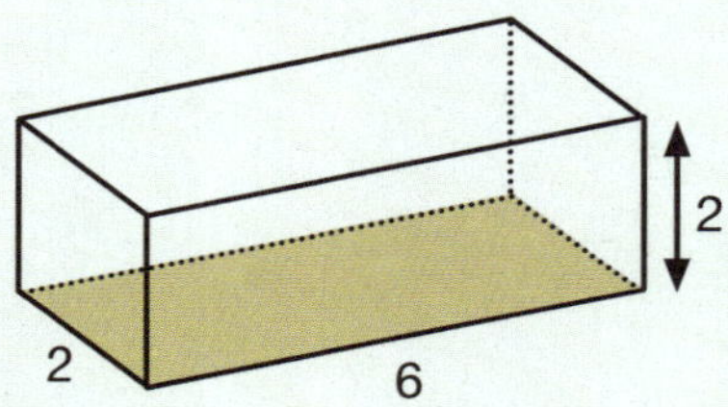

Base area: ________ sq. in.

Volume: __________ cu. in.

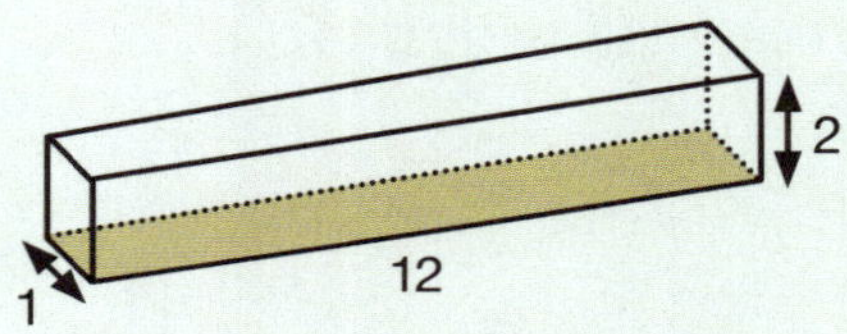

Base area: ________ sq. in.

Volume: __________ cu. in.

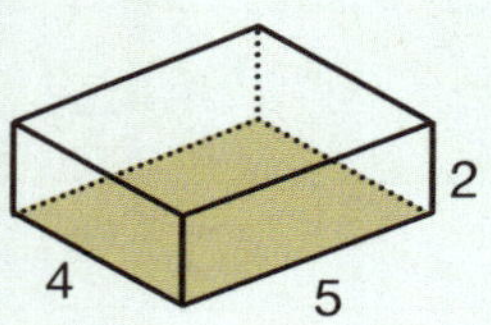

Base area: ________ sq. in.

Volume: __________ cu. in.

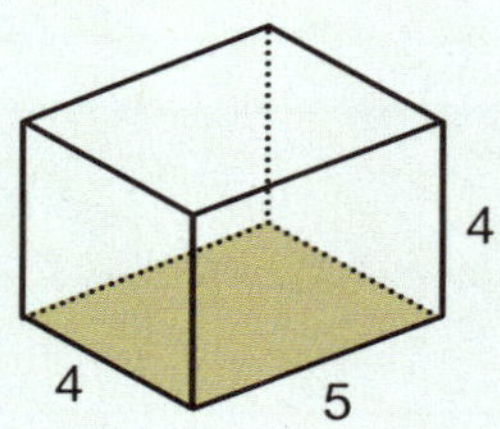

Base area: ________ sq. in.

Volume: __________ cu. in.

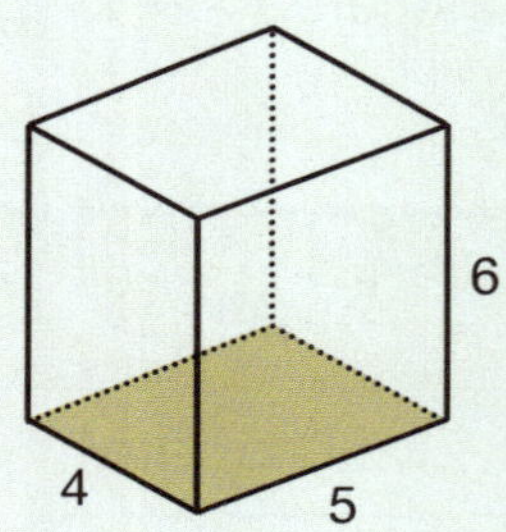

Base area: ________ sq. in.

Volume: __________ cu. in.

Review

Color the pictures to match the fractions. Then, use the pictures to complete the equivalent fractions.

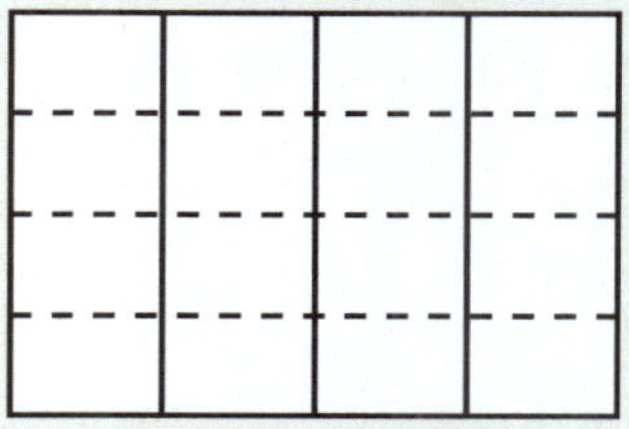

$\frac{1}{4} = \frac{}{16}$

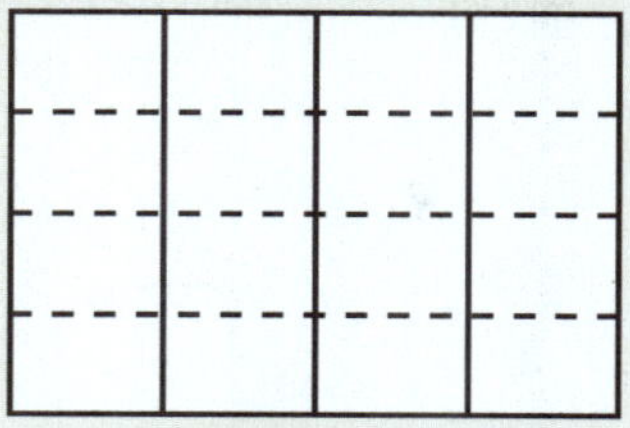

$\frac{2}{4} = \frac{}{16}$

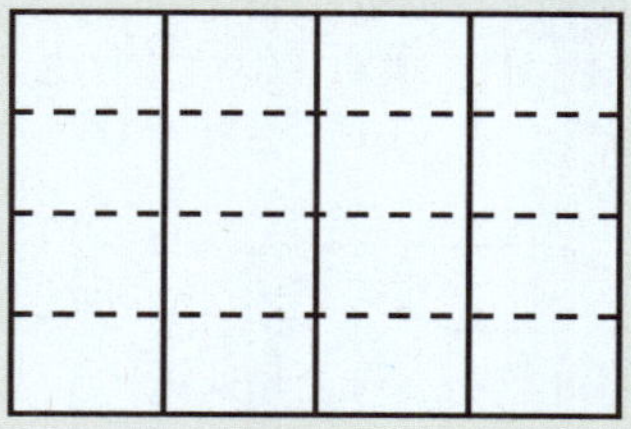

$\frac{3}{4} = \frac{}{16}$

Find the product.

$$\begin{array}{r} 541 \\ \times \quad 73 \\ \hline \end{array}$$

Use mental math to complete.

128 + 100 = ______

128 + 170 = ______

128 + 172 = ______

319 + 200 = ______

319 + 210 = ______

319 + 216 = ______

984 – 100 = ______

984 – 110 = ______

984 – 113 = ______

773 – 500 = ______

773 – 540 = ______

773 – 545 = ______

Use Megan's time card from the ski competition to answer the questions. Write the equations you use.

Run 1	Run 2	Run 3
37.14 seconds	36.05 seconds	35.92 seconds

What was the total time for all 3 of Megan's runs?

How much faster was Run 3 than Run 1?

Lesson Activities

A

The storage chest is 3 ft. high.
Its base has an area of 10 sq. ft.
What is the volume of the chest?

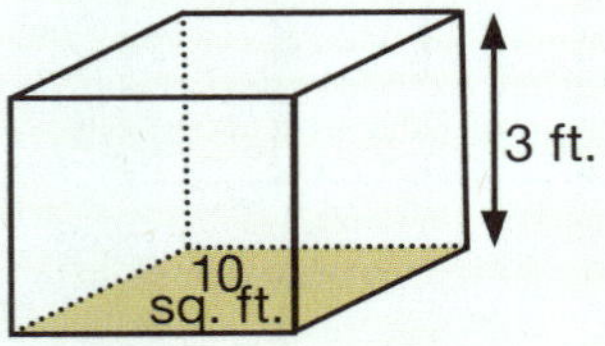

The jewelry box is 10 in. high.
It covers an area of 64 sq. in.
What is the volume of the jewelry box?

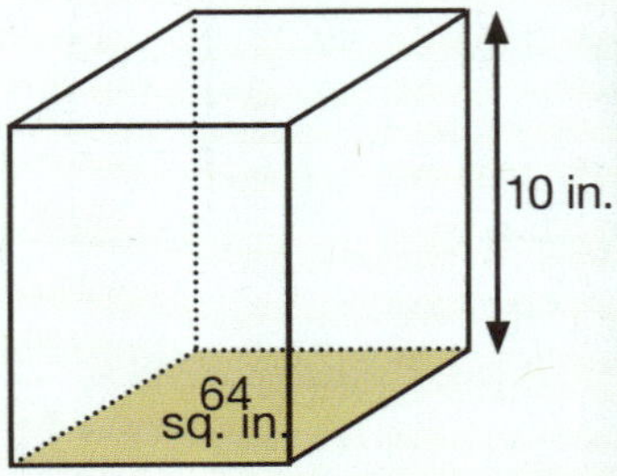

B

How to use Volume to Find Base Area or Height

If you know the volume of a rectangular prism and its height, you can divide the volume by the height to find the area of the base.

Ex. The box's volume is 20 cu. cm.
Its height is 5 cm.
What is the area of its base?

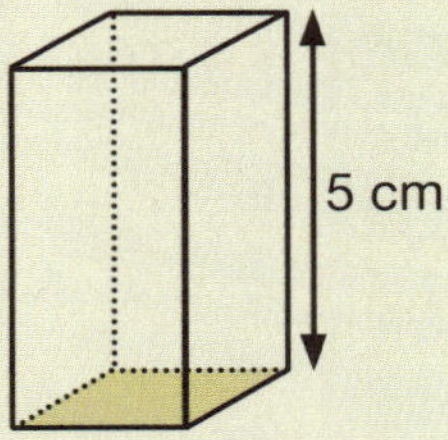

base area × height = volume

______ × 5 = 20

20 ÷ 5 = **4 sq. cm**

If you know the volume of a rectangular prism and the area of its base, you can divide the volume by the area of the base to find the height.

Ex. The box's volume is 40 cu. cm.
Its base has an area of 8 sq. cm.
What is its height?

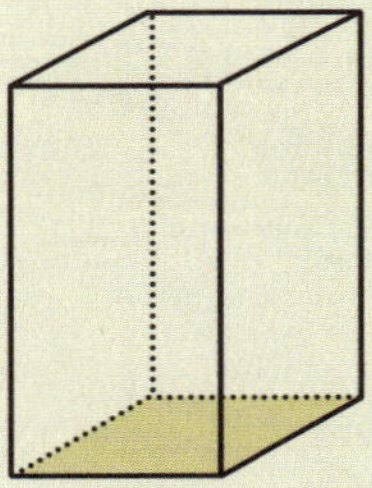

base area × height = volume

8 × ______ = 40

40 ÷ 8 = **5 cm**

Isabella builds a raised garden bed that covers 9 sq. ft. She pours 18 cu. ft. of dirt into the garden bed and smooths it flat. How many feet high is the dirt?

Will wants to build a large wall cabinet that will provide 80 cu. ft. of storage. He wants the cabinet to be 4 ft. tall. How much floor area will the cabinet cover?

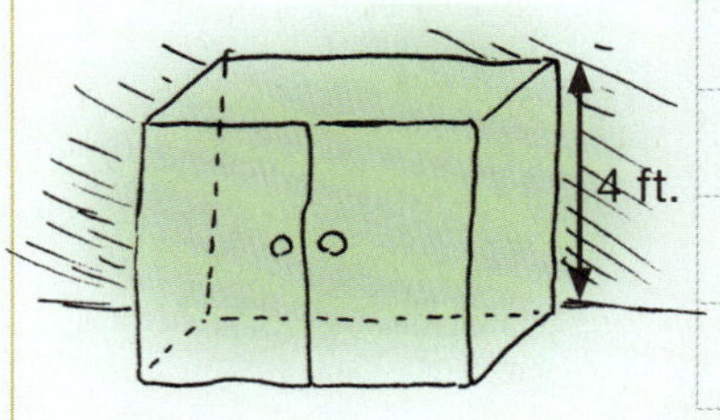

Practice

Find the height or base area of each solid.
Make sure to include the correct units in your answers.

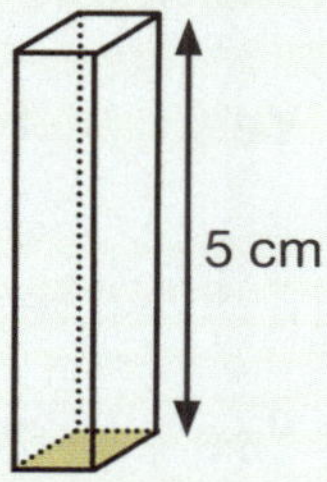

Volume: 5 cu. cm

Base area: ____sq. cm____

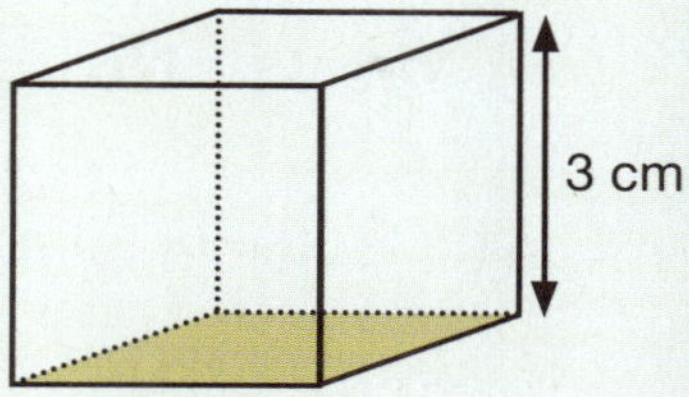

Volume: 27 cu. cm

Base area: ____________

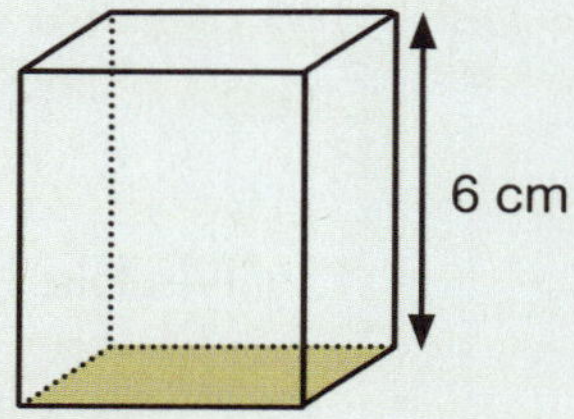

Volume: 60 cu. cm

Base area: ____________

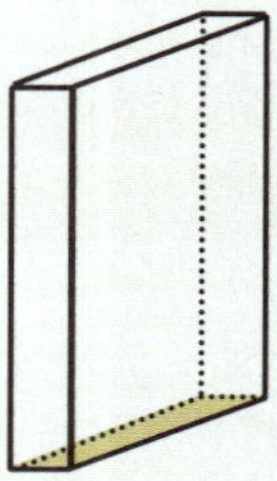

Base area:
3 sq. cm

Volume: 18 cu. cm

Height: ____________

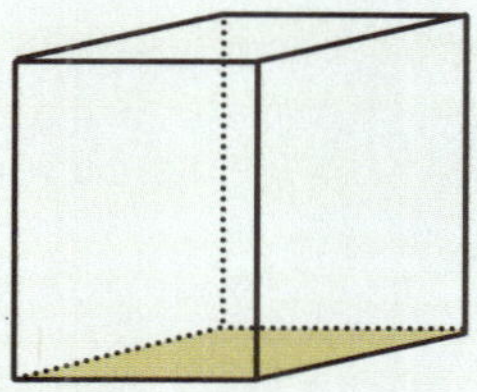

Base area:
9 sq. cm

Volume: 36 cu. cm

Height: ____________

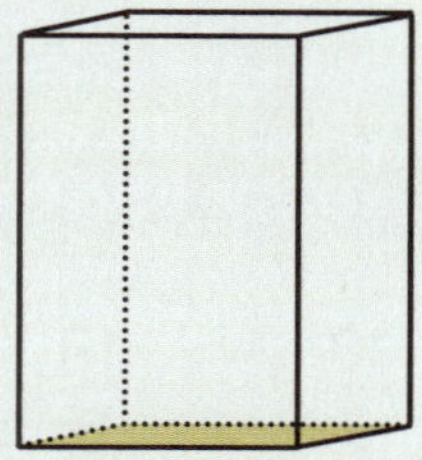

Base area:
8 sq. cm

Volume: 48 cu. cm

Height: ____________

Solve. Write the equations you use.

Oliver is making a centerpiece. He pours 100 cu. in. of pebbles into the dish. What is the depth of the pebbles?

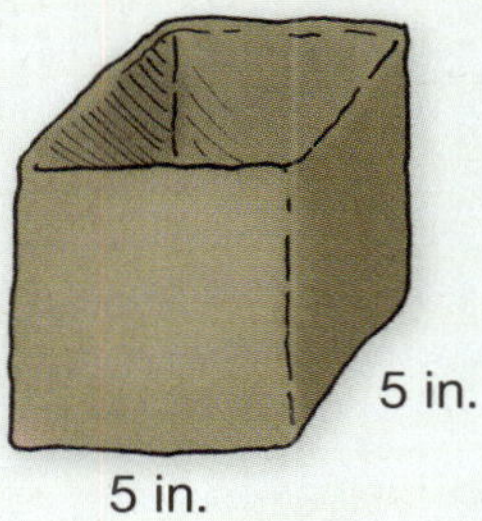

Aliyah fills the ball pit 3 ft. high. She uses 90 cu. ft. of balls.

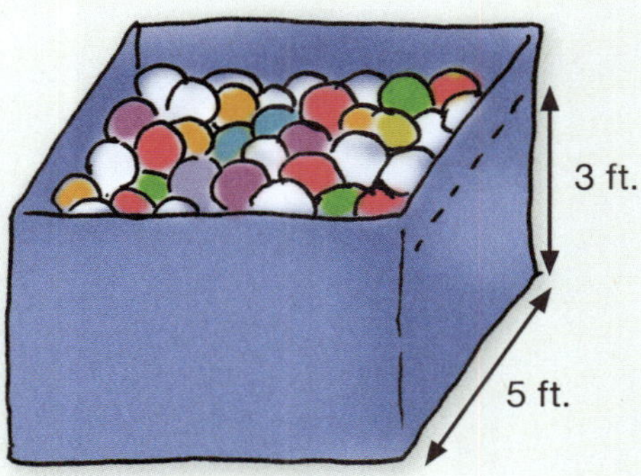

What is the area of the bottom of the ball pit?

What is the length of the ball pit?

Review

Circle yes or no to answer the questions.

Is 15 divisible by 3? **Yes | No**	Is 36 divisible by 2? **Yes | No**	Is 17 divisible by 2? **Yes | No**
Is 15 divisible by 5? **Yes | No**	Is 36 divisible by 4? **Yes | No**	Is 17 divisible by 3? **Yes | No**
Is 15 divisible by 6? **Yes | No**	Is 36 divisible by 5? **Yes | No**	Is 17 divisible by 4? **Yes | No**

Write each fraction as a whole number or mixed number. Use the number line to help.

$\frac{17}{6}$ $\frac{18}{6}$ $\frac{19}{6}$ $\frac{20}{6}$ $\frac{21}{6}$ $\frac{22}{6}$ $\frac{23}{6}$ $\frac{24}{6}$ $\frac{25}{6}$ $\frac{26}{6}$

3 (at $\frac{18}{6}$) 4 (at $\frac{24}{6}$)

$\div \frac{19}{6} = 3\frac{1}{6}$

$\frac{20}{6}$ = ____________

$\frac{21}{6}$ = ____________

$\frac{22}{6}$ = ____________

$\frac{23}{6}$ = ____________

$\frac{17}{6}$ = ____________

Find the quotient.

$7 \overline{)546}$

Evaluate.

$50 + 10 \times 3$

$30 \div 3 + 7$

$(50 + 10) \times 3$

$(30 \div 3) + 7$

Unit Wrap-Up

Choose the more sensible measurement for each volume.

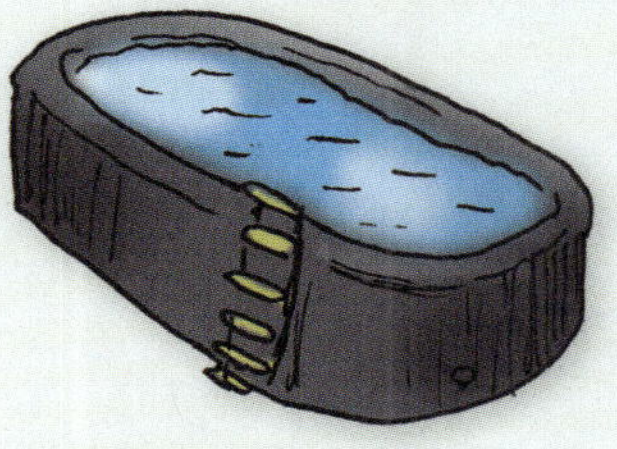

Volume of a pool

15 cu. cm | 15 cu. m

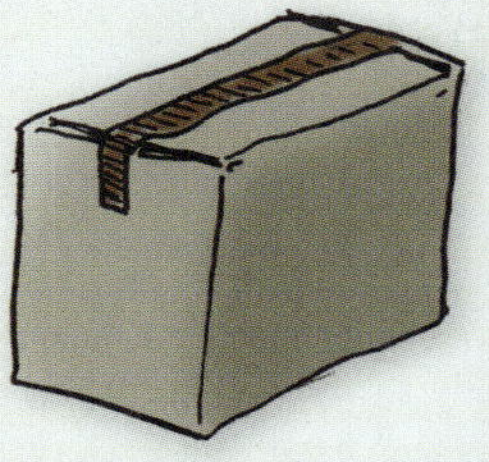

Volume of a moving box

3 cu. in. | 3 cu. ft.

Volume of a box of rice

48 cu. in. | 48 cu. ft.

Find the missing information for each solid.
Make sure to include the correct units in your answers.

Each cube has a volume of 1 cu. cm.

Volume: ______________

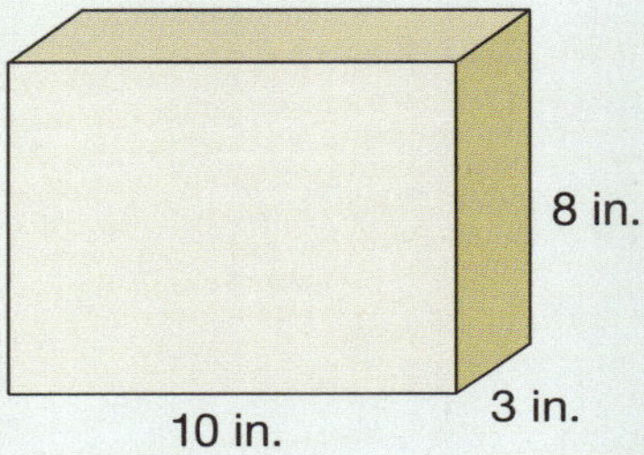

Volume: ______________

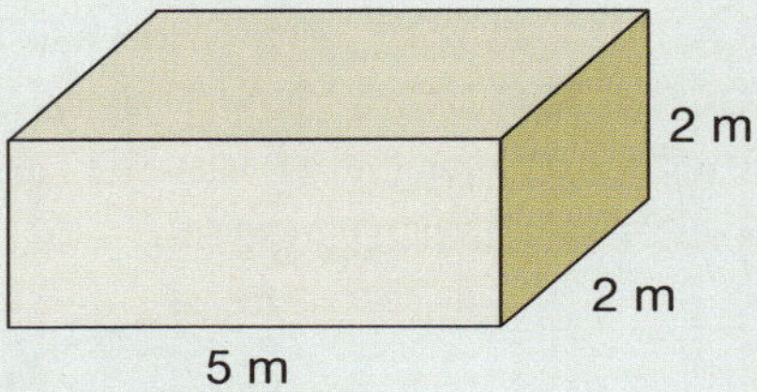

Volume: ______________

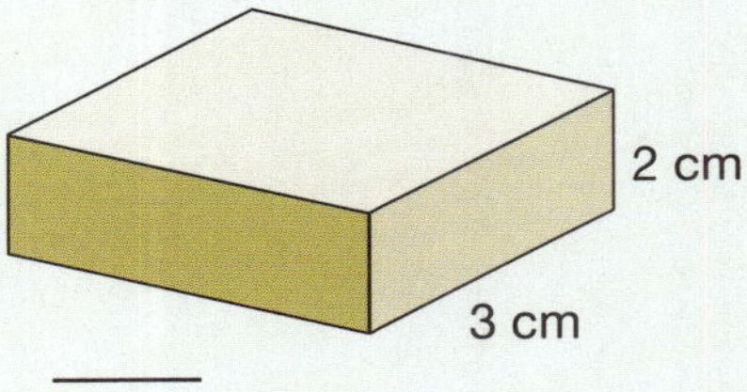

Volume: 36 cu. cm

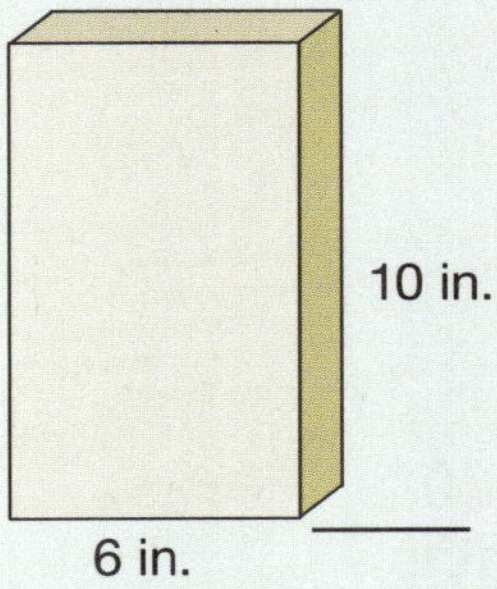

Volume: 60 cu. in.

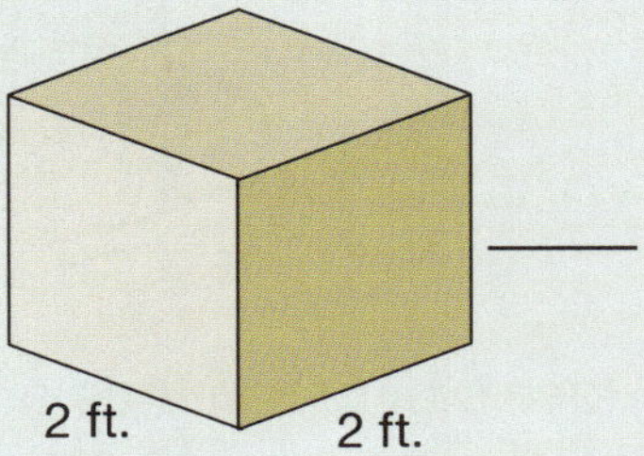

Volume: 8 cu. ft.

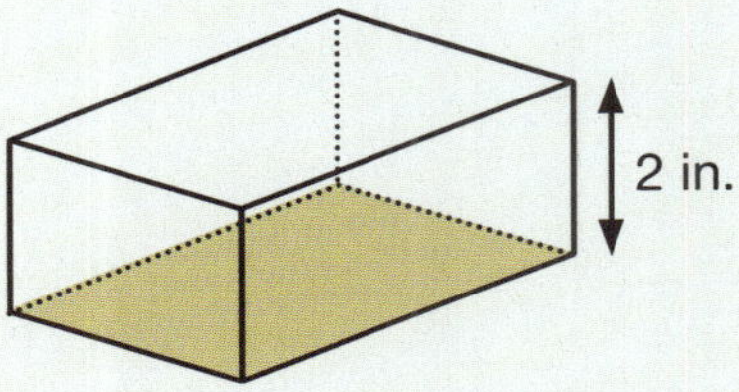

Base area: ______________

Volume: 24 cu. in.

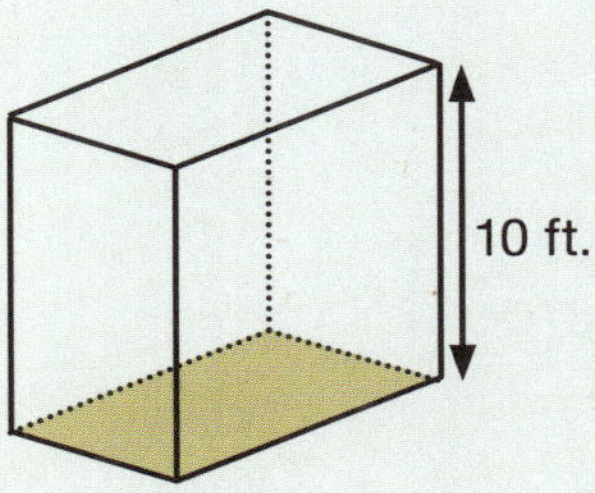

Base area: 60 sq. ft.

Volume: ______________

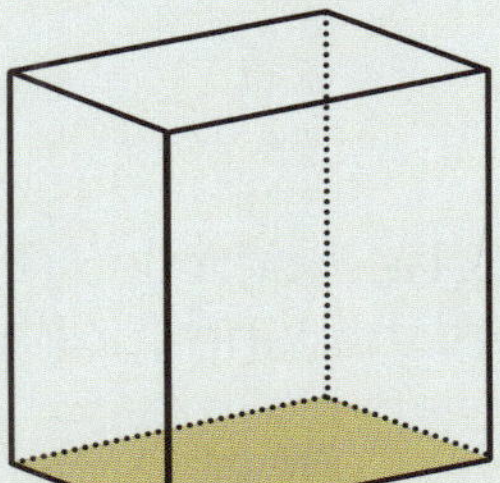

Base area: 8 sq. cm

Height: ______________

Volume: 40 cu. cm

Unit Wrap-Up

Solve. Write the equations you use.

Zaidee fills the aquarium to a depth of 10 in. What is the volume of the water?

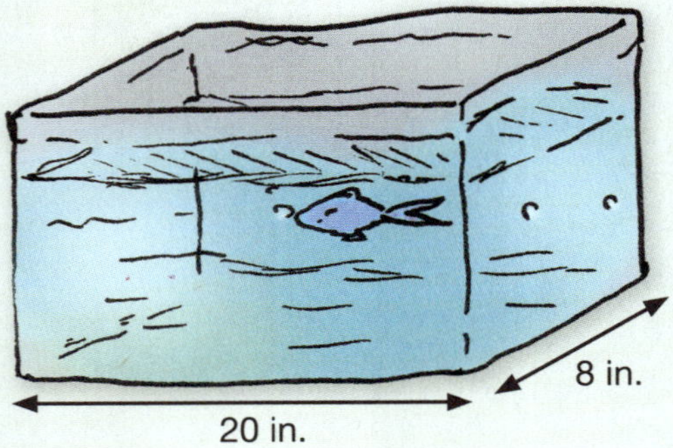

Quintin builds and sells scratching posts for cats. How many cubic inches of wood does he need for each scratching post?

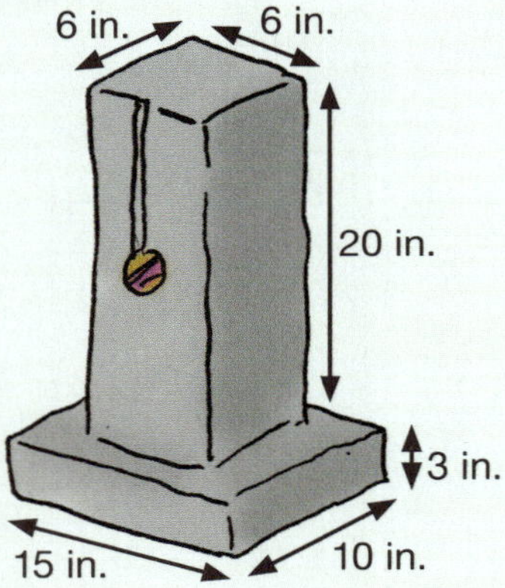

Rose's bedroom has a volume of 1,200 cu. ft. The ceilings are 8 ft. high. What is the area of the floor of her bedroom?

★ Rose's bedroom is 10 ft. wide. What is the length of her bedroom?

Lesson Activities

A

halves ▭ thirds ▭

fourths ▭ sixths ▭

eighths ▭ twelfths ▭

B

Fractions

Fractions are numbers that represent part of a whole.

The numerator tells the number of parts. The denominator tells how many equal parts the whole was split into.

Ex. What fraction of the cake has green frosting?

$\frac{2}{5}$

Numerator Number of parts

Denominator How many equal parts the whole was split into

______ 

______ 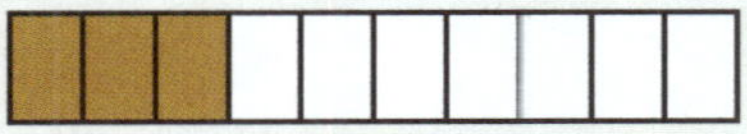

______ 

$\frac{2}{3}$ ▭

$\frac{3}{4}$ ▭

$\frac{5}{8}$ ▭

C

Hit the Target (2-Player Game)

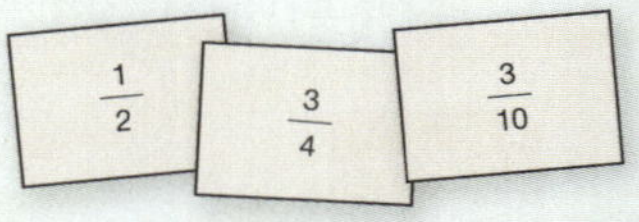

	1	1	0	0	$\frac{1}{2}$	$\frac{1}{2}$
Player 1						
Player 2						

5.1

Practice

Color the bars to match the fractions. Then, use the bars to compare the fractions.

$\frac{1}{2}$ ▭▭	$\frac{1}{5}$ ▭▭▭▭▭
$\frac{7}{8}$ ▭▭▭▭▭▭▭▭	$\frac{2}{5}$ ▭▭▭▭▭
$\frac{2}{4}$ ▭▭▭▭	$\frac{6}{6}$ ▭▭▭▭▭▭

$\frac{1}{2}$ ○ $\frac{7}{8}$	$\frac{1}{2}$ ○ $\frac{1}{5}$	$\frac{1}{2}$ ○ $\frac{2}{4}$
$\frac{1}{5}$ ○ $\frac{2}{5}$	$\frac{2}{4}$ ○ $\frac{2}{5}$	$\frac{7}{8}$ ○ $\frac{2}{5}$
$\frac{1}{2}$ ○ $\frac{6}{6}$	$\frac{7}{8}$ ○ $\frac{6}{6}$	$\frac{2}{5}$ ○ $\frac{6}{6}$

Write the missing fraction in each equation.

$\frac{3}{4}$ + ________ = 1	$\frac{1}{2}$ + ________ = 1	$\frac{2}{3}$ + ________ = 1
$\frac{5}{6}$ + ________ = 1	$\frac{7}{12}$ + ________ = 1	$\frac{1}{12}$ + ________ = 1

Match each fraction to its dot on the number line.

$\frac{1}{2}$ $\frac{1}{3}$ $\frac{1}{10}$ $\frac{3}{4}$ $\frac{9}{10}$ $\frac{7}{12}$

Review

Complete.

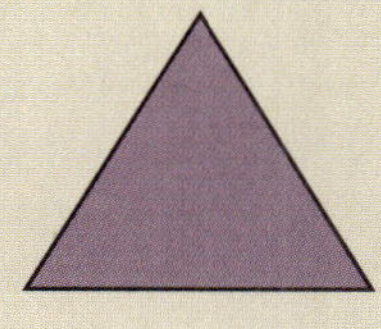

___0___ right angle(s)
___0___ obtuse angle(s)
___3___ acute angle(s)

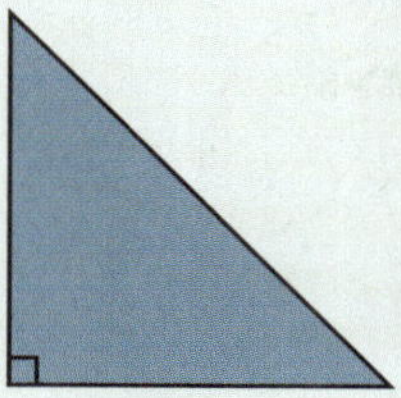

________ right angle(s)
________ obtuse angle(s)
________ acute angle(s)

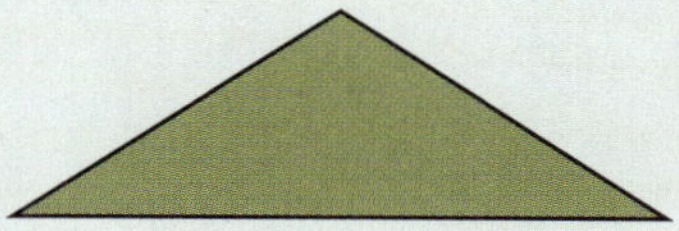

________ right angle(s)
________ obtuse angle(s)
________ acute angle(s)

Use mental math to complete.

$125 \times 2 =$ ____________

$125 \times 4 =$ ____________

$300 \times 4 =$ ____________

$301 \times 4 =$ ____________

$500 \times 5 =$ ____________

★ $499 \times 5 =$ ____________

Solve. Write your equations in the work space.

Michelle practiced piano for 270 minutes this week. She practiced 6 times, and she practiced the same amount each time. How long was each practice session?

Katherine practiced piano for 245 minutes this week. She practiced 7 times, and she practiced the same amount each time. How long was each practice session?

Who practiced more minutes in all?

Whose practice sessions were longer?

WORK SPACE

5.2

Lesson Activities

A

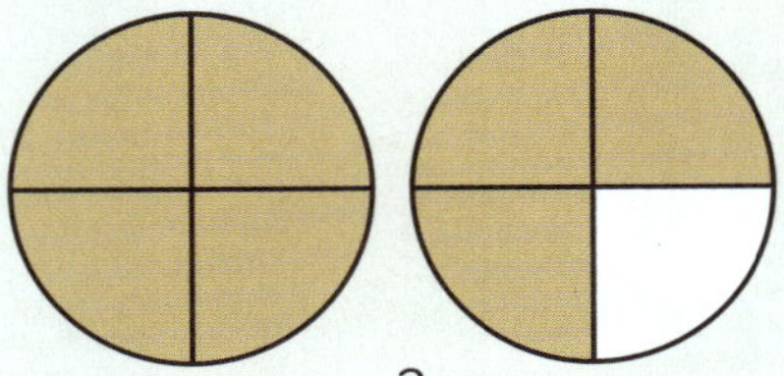

$1\frac{3}{4}$

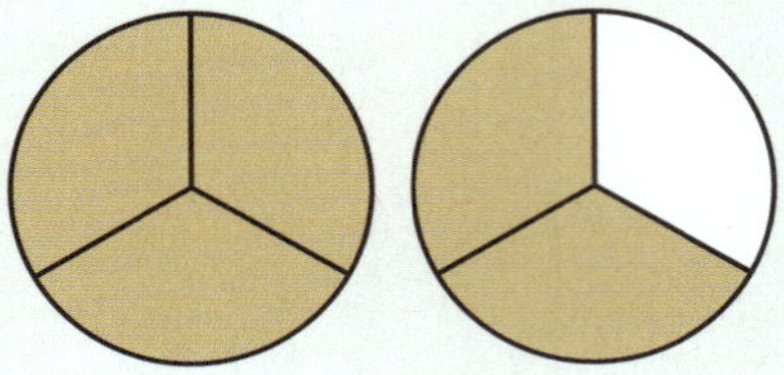

______

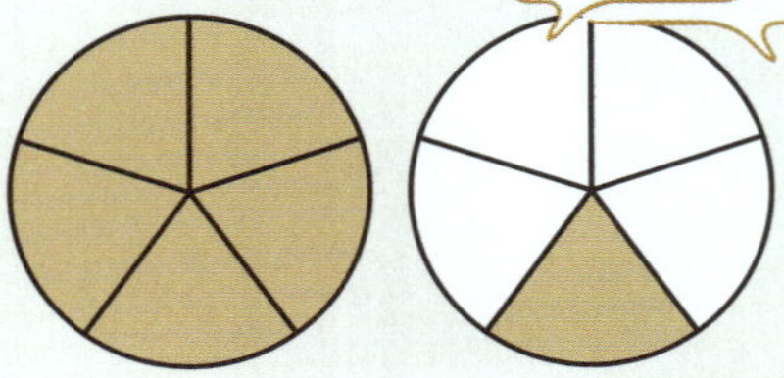

______

B

Mixed Numbers

A mixed number is a combination of a whole number and a fraction.

To convert a fraction to a mixed number, divide the numerator by the denominator.

Ex. Write $\frac{9}{4}$ as a mixed number.

$9 \div 4 = 2 \text{ R}1$

$\div \; \frac{9}{4} = \mathbf{2\frac{1}{4}}$

To convert a mixed number to a fraction, multiply the denominator by the whole number and add the numerator.

Ex. Write $2\frac{3}{5}$ as a fraction.

$5 \times 2 + 3 = 13$

$2\frac{3}{5} = \mathbf{\frac{13}{5}}$ (+, ×)

$\frac{6}{5} =$

$\frac{8}{5} =$

$1\frac{1}{12} =$

$1\frac{1}{4} =$

C

Four in a Row (2-Player Game)

$3\frac{1}{2}$	$\frac{23}{12}$	$2\frac{5}{12}$	$\frac{27}{10}$	$2\frac{3}{6}$
$\frac{11}{8}$	$1\frac{3}{10}$	$\frac{7}{3}$	$1\frac{5}{6}$	$\frac{14}{5}$
$2\frac{7}{10}$	$\frac{11}{6}$	$3\frac{3}{4}$	$\frac{29}{12}$	$1\frac{3}{8}$
$\frac{15}{4}$	$2\frac{1}{3}$	$\frac{7}{2}$	$2\frac{7}{8}$	$\frac{13}{10}$
$2\frac{4}{5}$	$\frac{23}{8}$	$1\frac{11}{12}$	$\frac{15}{6}$	$1\frac{4}{10}$

Practice

Complete the missing numbers in the chart. Use the circles to help.

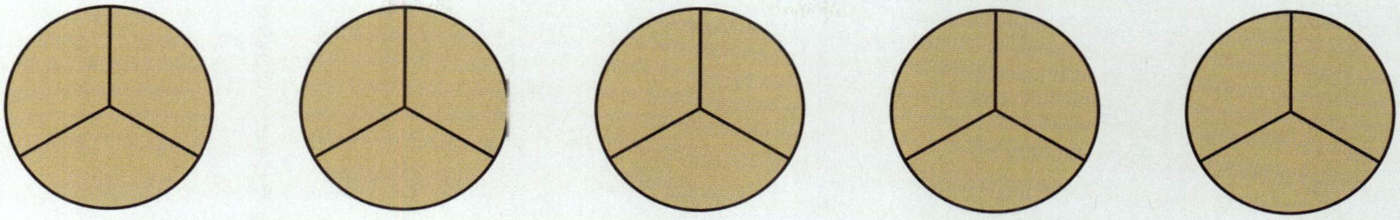

Whole Number or Mixed Number	2				$3\frac{1}{3}$	$3\frac{2}{3}$			$4\frac{2}{3}$
Fraction	$\frac{6}{3}$	$\frac{7}{3}$	$\frac{8}{3}$	$\frac{9}{3}$			$\frac{12}{3}$	$\frac{13}{3}$	

Write each mixed number as a fraction. Write each fraction as a mixed number.

$2\frac{5}{8} =$	$1\frac{2}{12} =$	$1\frac{9}{10} =$	$5\frac{1}{2} =$
$\frac{7}{5} =$	$\frac{7}{6} =$	$\frac{25}{10} =$	$\frac{17}{8} =$

Solve. Write the equations you use.

Edith makes 4 loaves of pumpkin bread. She cuts each loaf into eighths. How many slices of pumpkin bread does she have?

Levi's family has $1\frac{7}{8}$ pies left over after Thanksgiving. Each pie is cut into eighths. How many slices of pie do they have left?

Noah has 8 pieces of ribbon. Each piece of ribbon is $\frac{1}{3}$ of a meter long.

- How much ribbon does he have? Write your answer as a fraction.
- How much ribbon does he have? Write your answer as a mixed number.

The track is $\frac{1}{4}$ mile long. Jordyn runs 13 laps.

- How far does she run? Write your answer as a fraction.
- How far does she run? Write your answer as a mixed number.

5.2

Review

Find the volume of each solid.
Make sure to include the correct units in your answers.

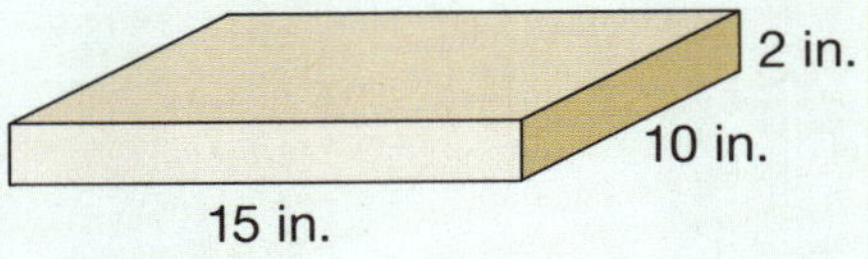

Volume: ____________

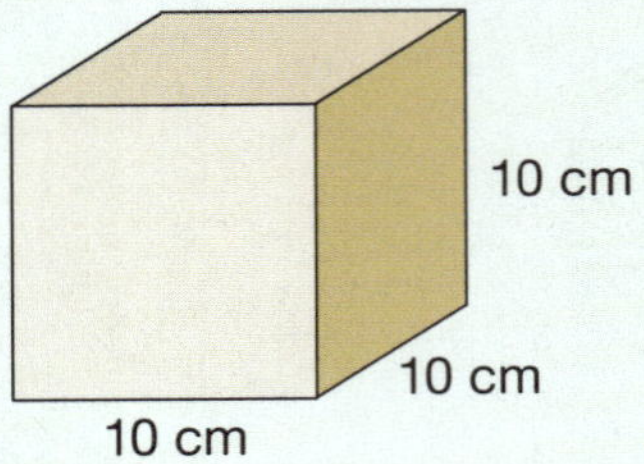

Volume: ____________

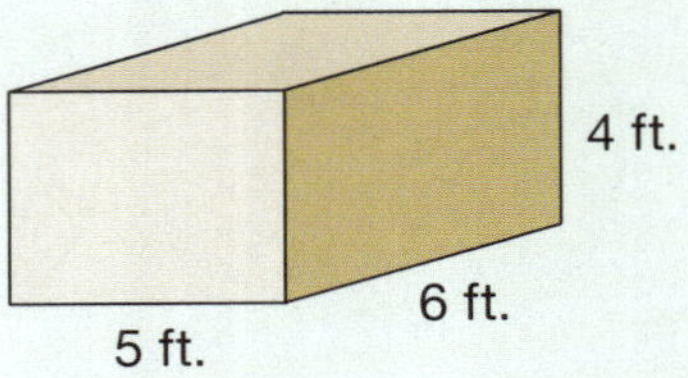

Volume: ____________

Use the printed rulers to measure the lines. Write each length as a mixed number.

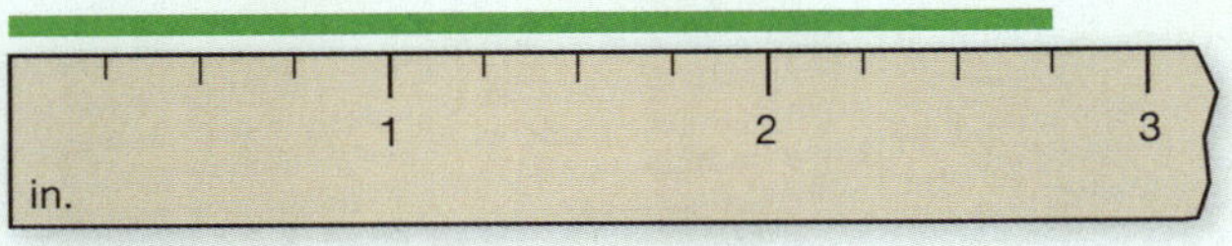

____________ in.

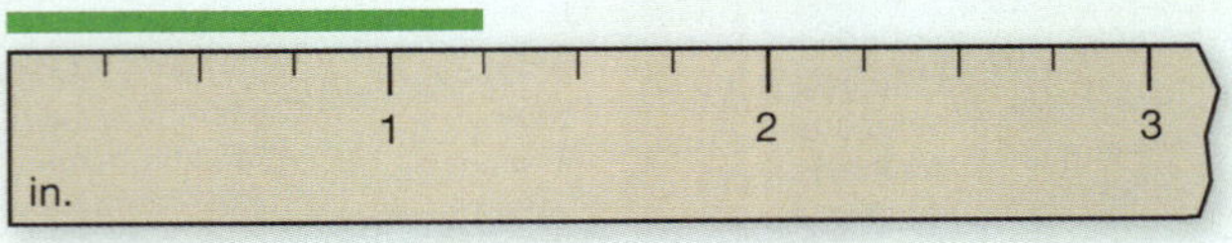

____________ in.

Solve. Write the equations you use.

Carpet costs $6 per square foot.
How much does it cost to carpet the room?

The perimeter of the garden is 92 feet.
Each side is the same length.
What is the length of each side?

Lesson Activities

A

Equivalent Fractions

Equivalent fractions are fractions that have different numerators and denominators but are equal to the same value.

One way to create an equivalent fraction is to make each fractional part into more equal parts. Multiply the numerator and denominator by the same number to find the equivalent fraction.

Ex. Trina has $\frac{1}{2}$ of a pizza.
She cuts the pizza into 4 equal slices.
What equivalent fraction does she create?

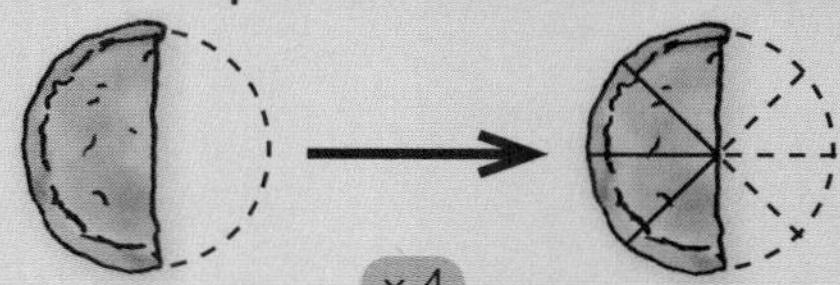

$$\frac{1}{2} \underset{\times 4}{\overset{\times 4}{=}} \frac{4}{8}$$

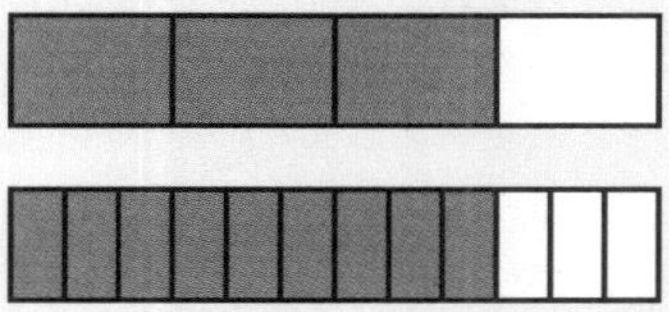

$$\frac{3}{4} \underset{\times 3}{\overset{\times 3}{=}} \frac{\quad}{\quad}$$

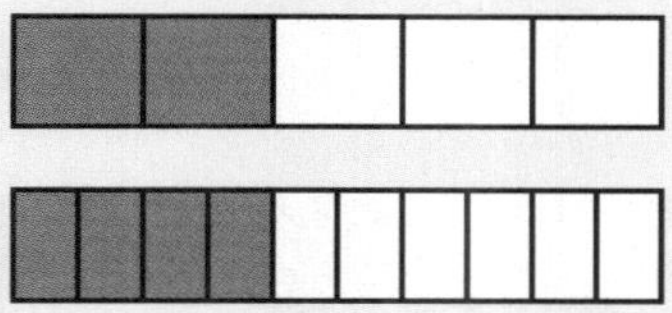

$$\frac{2}{5} \underset{\times 2}{\overset{\times 2}{=}} \frac{\quad}{\quad}$$

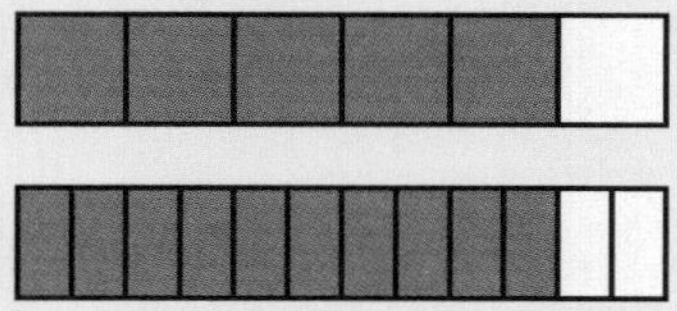

$$\frac{5}{6} \underset{\times 2}{\overset{\times 2}{=}} \frac{\quad}{\quad}$$

B

Ex. $\frac{2}{3} = \frac{?}{12}$

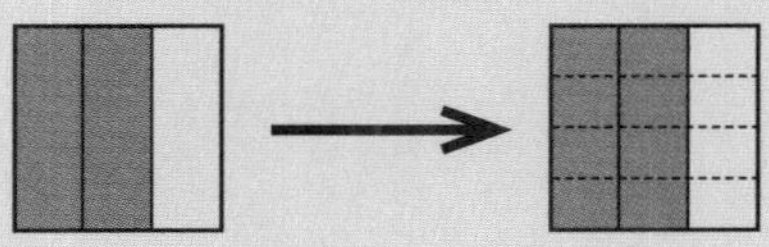

$$\frac{2}{3} \underset{\times 4}{\overset{\times 4}{=}} \frac{\mathbf{8}}{12}$$

Ex. $\frac{2}{5} = \frac{6}{?}$

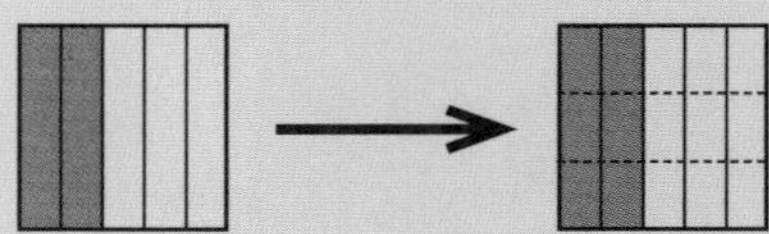

$$\frac{2}{5} \underset{\times 3}{\overset{\times 3}{=}} \frac{6}{\mathbf{15}}$$

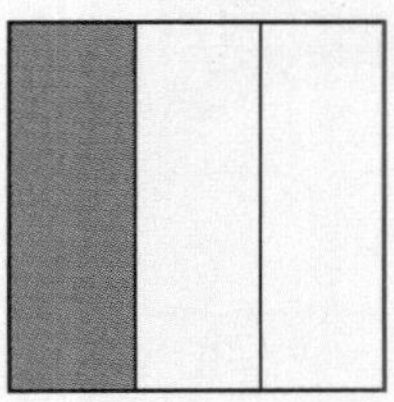

$$\frac{1}{3} = \frac{2}{\quad}$$

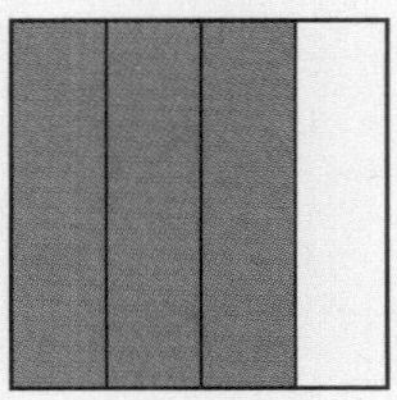

$$\frac{3}{4} = \frac{\quad}{16}$$

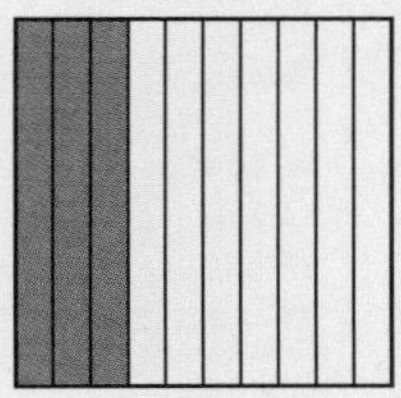

$$\frac{3}{10} = \frac{\quad}{20}$$

C

Fill the Fractions (2-Player Game)

$\frac{7}{8} = \frac{}{24}$	$\frac{1}{2} = \frac{8}{}$	$\frac{4}{5} = \frac{}{25}$
$\frac{2}{5} = \frac{8}{}$	$\frac{3}{8} = \frac{9}{}$	$\frac{5}{12} = \frac{}{24}$
$\frac{1}{3} = \frac{}{30}$	$\frac{6}{10} = \frac{12}{}$	$\frac{9}{12} = \frac{18}{}$
$\frac{2}{3} = \frac{10}{}$	$\frac{3}{6} = \frac{}{18}$	$\frac{1}{2} = \frac{}{40}$

Practice

Complete the missing number in each pair of equivalent fractions. Then, find the blanks that match the answer for each problem. Write the matching letter in the blanks to solve the riddle.

V $\frac{2}{3} = \frac{6}{}$	Y $\frac{1}{2} = \frac{40}{}$	I $\frac{7}{8} = \frac{}{16}$
R $\frac{3}{8} = \frac{6}{}$	G $\frac{1}{4} = \frac{}{8}$	S $\frac{4}{5} = \frac{80}{}$
O $\frac{5}{10} = \frac{}{100}$	T $\frac{5}{6} = \frac{}{12}$	N $\frac{3}{4} = \frac{15}{}$
D $\frac{4}{4} = \frac{36}{}$	E $\frac{1}{3} = \frac{}{21}$	

Why did the obtuse angle go to the beach?
Because it was...

50	9	7	16

20	14	20	7	10	80

36	7	2	16	7	7	100

Review

Find the least common multiple for each pair of numbers.

LCM of 3 and 2: ________

LCM of 3 and 4: ________

LCM of 3 and 5: ________

LCM of 4 and 5: ________

LCM of 4 and 6: ________

LCM of 4 and 8: ________

Complete the chart.

	Half
10	5
16	
20	
30	
32	
100	

Complete the circles with <, >, or =.

$\frac{1}{12} \bigcirc \frac{5}{12}$

$\frac{3}{6} \bigcirc \frac{7}{6}$

$\frac{4}{5} \bigcirc \frac{2}{5}$

$\frac{3}{8} \bigcirc \frac{8}{3}$

$\frac{5}{4} \bigcirc \frac{5}{5}$

$3\frac{3}{8} \bigcirc 2\frac{7}{8}$

$1\frac{9}{10} \bigcirc 1\frac{8}{10}$

$2\frac{1}{2} \bigcirc 2\frac{2}{4}$

$2 \bigcirc \frac{12}{6}$

$2 \bigcirc \frac{13}{6}$

Solve. Write the equations you use.

The playground is 38 meters long and 24 meters wide. What is its perimeter?

The playground is 38 meters long and 24 meters wide. What is its area?

Lesson Activities

A

LCM of 5 and 2: ________

LCM of 4 and 8: ________

LCM of 4 and 10: ________

B

Use Common Denominators to Compare Fractions

When fractions have different denominators, we first find a common denominator. Then, it's easier to compare the fractions.

1. Find the least common multiple of both denominators.
2. Write an equivalent fraction for each fraction you are comparing. Use the LCM as the denominator for both equivalent fractions.
3. Compare the equivalent fractions.

Ex. Which head of lettuce weighs more?

The denominators are 3 and 4.

The LCM of 3 and 4 is 12. Use 12 as the common denominator.

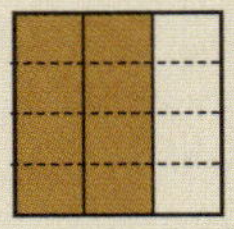

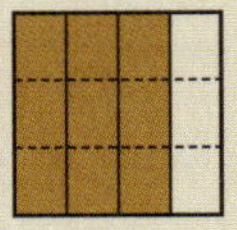

$\frac{2}{3} = \frac{8}{12}$ (× 4)

$\frac{3}{4} = \frac{9}{12}$ (× 3)

$\frac{9}{12}$ is greater than $\frac{8}{12}$, so $\frac{3}{4}$ is greater than $\frac{2}{3}$.

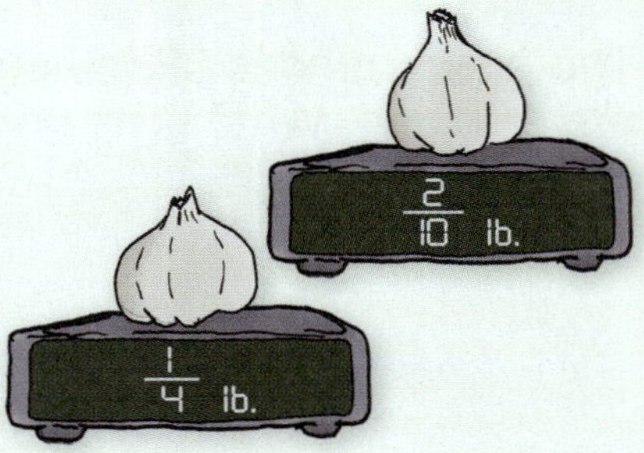

$\frac{2}{5}$ ◯ $\frac{1}{2}$

$\frac{3}{4}$ ◯ $\frac{5}{8}$

$\frac{1}{4}$ ◯ $\frac{2}{10}$

C

Fraction War 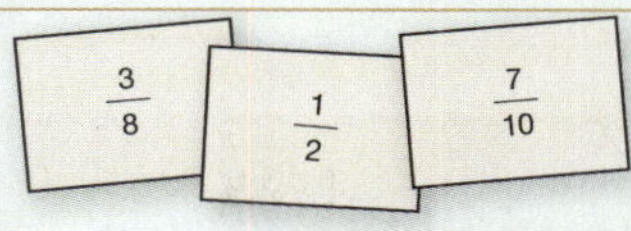

(2-Player Game)

Player 1					
Player 2					

Practice

Find the least common multiple for each pair of numbers.

LCM of 3 and 8: ________

LCM of 4 and 16: ________

LCM of 6 and 15: ________

Write equivalent fractions with common denominators for each pair of fractions. Use the LCMs (above) to help find the common denominators. Then, write <, >, or = to compare the fractions.

$\frac{3}{8} \bigcirc \frac{1}{3}$

$\frac{7}{16} \bigcirc \frac{3}{4}$

$\frac{2}{6} \bigcirc \frac{5}{15}$

Solve. Write the equivalent fractions you use to answer the questions.

Sammy ran $\frac{2}{5}$ of a kilometer. Mina ran $\frac{3}{10}$ of a kilometer. Who ran farther?

Milo has $\frac{2}{3}$ cup of sugar. He needs $\frac{3}{4}$ cup to make cookies. Does he have enough sugar?

5.4

Review

Use the clues to complete the chart.

- The platypus weighs 1 kg.
- The koala weighs 11 kg more than the platypus.
- The emu's weight is 4 times the koala's weight.
- The kangaroo weighs twice as much as the emu.

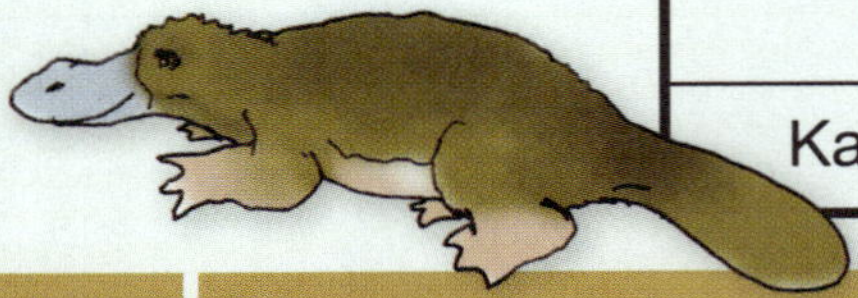

Animal	Weight (kg)
Platypus	
Koala	
Emu	
Kangaroo	

Round to the underlined digit.

$\underline{4}.579 \approx$ ______

$4.\underline{5}79 \approx$ ______

$4.5\underline{7}9 \approx$ ______

$\underline{2}97{,}845 \approx$ ______

$2\underline{9}7{,}845 \approx$ ______

$29\underline{7}{,}845 \approx$ ______

Use mental math to complete.

63 ÷ 9 = ______	54 ÷ 9 = ______
630 ÷ 9 = ______	540 ÷ 9 = ______
6,300 ÷ 9 = ______	5,400 ÷ 9 = ______
40 ÷ 8 = ______	30 ÷ 5 = ______
400 ÷ 8 = ______	300 ÷ 5 = ______
4,000 ÷ 8 = ______	3,000 ÷ 5 = ______

Find the volume of the solid. Write the equations you use.

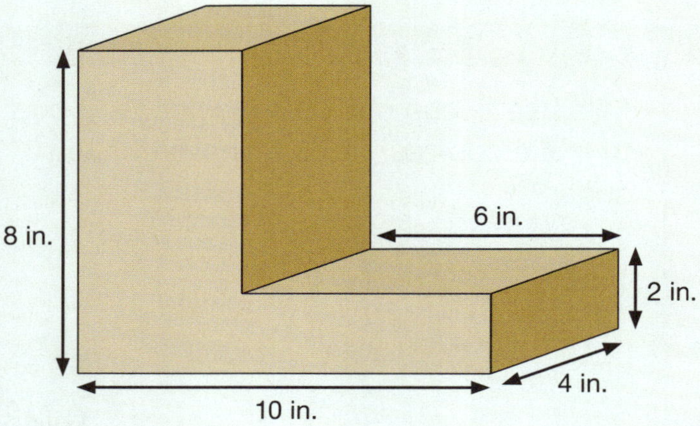

Volume: ______

Lesson Activities

A

$\frac{3}{8} + \frac{2}{8} =$

$\frac{6}{10} + \frac{3}{10} =$

$\frac{4}{12} + \frac{1}{12} =$

B

How to Use Common Denominators to Add Fractions

1. Find the least common multiple (LCM) of both denominators. You will use this number for the common denominator.
2. Rewrite each fraction as an equivalent fraction with the common denominator.
3. Add the fractions.

Ex. $\frac{2}{3} + \frac{1}{6} = ?$

The denominators are 3 and 6.

The LCM of 3 and 6 is 6.

So, use 6 as the common denominator.

$\frac{2}{3} + \frac{1}{6}$

$\downarrow \quad \downarrow$

$\frac{4}{6} + \frac{1}{6} = \mathbf{\frac{5}{6}}$

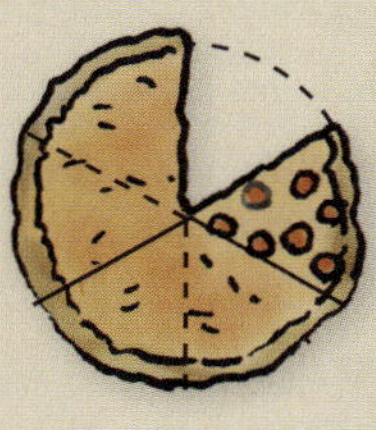

$\frac{1}{4} + \frac{3}{8}$

$\frac{3}{4} + \frac{1}{6}$

$\frac{1}{5} + \frac{1}{2}$

C

Fraction Addition War

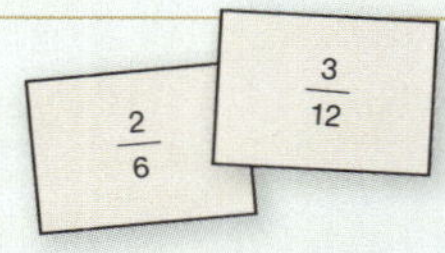

(2-Player Game)

Player 1	— + —	— + —	— + —
Player 2	— + —	— + —	— + —

Practice

Find the sum.

$\frac{3}{10} + \frac{2}{5}$

$\frac{1}{4} + \frac{1}{8}$

$\frac{1}{2} + \frac{1}{3}$

Describe the mistake in each problem. Then, solve it correctly.

incorrect

$\frac{3}{8} + \frac{1}{2}$

$\downarrow \quad \downarrow$

$\frac{3}{8} + \frac{1}{8} = \frac{4}{8}$

What is the mistake?

Correct solution:

incorrect

$\frac{2}{5} + \frac{1}{3}$

$\downarrow \quad \downarrow$

$\frac{6}{15} + \frac{5}{15} = \frac{11}{30}$

What is the mistake?

Correct solution:

Solve. Write the equations you use.

Ava makes granola with $\frac{2}{3}$ cup of dried cherries and $\frac{1}{4}$ cup of dried cranberries. How much dried fruit does she use in all?

Gideon makes a smoothie with $\frac{1}{6}$ pound of blueberries and $\frac{1}{4}$ pound of chopped pineapple. How much fruit does he put in the smoothie in all?

Review

Draw a triangle that matches each description.

1 right angle

1 obtuse angle

3 acute angles

Write the numbers in order from least to greatest.

1.01 0.999
1 0.90

________ least ________ ________ ________ greatest

0.04 0.041
0.004 0.40

________ least ________ ________ ________ greatest

**Circle the words that describe the answer to each problem.
You do not need to find the exact answers.**

358 + 315		217 + 345		153 + 439	
less than 600	greater than 600	less than 600	greater than 600	less than 600	greater than 600
642 – 96		**975 – 507**		**850 – 328**	
less than 500	greater than 500	less than 500	greater than 500	less than 500	greater than 500

Lesson Activities

A

$\frac{5}{6} - \frac{3}{6} =$

$\frac{3}{8} - \frac{1}{8} =$

$\frac{11}{12} - \frac{3}{12} =$

B

How to Use Common Denominators to Subtract Fractions

1. Find the least common multiple (LCM) of both denominators. You will use this number for the common denominator.
2. Rewrite each fraction as an equivalent fraction with the common denominator.
3. Subtract the fractions.

Ex. $\frac{7}{8} - \frac{1}{4} = ?$

The denominators are 8 and 4.
The LCM of 8 and 4 is 8.
So, use 8 as the common denominator.

$\frac{7}{8} - \frac{1}{4}$

$\downarrow \quad \downarrow$

$\frac{7}{8} - \frac{2}{8} = \mathbf{\frac{5}{8}}$

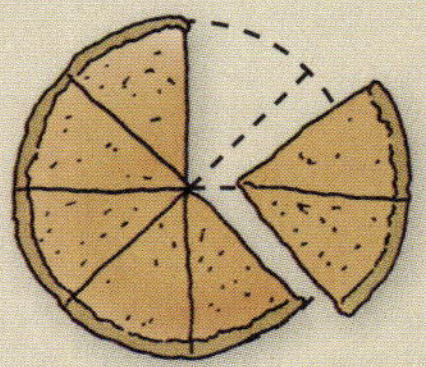

$\frac{1}{2} - \frac{1}{6}$

$\frac{4}{5} - \frac{3}{10}$

$\frac{2}{3} - \frac{1}{4}$

C

Fraction Difference War

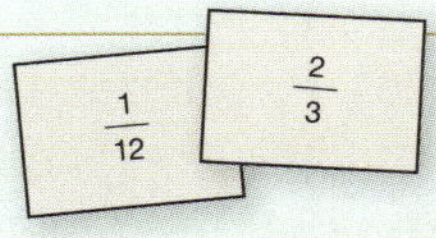

(2-Player Game)

Player 1	$\frac{\square}{\square} - \frac{\square}{\square}$	$\frac{\square}{\square} - \frac{\square}{\square}$	$\frac{\square}{\square} - \frac{\square}{\square}$
Player 2	$\frac{\square}{\square} - \frac{\square}{\square}$	$\frac{\square}{\square} - \frac{\square}{\square}$	$\frac{\square}{\square} - \frac{\square}{\square}$

Practice

Find the difference.

$\frac{5}{8} - \frac{1}{4}$

$\frac{8}{10} - \frac{1}{2}$

$\frac{2}{3} - \frac{1}{12}$

Find the missing numbers to complete the problems.

$\frac{2}{3} - \frac{1}{9}$

$\downarrow \quad \downarrow$

$\frac{\square}{9} - \frac{1}{9} = \frac{\square}{9}$

★

$\frac{1}{\square} - \frac{\square}{5}$

$\downarrow \quad \downarrow$

$\frac{5}{10} - \frac{2}{10} = \frac{\square}{10}$

★

$\frac{\square}{4} - \frac{\square}{5}$

$\downarrow \quad \downarrow$

$\frac{15}{20} - \frac{\square}{20} = \frac{11}{20}$

Use the clues to find the missing weights for the bars of soap. Write the equations you use.

- The lavender soap weighs $\frac{1}{3}$ lb. less than the rosemary soap.
- The lemon soap weighs $\frac{1}{6}$ lb. more than the lavender soap.
- The peppermint soap weighs $\frac{1}{4}$ lb. less than the lemon soap.

5.6

Review

Connect each number to its position on the number line.

$1\frac{2}{6}$ $1\frac{1}{6}$ $1\frac{4}{6}$ $2\frac{2}{6}$ $2\frac{3}{6}$

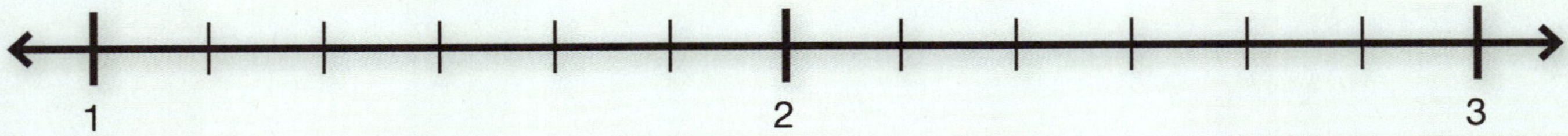

$\frac{9}{6}$ $\frac{6}{6}$ $\frac{7}{6}$ $\frac{13}{6}$ $\frac{12}{6}$

Use long division to solve.

$4\overline{)67}$ $7\overline{)109}$ $4\overline{)571}$ $5\overline{)538}$

Solve. Write the equations you use.

The storage unit is 15 feet long, 12 feet wide and 8 feet tall. What is the volume of the storage unit?

Zachary has 3 kg of rice. Then, he uses 1.7 kg. How much rice is left?

Lesson Activities

A

If the sum of two fractions is an improper fraction, convert the fraction to a mixed number.

Ex. $\frac{1}{2} + \frac{5}{8} = ?$

$\downarrow \quad \downarrow$

$\frac{4}{8} + \frac{5}{8} = \frac{9}{8} = 1\frac{1}{8}$

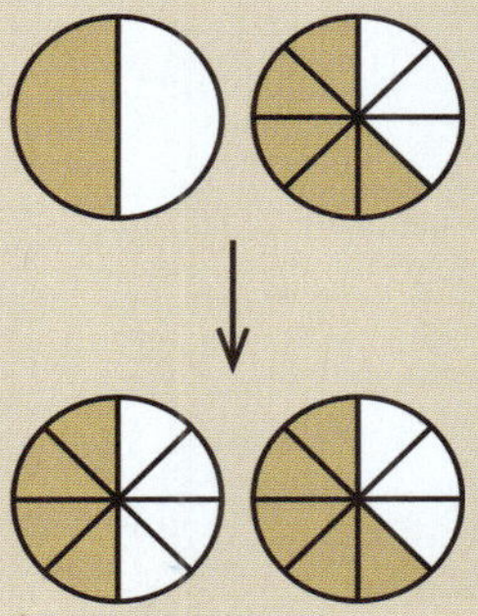

One way to subtract a fraction from a mixed number is to convert the mixed number to an improper fraction.

Ex. $1\frac{1}{6} - \frac{1}{3} = ?$

$\downarrow \quad \downarrow$

$\frac{7}{6} - \frac{1}{3}$

$\downarrow \quad \downarrow$

$\frac{7}{6} - \frac{2}{6} = \frac{5}{6}$

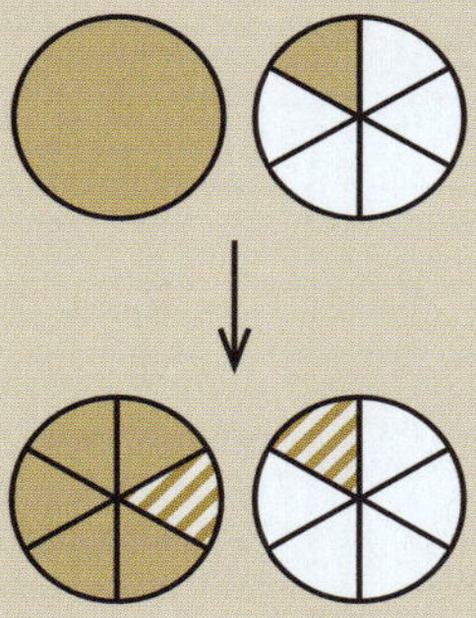

$\frac{3}{4} + \frac{7}{8}$

$1\frac{1}{2} - \frac{5}{6}$

$1\frac{1}{6} - \frac{7}{12}$

B

Close to 1

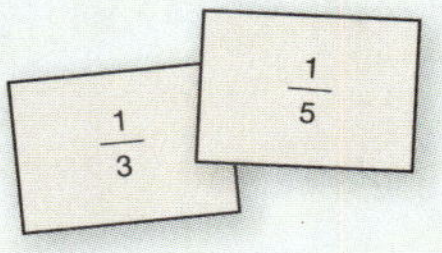

(2-Player Game)

Player 1	— + —	— + —	— + —
Player 2	— + —	— + —	— + —

5.7

Practice

Circle the fractions that match the description.
X the fractions that do not match the description.

Less than 1	Equal to 1	Greater than 1
$\frac{3}{4}$ $\frac{8}{7}$ $\frac{6}{6}$	$\frac{5}{5}$ $\frac{5}{6}$ $\frac{6}{5}$	$\frac{10}{10}$ $\frac{11}{10}$ $\frac{9}{10}$
$\frac{4}{3}$ $\frac{8}{10}$ $\frac{10}{8}$	$\frac{10}{9}$ $\frac{8}{9}$ $\frac{4}{4}$	$\frac{3}{2}$ $\frac{5}{3}$ $\frac{8}{8}$

Find the sum or difference.

$\frac{3}{5} + \frac{9}{10}$

$1\frac{1}{4} - \frac{5}{12}$

$1\frac{1}{3} - \frac{11}{12}$

Use the recipe to answer the questions. Write the equations you use.

What is the total amount of raisins and flaked coconut called for in the recipe?

How many more cups of oats than raisins does the recipe call for?

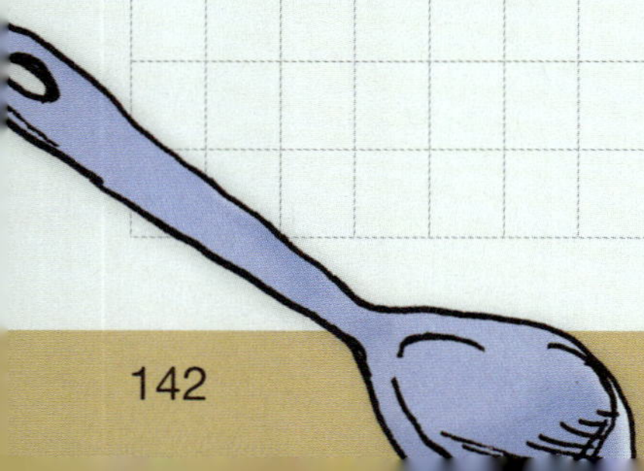

Oatmeal Raisin Cookies

$\frac{3}{4}$ cup all-purpose flour
$\frac{1}{2}$ teaspoon baking soda
$\frac{1}{2}$ teaspoon salt
$\frac{1}{2}$ cup butter
$\frac{3}{8}$ cup brown sugar
$\frac{3}{8}$ cup white sugar
$1\frac{1}{4}$ cups oats
1 egg
$\frac{2}{3}$ cup raisins
$\frac{1}{2}$ cup flaked coconut

Review

Find the missing information for each rectangular prism. Make sure to include the correct units.

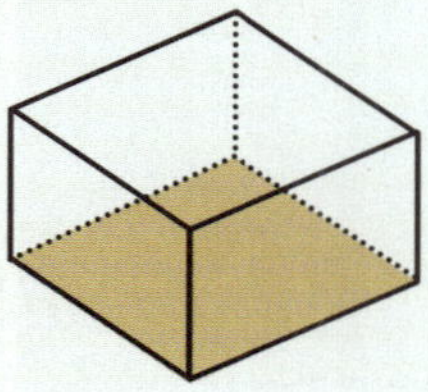

Base area: 9 sq. cm

Height: 4 cm

Volume: ________________

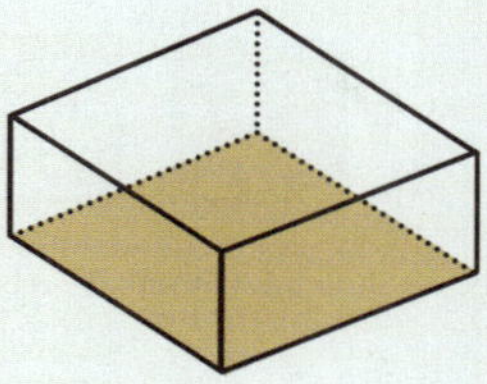

Base area: 30 sq. ft.

Height: ________________

Volume: 90 cubic ft.

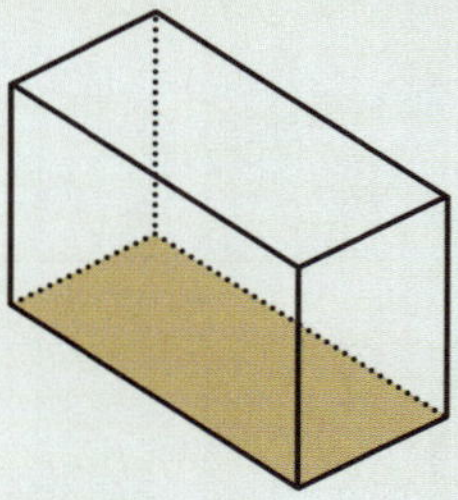

Base area: ________________

Height: 4 m

Volume: 40 cubic m

Find the product.

$$\begin{array}{r} 749 \\ \times \quad 58 \\ \hline \end{array}$$

Write each decimal as a mixed number.

3.2 = $3\frac{2}{10}$

1.54 = ________________

3.02 = ________________

1.837 = ________________

3.020 = ________________

2.019 = ________________

Solve. Write the equations you use.

Seth ran the race in 20.74 seconds. Ian ran the race in 23.06 seconds. How many seconds shorter was Seth's time than Ian's time?

The fund-raising committee wants to raise $20,000 for new playground equipment. They have raised $12,675 so far. How much money do they have left to raise?

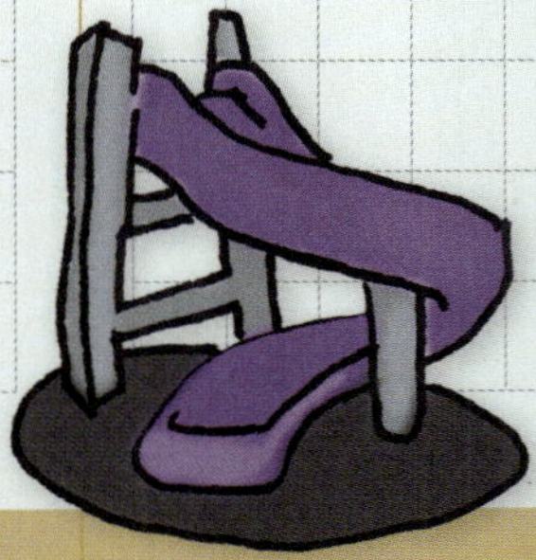

Lesson Activities

A

$$\begin{array}{r} 1\frac{1}{6} \\ +\ 2\frac{4}{6} \\ \hline \end{array}$$

$$\begin{array}{r} 2\frac{4}{5} \\ +\ 1\frac{3}{5} \\ \hline \end{array}$$

B

Use Common Denominators to Add Mixed Numbers

1. Rewrite the problem. Keep the whole numbers the same. Write the fractions as equivalent fractions with common denominators.
2. Add the fractions. Then, add the whole numbers.
3. If you have an improper fraction in the sum, convert the improper fraction to a mixed number. Add it to the whole number.

Ex.

$$\begin{array}{rcl} 1\frac{2}{3} & = & 1\frac{4}{6} \\ +\ 2\frac{1}{2} & = & 2\frac{3}{6} \\ \hline \end{array} \longrightarrow \begin{array}{rcl} 1\frac{2}{3} & = & 1\frac{4}{6} \\ +\ 2\frac{1}{2} & = & 2\frac{3}{6} \\ \hline & & 3\frac{7}{6} \end{array} \longrightarrow \begin{array}{rcl} 1\frac{2}{3} & = & 1\frac{4}{6} \\ +\ 2\frac{1}{2} & = & 2\frac{3}{6} \\ \hline & & 3\frac{7}{6} = 4\frac{1}{6} \end{array}$$

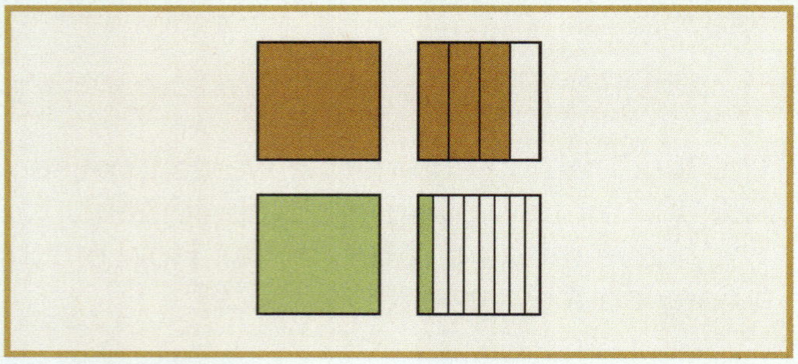

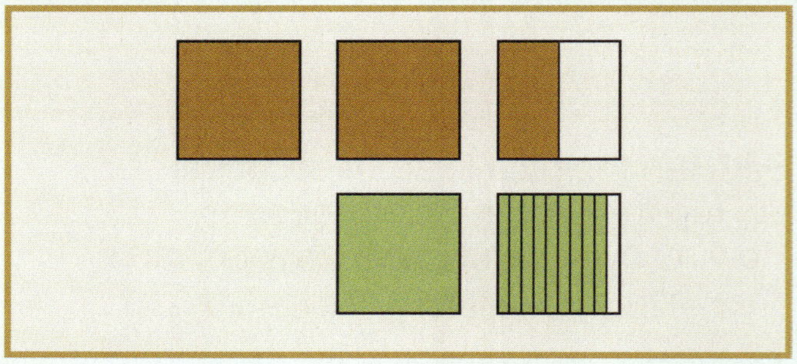

$$\begin{array}{r} 1\frac{3}{4} \\ +\ 1\frac{1}{8} \\ \hline \end{array}$$

$$\begin{array}{r} 2\frac{1}{2} \\ +\ 1\frac{9}{10} \\ \hline \end{array}$$

C

SPIN TO WIN!

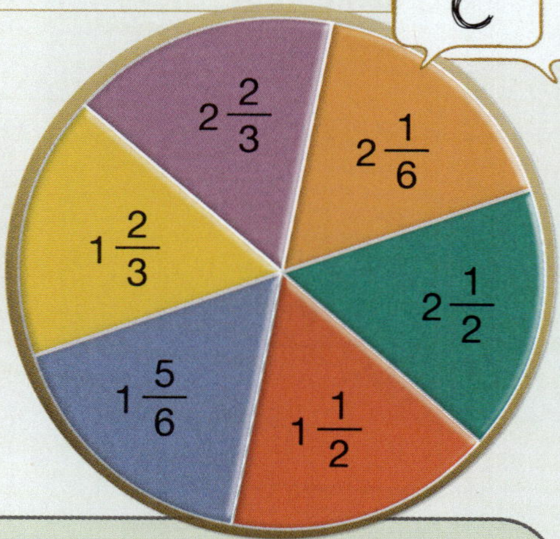

Player 1	Player 2
+	+
+	+
+	+

Practice

Complete.

$$3\frac{2}{5} + 1\frac{3}{10} = \underline{\qquad}$$

$$2\frac{2}{3} + 3\frac{5}{6} = \underline{\qquad}$$

$$1\frac{7}{8} + 2\frac{1}{4} = \underline{\qquad}$$

Review

Label the numbers on the number line.

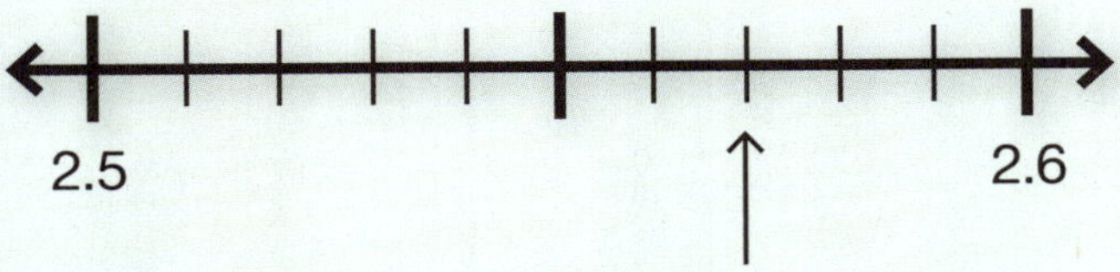

______

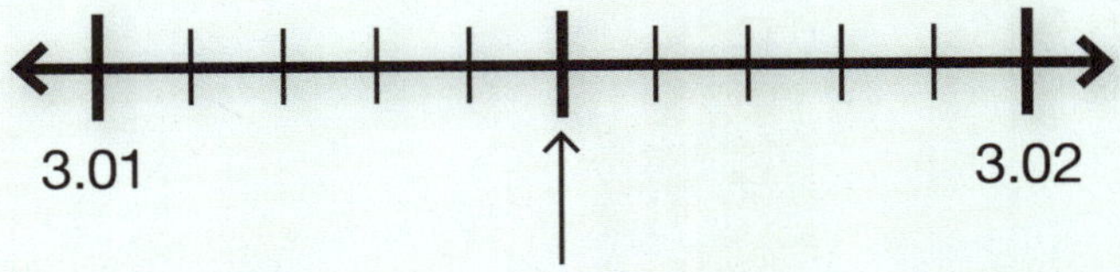

______

Find the missing dimension for each solid. All measurements are in centimeters.

Volume: 36 cubic cm

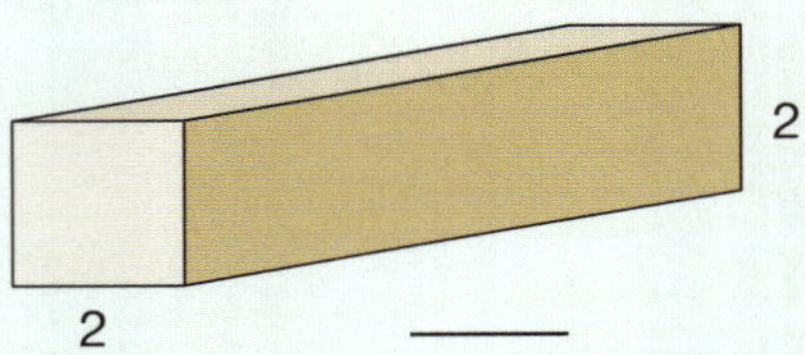

Volume: 36 cubic cm

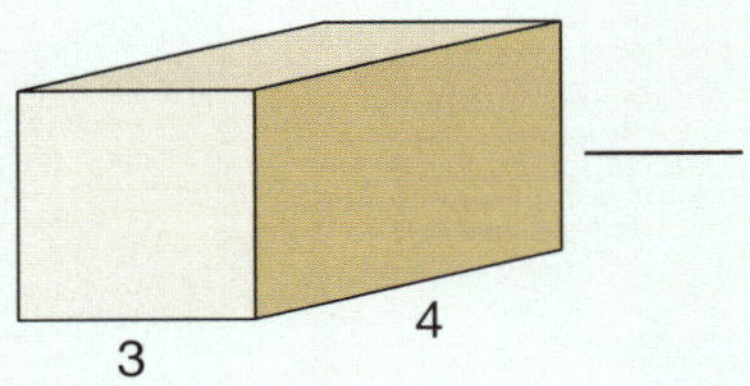

Volume: 36 cubic cm

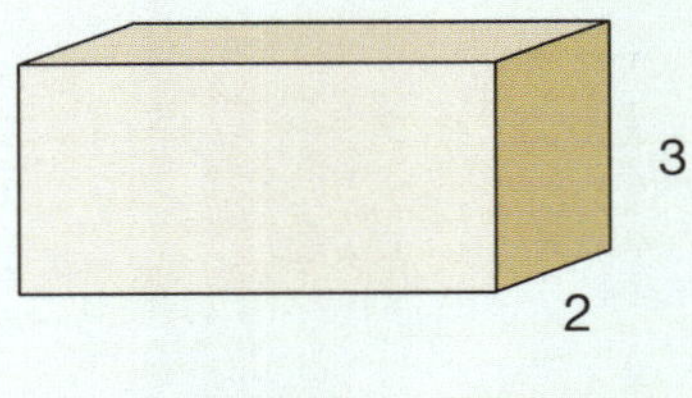

Solve. Write the equations you use.

Caleb has a block of clay that weighs 3 kilograms. He splits the clay into 5 equal balls. How heavy is each ball in grams? (1 kg equals 1,000 grams.)

The art teacher buys 4 cases of markers. Each case holds 10 boxes. Each box holds 8 markers. How many markers does the art teacher buy?

Lesson Activities

A

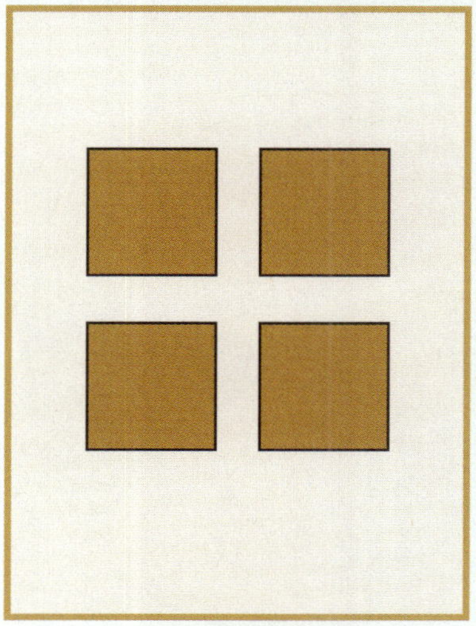

$$\begin{array}{r} 4 \\ - \; 2\frac{2}{3} \\ \hline \end{array}$$

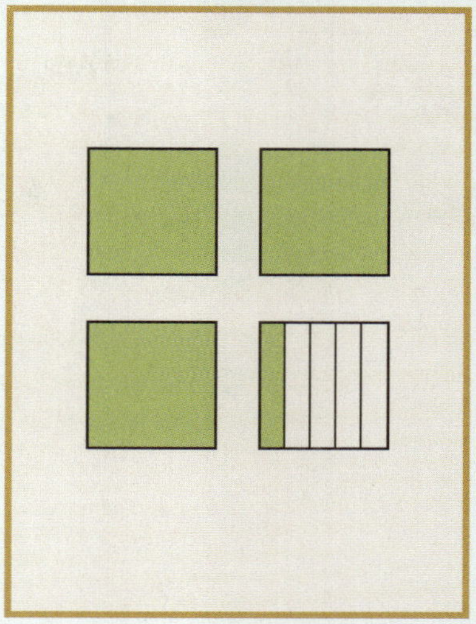

$$\begin{array}{r} 3\frac{1}{5} \\ - \; 1\frac{4}{5} \\ \hline \end{array}$$

B

Use Common Denominators to Subtract Mixed Numbers

1. Rewrite the problem. Keep the whole numbers the same. Write the fractions as equivalent fractions with common denominators.
2. If the top fraction is less than the bottom fraction, trade 1 whole for fractional parts.
3. Subtract the fractions. Then, subtract the whole numbers.

Ex.

$$\begin{array}{rcl} 3\frac{1}{2} & = & 3\frac{3}{6} \\ -\;1\frac{5}{6} & = & 1\frac{5}{6} \\ \hline \end{array} \longrightarrow \begin{array}{rcl} & & 2\frac{9}{6} \\ 3\frac{1}{2} & = & \not{3}\,\frac{\not{3}}{6} \\ -\;1\frac{5}{6} & = & 1\frac{5}{6} \\ \hline \end{array} \longrightarrow \begin{array}{rcl} & & 2\frac{9}{6} \\ 3\frac{1}{2} & = & \not{3}\,\frac{\not{3}}{6} \\ -\;1\frac{5}{6} & = & 1\frac{5}{6} \\ \hline & & \mathbf{1\frac{4}{6}} \end{array}$$

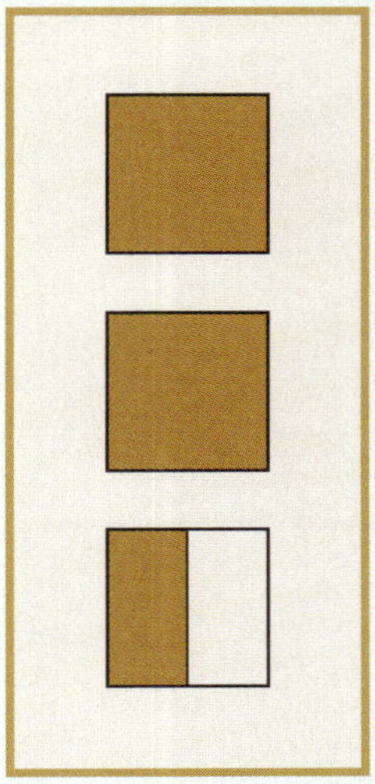

$$\begin{array}{r} 2\frac{1}{2} \\ - \; 1\frac{1}{4} \\ \hline \end{array}$$

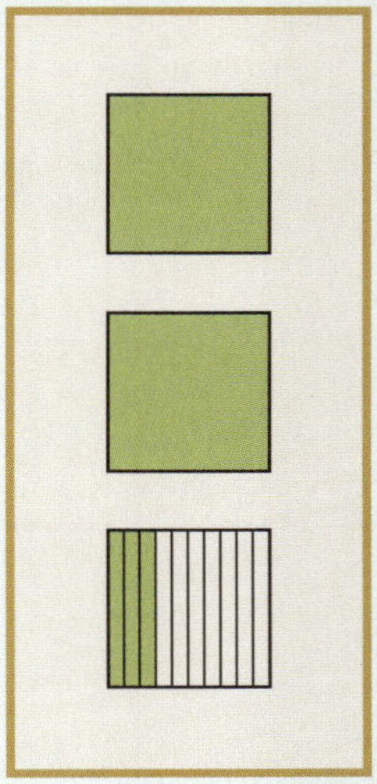

$$\begin{array}{r} 2\frac{3}{10} \\ - \; 1\frac{3}{5} \\ \hline \end{array}$$

SPIN TO WIN!

C

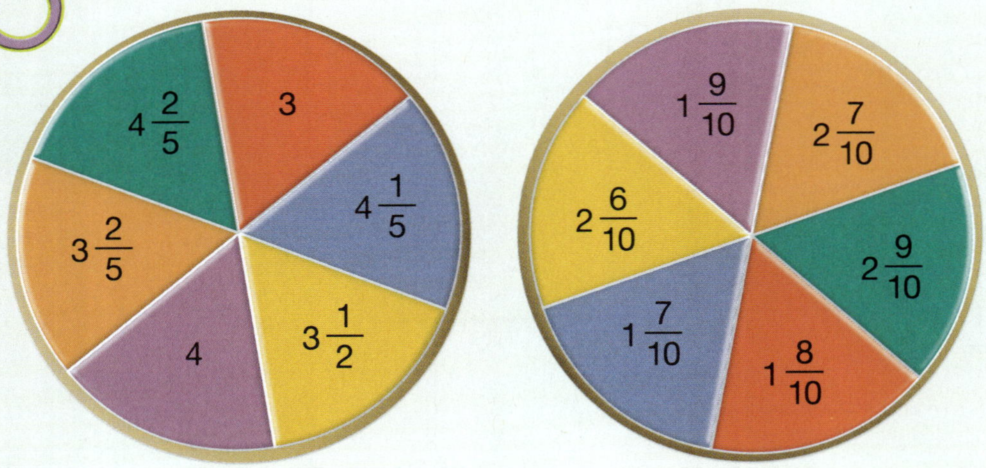

Player 1

−

−

−

Player 2

−

−

−

Practice

Complete.

$$3\frac{1}{2} - 1\frac{3}{4} = \underline{\qquad}$$

$$4\frac{1}{3} - 1\frac{5}{6} = \underline{\qquad}$$

$$5 - 2\frac{2}{3} = \underline{\qquad}$$

Review

Answer the questions about the numbers. Write your answers as whole numbers or decimals.

3,489,620

What is the value of the 9? *9,000*

What is the value of the 4? ______

What is the value of the 8? ______

What is the value of the 3? ______

2.751

What is the value of the 7? *0.7*

What is the value of the 5? ______

What is the value of the 2? ______

What is the value of the 1? ______

Solve. Write the equations you use.

Windsor's family hiked 4 miles through the forest. How long was their hike in feet? (1 mile equals 5,280 feet.)

Daniel's family has 2 gallons of milk. They drink 2 quarts of milk per day. How many days will their milk last? (1 gallon equals 4 quarts.)

Lesson Activities

A

$2\frac{1}{4}$ $2\frac{7}{8}$ $2\frac{1}{10}$ $3\frac{1}{4}$ $3\frac{3}{4}$ $3\frac{2}{3}$

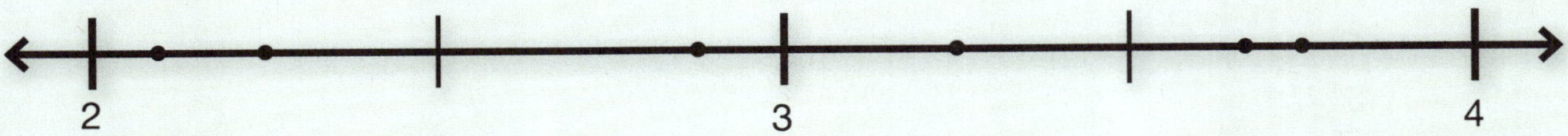

$2\frac{1}{4} \approx$ ______ $2\frac{7}{8} \approx$ ______ $2\frac{1}{10} \approx$ ______

$3\frac{1}{4} \approx$ ______ $3\frac{3}{4} \approx$ ______ $3\frac{2}{3} \approx$ ______

B

Estimate

+ ______

$$\begin{array}{r} 2\frac{7}{8} \\ +\ 3\frac{3}{4} \\ \hline \end{array}$$

Estimate

− ______

$$\begin{array}{r} 3\frac{1}{4} \\ -\ 2\frac{1}{10} \\ \hline \end{array}$$

C

Elliot uses $2\frac{1}{4}$ cups of strawberries and $3\frac{2}{3}$ cups of melon to make fruit salad. How many cups of fruit does he use in all?

Mckenzie filled her water bottle with $1\frac{3}{4}$ liters of water. After she drank some, she had $\frac{5}{6}$ liters left. How much water did she drink?

Practice

Round each number to the nearest whole number. Then, circle the better estimate for the sum or difference. You do not need to find the exact answers.

$1\frac{7}{8} + 1\frac{5}{6}$

3	4

$2\frac{1}{10} + 2\frac{1}{5}$

4	5

$1\frac{1}{4} + 1\frac{11}{12}$

3	4

$5 - 2\frac{10}{12}$

2	3

$5\frac{1}{5} - 2\frac{1}{8}$

2	3

$5\frac{1}{5} - 2\frac{7}{8}$

2	3

Solve. Write the equations you use.

Aaron and Lewis ran a relay race together. Aaron ran $1\frac{8}{10}$ km, and Lewis ran the rest of the race. The total length of the race was $5\frac{1}{5}$ km. How far did Lewis run?

Owen's pet turtle weighs $2\frac{3}{8}$ pounds. His pet guinea pig weighs $\frac{3}{4}$ pounds less than his turtle. How much does his guinea pig weigh?

5.10

Review

Complete the chart.

Cups	1	5	10	20	25	40	50	100
Fluid Ounces	8							

Find the volume of each solid. Make sure to include the correct units.

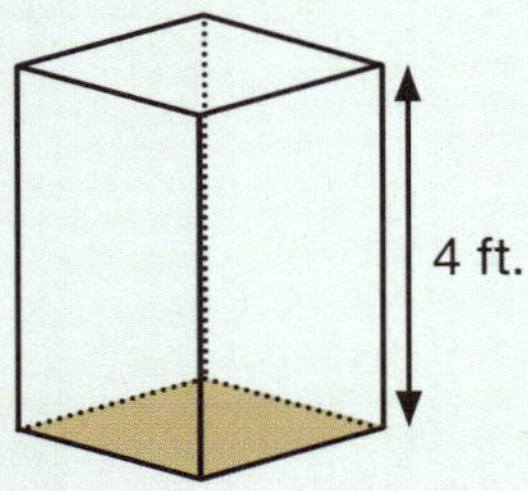

Base area: 4 sq. ft.

Volume: ___________________

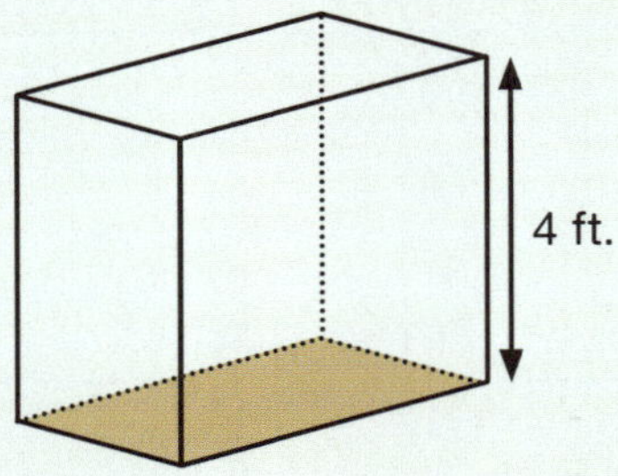

Base area: 8 sq. ft.

Volume: ___________________

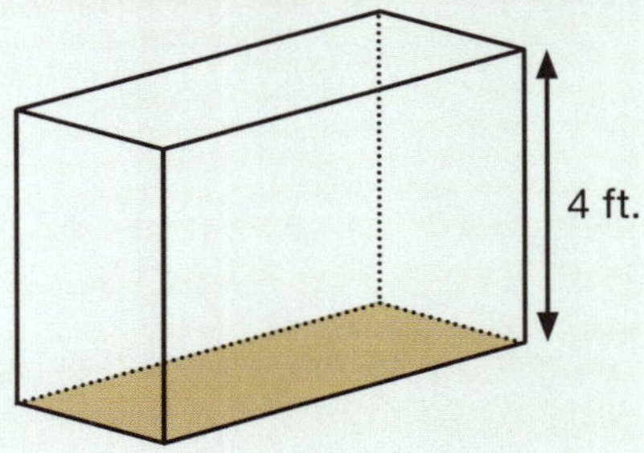

Base area: 10 sq. ft.

Volume: ___________________

Draw a line to connect the numbers in order from Start to End. Follow the rule.

Rule: Add 0.3

Start →

0.4	0.7	1.0	1.7	2.0
0.3	0.2	1.3	2.4	2.5
0.5	0.6	1.6	1.9	2.2
0.8	1.4	2.0	2.3	2.5
1.5	1.8	2.2	2.7	2.8

END

Rule: Subtract 0.4

Start →

5.8	5.5	2.6	2.2	1.8
5.4	5.1	3.0	1.9	1.4
5.0	4.5	3.4	3.5	1.0
4.6	4.2	3.8	0.7	0.6
4.4	3.9	3.6	0.4	0.2

END

Write one pair of parentheses in each equation to make the equation true.

★ $6 + 8 \div 1 \times 2 = 22$

★ $6 + 8 \div 1 \times 2 = 10$

★ $6 + 8 \div 1 \times 2 = 28$

Unit Wrap-Up

Use the words from the word bank to complete the sentence.

A ____________________ is a number with a whole number and a fraction.

____________________ fractions look different but have the same value.

The ____________________ is the top number in a fraction.

The ____________________ is the bottom number in a fraction.

Word bank
denominator
mixed number
numerator
equivalent

Write equivalent fractions with common denominators for each pair of fractions. Then, write <, >, or = to compare the fractions.

$\frac{7}{12} \bigcirc \frac{2}{3}$

$\frac{7}{10} \bigcirc \frac{3}{5}$

$\frac{2}{5} \bigcirc \frac{1}{4}$

Find the sum or difference.

$\frac{3}{8} + \frac{3}{4}$

$\frac{9}{10} - \frac{2}{5}$

$\frac{5}{6} - \frac{1}{4}$

Round each number to the nearest whole number. Then, circle the better estimate for the sum or difference.

$3\frac{2}{3} + 2\frac{3}{4}$

6 | 7

$1\frac{1}{4} + 2\frac{5}{8}$

3 | 4

$2\frac{1}{8} - 1\frac{1}{10}$

1 | 2

Unit Wrap-Up

Miri wants to make this quilt.
Use the quilt pattern to answer the questions.

Star Quilt Pattern

Fabric at the fabric store comes in rolls. You'll need the following lengths of each color of fabric.

- $\frac{3}{4}$ yd. dark blue fabric
- $1\frac{5}{8}$ yd. light blue fabric
- $3\frac{1}{4}$ yd. white fabric
- $1\frac{2}{3}$ yd. green fabric
- $4\frac{5}{6}$ yd. gray fabric for the back of the quilt

How much blue fabric does Miri need in all? (Include both the dark blue fabric and light blue fabric.)

Miri already has two pieces of gray fabric. One piece is $1\frac{1}{2}$ yd. long. The other piece is $3\frac{2}{3}$ yd. long. Does she have enough gray fabric?

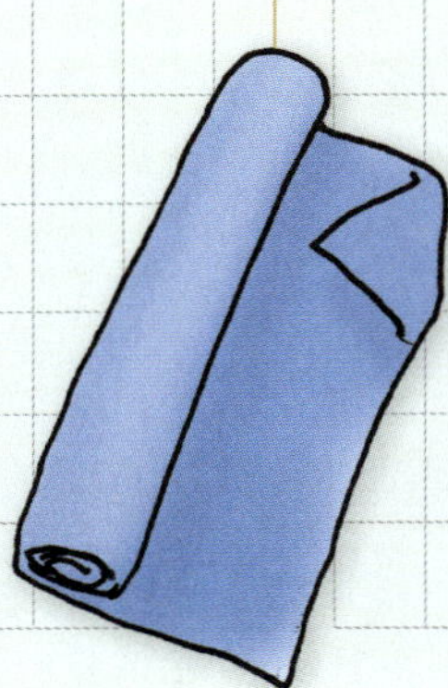

How much more white fabric than green fabric does Miri need?

Miri already has $2\frac{1}{3}$ yd. of white fabric. How much more white fabric does she need?

Lesson Activities

A

Number of Tickets	1	2	3	4	5	6	7	8
15	*15*	*30*						
25								
35								

B

Mental Division

We can use skip-counting to mentally divide by numbers like 15, 25, and 35.
Or, we can think about equal groups within the dividend.

Ex. Andrew wants to buy a prize that costs 60 points. How many 15-point tickets does he need?

Skip-Counting

60 ÷ 15 = ?

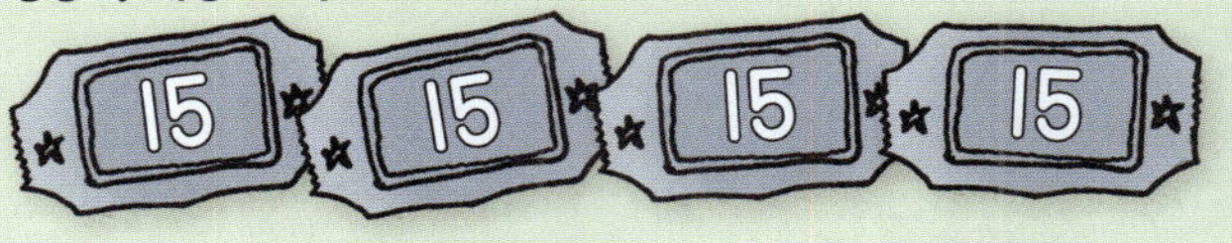

15 30 45 60

60 is the fourth multiple of 15.
So, there are 4 groups of 15 in 60.
60 ÷ 15 = **4**

Think about Equal Groups

60 ÷ 15 = ?

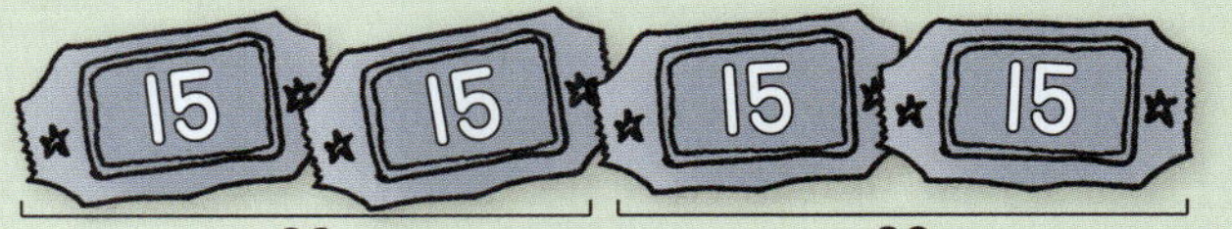

30 30
60

2 groups of 15 equal 30.
2 groups of 30 equal 60.
So, there are 4 groups of 15 in 60.
60 ÷ 15 = **4**

How many 35-point tickets do you need to buy a dinosaur?

How many 15-point tickets do you need to buy a box of candy?

How many 25-point tickets do you need to buy a teddy bear?

★ How many 250-point tickets do you need to buy a speaker?

6.1

Practice

Find the quotients.

15 ÷ 15 = ______

30 ÷ 15 = ______

45 ÷ 15 = ______

60 ÷ 15 = ______

25 ÷ 25 = ______

50 ÷ 25 = ______

75 ÷ 25 = ______

100 ÷ 25 = ______

35 ÷ 35 = ______

70 ÷ 35 = ______

105 ÷ 35 = ______

140 ÷ 35 = ______

120 ÷ 15 = ______

150 ÷ 15 = ______

180 ÷ 15 = ______

200 ÷ 25 = ______

300 ÷ 25 = ______

400 ÷ 25 = ______

★ 90 ÷ 45 = ______

★ 180 ÷ 45 = ______

★ 270 ÷ 45 = ______

Write the missing dividend in each division problem.

______ ÷ 25 = 6

______ ÷ 15 = 5

★ ______ ÷ 45 = 3

Solve. Write the equations you use.

There are 175 children at softball camp. The coaches split them into teams of 25. How many teams do they make?

Jazz dance lessons cost $105 for the winter term. Each lesson costs $15. How many lessons are in the winter term?

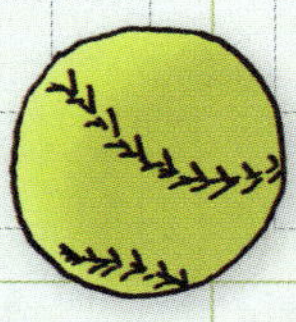

The library has $115 to buy board games. Each board game costs $25. How many board games can they buy?

How much money will they have left?

Asher's family set aside $150 to buy tickets to a show. Each ticket costs $35. How many tickets can they buy?

How much money will they have left?

Review

Find the products. Use the completed product to help.

$30 \times 3 =$ 90	$50 \times 4 =$ 200	$70 \times 5 =$ 350
$31 \times 3 =$ 93	$49 \times 4 =$ ______	$72 \times 5 =$ ______
$32 \times 3 =$ ______	$48 \times 4 =$ ______	$74 \times 5 =$ ______
$34 \times 3 =$ ______	$45 \times 4 =$ ______	$76 \times 5 =$ ______

Complete the chart.

	× 2
25	50
35	
55	
75	
45	
65	
85	

Find the sum or difference. If your answer is an improper fraction, convert the improper fraction to a mixed number.

$\frac{1}{6} + \frac{11}{12}$

$\frac{3}{4} - \frac{1}{6}$

$\frac{7}{9} - \frac{1}{3}$

$\frac{7}{10} + \frac{3}{5}$

Find the volume of the box. Write the equations you use in the work space.

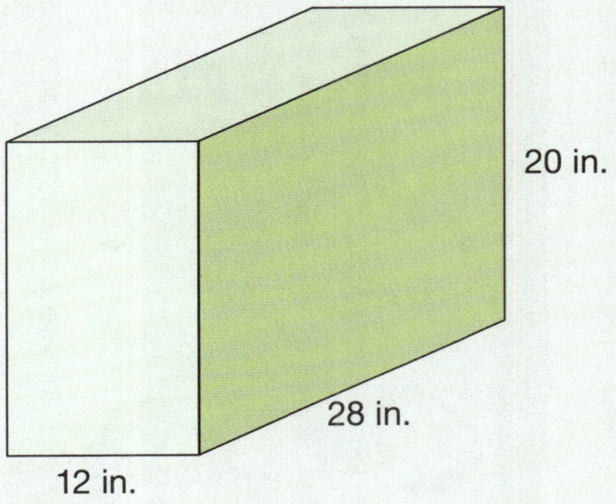

WORK SPACE

6.2

Lesson Activities

A

I have 20 ft. of rope. I cut the rope into 5 equal pieces. How long is each piece?

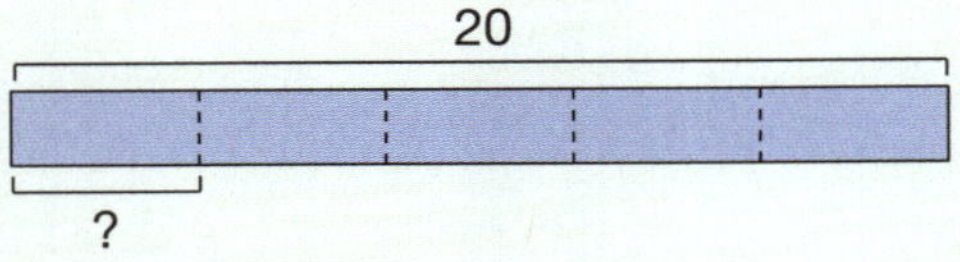

20 ÷ 5 = __________

I have 20 ft. of rope. I cut the rope into pieces that are each 5 ft. long. How many pieces do I make?

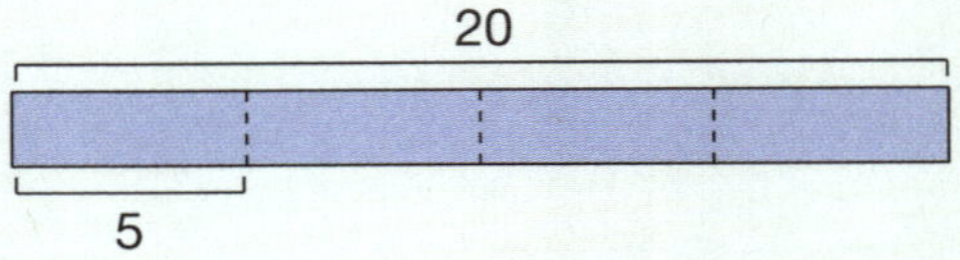

20 ÷ 5 = __________

B

Divide by 2 or 5

A number is divisible by 2 if it is even.

To mentally divide a number by 2, break the number into parts and split each part in half.

Ex. Simon won 38 tickets at the arcade. He shared the tickets equally with his brother. How many did they each get?

38 ÷ 2 = ?

Half of 30 → 15

Half of 8 → 4

19

38 ÷ 2 = **19 tickets**

A number is divisible by 5 if it has 0 or 5 in its ones-place.

To mentally divide a number by 5, write the problem as a missing factor problem. Then, multiply and adjust to find the missing factor.

Ex. Isabella won 65 tickets at the arcade. Each bracelet costs 5 tickets. How many bracelets can she buy?

65 ÷ 5 = ? → _____ × 5 = 65

10 × 5 = 50. Too low.
11 × 5 = 55. Too low.
12 × 5 = 60. Too low.
13 × 5 = 65. Just right!

65 ÷ 5 = **13 bracelets**

If you have 105 tickets, how many prizes can you get?

If you have 90 tickets, how many prizes can you get?

Practice

Circle the numbers that match the description.
X the numbers that do not match the description.

Divisible by 2		
85	90	92
95	100	105

Divisible by 5		
85	90	92
95	100	105

Divisible by 10		
85	90	92
95	100	105

Complete.

80 $\xrightarrow{\div 2}$ 40 $\xrightarrow{\div 2}$ ______ $\xrightarrow{\div 2}$ ______ $\xrightarrow{\div 2}$ ______

144 $\xrightarrow{\div 2}$ ______ $\xrightarrow{\div 2}$ ______ $\xrightarrow{\div 2}$ ______ $\xrightarrow{\div 2}$ ______

400 $\xrightarrow{\div 2}$ ______ $\xrightarrow{\div 2}$ ______ $\xrightarrow{\div 2}$ ______ $\xrightarrow{\div 2}$ ______

Use mental math to find the quotient.

$70 \div 5 =$ ______

$85 \div 5 =$ ______

$120 \div 5 =$ ______

Solve. Write the equations you use.

Abigail bakes 103 cookies to give away.
She packs 5 cookies in each box.
How many boxes does she fill?

How many cookies does she have left?

The books at the library sale cost $5 each.
Carlos has $67 to spend on books.
How many books can he buy?

If he buys as many books as possible,
how much money will he have left?

6.2

Review

Complete.

$$2\frac{1}{3} + 1\frac{1}{4} = \underline{\quad\quad}$$

$$3\frac{4}{5} + 2\frac{7}{10} = \underline{\quad\quad}$$

$$4\frac{1}{2} + 5\frac{7}{8} = \underline{\quad\quad}$$

Draw a line that connects the numbers in order from Start to End. Follow the rule.

Rule: Add 0.07

Start → 0.07 … END (after 0.77)

0.07	0.14	0.3	0.70	0.77
0.014	0.21	0.25	0.63	0.69
0.24	0.28	0.41	0.56	0.6
0.32	0.35	0.42	0.49	0.55
0.36	0.4	0.19	0.52	0.38

Rule: Subtract 0.03

Start → 0.8 … END (after 0.56)

0.8	0.77	0.74	0.69	0.38
0.07	0.7	0.71	0.54	0.44
0.79	0.75	0.68	0.4	0.5
0.83	0.86	0.65	0.57	0.53
0.99	0.84	0.62	0.59	0.56

Solve. Write the equations you use.

Elijah swam 45 laps on Monday. He swam 25 fewer laps on Tuesday than he swam on Monday. How many laps did he swim on Tuesday?

How many laps did he swim in all on Monday and Tuesday?

Katelyn played 3 times as many basketball games in November as she played in October. She played 18 basketball games in November. How many basketball games did she play in October?

How many more basketball games did she play in November than October?

Lesson Activities

A

Multiple of 3	3	6	9	12	15	18	21	24	27	30
Sum of digits	*3*	*6*	*9*	*3*						

Multiple of 3	33	36	39	42	45	48	51	54	57	60
Sum of digits										

B

Divide by 3

A number is divisible by 3 if the sum of its digits is divisible by 3.

Ex. Is 96 divisible by 3?

9 + 6 = 15

15 is divisible by 3, so 96 is divisible by 3.

To mentally divide a number by 3, write the problem as a missing factor problem. Then, multiply and adjust to find the missing factor.

Ex. Sasha has 57 tickets. Each game at the fair costs 3 tickets. How many games can he play?

57 ÷ 3 = ? → _____ × 3 = 57

20 × 3 = 60. Too high.
19 × 3 = 57. Just right!

57 ÷ 3 = **19 games**

72 ÷ 3 = ___________

93 ÷ 3 = ___________

84 ÷ 3 = ___________

C

Division Tic-Tac-Toe (2-Player Game)

66	75	100	76
81	70	72	102
96	68	99	90
87	105	80	86

Practice

**Circle the numbers that are divisible by 3.
X the numbers that are not divisible by 3.**

49	51	37	75	96	97
267	672	101	102	1,001	1,002

Find the quotients.

60 ÷ 3 = ____________

63 ÷ 3 = ____________

66 ÷ 3 = ____________

69 ÷ 3 = ____________

72 ÷ 3 = ____________

90 ÷ 3 = ____________

87 ÷ 3 = ____________

84 ÷ 3 = ____________

81 ÷ 3 = ____________

78 ÷ 3 = ____________

120 ÷ 3 = ____________

123 ÷ 3 = ____________

126 ÷ 3 = ____________

129 ÷ 3 = ____________

132 ÷ 3 = ____________

Complete the price chart. Use the completed box to help.

Number of tacos			50		
Total price	$144	$147	$150	$153	$156

Write a number that matches each description. (Many answers are possible.)

- This number has 3 digits.
- This number is greater than 200 and less than 500.
- This number is divisible by 2.
- This number is divisible by 3.

☐☐☐

- This number has 4 digits.
- This number is less than 2,000.
- This number is divisible by 5.
- Thie number is divisible by 3.

☐,☐☐☐

Review

Complete.

$$3\frac{4}{5} - 2\frac{3}{10} =$$

$$4\frac{1}{8} - 2\frac{1}{2} =$$

$$6 - 3\frac{5}{6} =$$

Circle the problems that equal the number in the star.

2	20	5	50
80 ÷ 4	80 ÷ 4	150 ÷ 3	150 ÷ 3
80 ÷ 40	80 ÷ 40	150 ÷ 30	150 ÷ 30
140 ÷ 7	140 ÷ 7	400 ÷ 8	400 ÷ 8
140 ÷ 70	140 ÷ 70	400 ÷ 80	400 ÷ 80

Find the least common multiple for each pair of numbers.

LCM of 5 and 6: ________

LCM of 5 and 7: ________

LCM of 5 and 10: ________

Lesson Activities

A

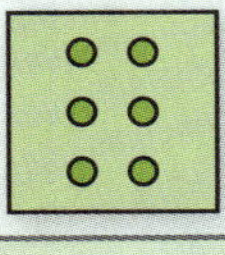
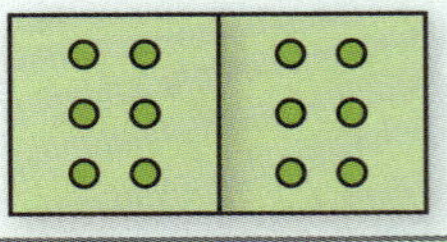

	6	12	18
Divisible by 2?			
Divisible by 3?			
Divisible by 6?			

B

Divide by 6

A number is divisible by 6 if it is divisible by 2 and divisible by 3.

Ex. Is 78 divisible by 6?

78 is an even number, so it is divisible by 2.

7 + 8 = 15. 15 is divisible by 3, so 78 is divisible by 3.

78 is divisible by both 2 and 3, so it is divisible by 6.

To mentally divide a number by 6, write the problem as a missing factor problem. Then, multiply and adjust to find the missing factor.

Ex. The bakery packs its products in boxes of 6. If they pack 78 donuts, how many boxes of donuts do they fill?

78 ÷ 6 = ? ➔ _____ × 6 = 78

10 × 6 = 60. Too low.
11 × 6 = 66. Too low.
12 × 6 = 72. Too low.
13 × 6 = 78. Just right!

78 ÷ 6 = **13**

132 ÷ 6 = __________

114 ÷ 6 = __________

Practice

Circle the numbers that match the description.
X the numbers that do not match the description.

Divisible by 2		
90	92	93
96	99	100
102	105	108

Divisible by 3		
90	92	93
96	99	100
102	105	108

Divisible by 6		
90	92	93
96	99	100
102	105	108

Arrange the digits to create a number that matches the description at the top of the column. (More than one answer is possible for some of the problems.)

	Divisible by 2	Divisible by 3	Divisible by 6
5 6 1	1 5 6	___ ___ ___	___ ___ ___
2 9 4	___ ___ ___	___ ___ ___	___ ___ ___
0 7 2	___ ___ ___	___ ___ ___	___ ___ ___

Use mental math to find the quotient.

$84 \div 6 =$ ____________

$126 \div 6 =$ ____________

★ $294 \div 6 =$ ____________

Review

Write equivalent fractions with common denominators for each pair of fractions. Then, write <, >, or = to compare the fractions.

$\frac{5}{12} \bigcirc \frac{1}{3}$

$\frac{6}{10} \bigcirc \frac{3}{5}$

$\frac{3}{5} \bigcirc \frac{3}{4}$

Use long division to solve.

$6 \overline{)397}$

Use mental math to solve.

23 × 2 = ________

23 × 4 = ________

4 × 8 × 2 = ________

4 × 8 × 4 = ________

51 × 2 = ________

51 × 4 = ________

2 × 15 × 6 = ________

4 × 15 × 6 = ________

75 × 2 = ________

75 × 4 = ________

2 × 25 × 8 = ________

4 × 25 × 8 = ________

Complete.

________ pair(s) of parallel sides

________ right angle(s)

________ pair(s) of parallel sides

________ right angle(s)

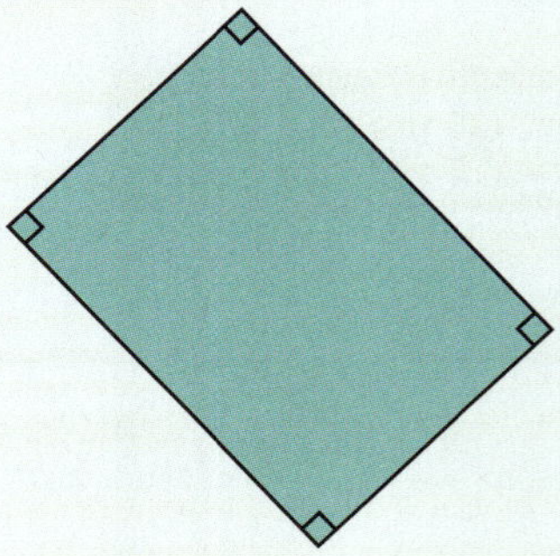

________ pair(s) of parallel sides

________ right angle(s)

Lesson Activities

A

Divide by 4

To mentally divide a number by 4, divide by 2 twice.

Ex. There are 60 children at lacrosse camp. The coaches split the children into 4 equal groups. How many children are in each group?

60 ÷ 4 = ?

60 ÷ 2 = 30

30 ÷ 2 = 15

60 ÷ 4 = **15 children**

60 → 30, 30; 30 → 15, 15; 30 → 15, 15

A number is divisible by 4 if you get an even number when you divide the number by 2.

Ex. Is 60 divisible by 4?

60 ÷ 2 = 30

30 is an even number. That means you can divide it by 2 and get another whole number.

So, 60 is divisible by 4.

84 ÷ 4 = ___________

208 ÷ 4 = ___________

B

Division Tic-Tac-Toe (2-Player Game)

51	52	53	54	55	56	57	58	59	60
61	62	63	64	65	66	67	68	69	70
71	72	73	74	75	76	77	78	79	80
81	82	83	84	85	86	87	88	89	90
91	92	93	94	95	96	97	98	99	100

Practice

**Circle the numbers that match the description.
X the numbers that do not match the description.**

Divisible by 2			
90	92	93	94
96	98	99	100
103	104	106	108

Divisible by 4			
90	92	93	94
96	98	99	100
103	104	106	108

Find the quotients.

48 ÷ 2 = ____________

48 ÷ 4 = ____________

68 ÷ 2 = ____________

68 ÷ 4 = ____________

84 ÷ 2 = ____________

84 ÷ 4 = ____________

100 ÷ 2 = ____________

100 ÷ 4 = ____________

116 ÷ 2 = ____________

116 ÷ 4 = ____________

★ 536 ÷ 2 = ____________

536 ÷ 4 = ____________

Use the numbers to solve the number riddles. You will use each number once.

75	90	109	130	140	162

- I am a two-digit number.
- I am divisible by 5.
- I am not divisible by 10.

- I am a two-digit number.
- I am divisible by 6.

- I am a three-digit number.
- I am divisible by 10.
- I am divisible by 4.

- I am a three-digit number.
- I am divisible by 10.
- I am not divisible by 4.

- I am a three-digit number.
- I am divisible by 6.

- I am a three-digit number.
- I am not divisible by 10.
- I am not divisible by 6.

Review

Circle yes or no to answer the questions.

Is 70 divisible by 7? **Yes | No**	Is 64 divisible by 8? **Yes | No**	Is 81 divisible by 9? **Yes | No**
Is 75 divisible by 7? **Yes | No**	Is 72 divisible by 8? **Yes | No**	Is 85 divisible by 9? **Yes | No**
Is 77 divisible by 7? **Yes | No**	Is 74 divisible by 8? **Yes | No**	Is 90 divisible by 9? **Yes | No**

Complete the circles with <, >, or =.

0.8 ◯ 0.08

0.7 ◯ 0.70

0.060 ◯ 0.06

0.005 ◯ 0.050

0.040 ◯ 0.04

Complete the missing factors in the factor pairs.

Factor Pairs of 30	Factor Pairs of 40
1 × ______	1 × ______
2 × ______	2 × ______
3 × ______	4 × ______
5 × ______	5 × ______

Solve. Write the equations you use.

The tennis coach has 164 tennis balls. She splits them evenly into 4 baskets. How many tennis balls are in each basket?

6 tennis lessons cost $216. How much does each lesson cost?

WORK SPACE

Lesson Activities

Factor Pairs of 24

1	2	3
4	5	6
7	8	9

A

Factor Pairs of 23

1	2	3
4	5	6
7	8	9

B

How to Find All Factors of a Number Less Than 100

To find all factors of a number less than 100, check to see whether the target number is divisible by the numbers 1 to 9.

If the target number is divisible by one of the numbers, write the matching factor pair.

Once you find all the factor pairs, write all the factors in order from least to greatest.

Ex. Find all the factors of 68.

68 ÷ 1 = 68. 1 × 68 is a factor pair.

68 ÷ 2 = 34. 2 × 34 is a factor pair.

68 is not divisible by 3, so 3 is not a factor of 68.

68 ÷ 4 = 17. 4 × 17 is a factor pair.

68 is not divisible by 5, 6, 7, 8, or 9. So, 5, 6, 7, 8, and 9 are not factors of 68.

Factors of 68: **1, 2, 4, 17, 34, and 68.**

Prime numbers have exactly 2 factors: 1 and the number itself.

Composite numbers have more than 2 factors.

Ex. Is 68 prime or composite?

68 has more than 2 factors, so it is composite.

Ex. Is 23 prime or composite?

23 has exactly 2 factors, so it is prime.

Rachel is helping set up 60 chairs for a concert. She wants to arrange them in equal rows and use all the chairs. How many chairs can she put in each row? Find all possible answers.

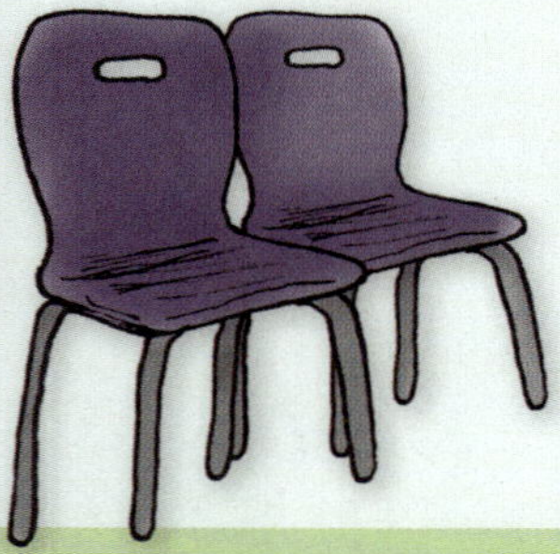

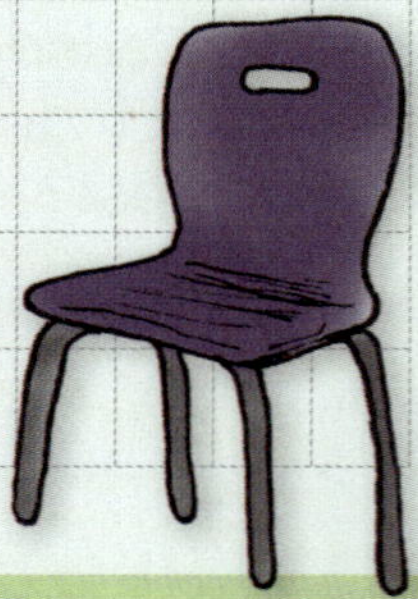

Practice

Find all factors of each number. Use mental or written division to check whether each number is divisible by the numbers from 1 to 9. Then, answer the questions.

Factor Pairs of 64

Is 64 prime or composite? ______________

Factor Pairs of 67

Is 67 prime or composite? ______________

Factor Pairs of 89

Is 89 prime or composite? ______________

Factor Pairs of 93

Is 93 prime or composite? ______________

Solve.

David baked 90 cookies to give away. He wants to pack the cookies in boxes, and he wants to put the same number of cookies in each box. How many cookies can he pack in each box? Find all possible answers.

6.6

Review

Complete the equivalent fractions. Then, write each fraction as a decimal. Use the pictures to help.

$\frac{1}{2} = \frac{5}{10} =$ *0.5*

$\frac{1}{4} = \frac{\quad}{100} =$ ______

$\frac{3}{4} = \frac{\quad}{100} =$ ______

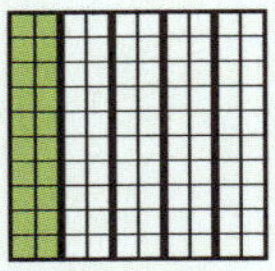

$\frac{1}{5} = \frac{\quad}{10} =$ ______

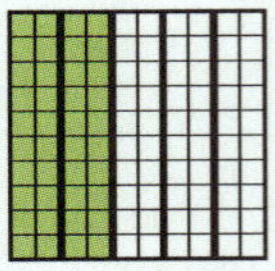

$\frac{2}{5} = \frac{\quad}{10} =$ ______

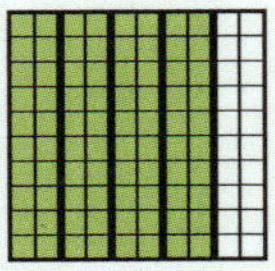

$\frac{4}{5} = \frac{\quad}{10} =$ ______

Complete.

$90 \times 90 =$ ______

$9 \times 900 =$ ______

$900 \times 900 =$ ______

$90 \times 9{,}000 =$ ______

$900 \times 90 =$ ______

$9{,}000 \times 9 =$ ______

Find the missing information for each rectangular prism.

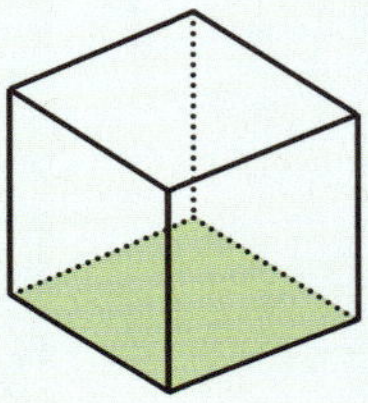

Volume: 64 cubic cm

Height: 4 cm

Base area: ______

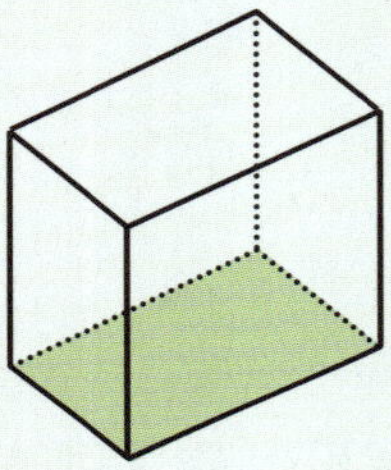

Volume: 75 cubic cm

Height: 5 cm

Base area: ______

Solve. Write the equations you use.

Moira had $3\frac{5}{12}$ chocolate bars. She gave $1\frac{2}{3}$ chocolate bars to her sister. How many chocolate bars did she have left?

Steven's baby sister weighed 5.45 kg. Then, she gained 0.87 kg. How much did she weigh then?

Lesson Activities

A

Hope made 24 lavender-scented candles for the craft fair. She wants to pack an equal number of candles in each box. How many candles can she pack in each box? Find all possible answers.

Hope also made 28 eucalyptus-scented candles. If she puts an equal number of these candles in each box, how many candles can she pack in each box? Find all possible answers.

B

Greatest Common Factor

The greatest common factor (GCF) of two numbers is the highest factor they have in common.

To find the greatest common factor:

1. Make a list of the factors of each number.
2. Look for the greatest factor they have in common.

Ex. Find the greatest common factor of 10 and 15.

Factor pairs of 10:	Factor pairs of 15:
1 × 10	1 × 15
2 × 5	3 × 5

The common factors of 10 and 15 are 1 and 5.

So, the greatest common factor of 10 and 15 is **5**.

Factor Pairs of 24	Factor Pairs of 28	Factor Pairs of 30

What factor(s) do 24 and 28 have in common?

GCF of 24 and 28: ________

What factor(s) do 28 and 30 have in common?

GCF of 28 and 30: ________

What factor(s) do 24 and 30 have in common?

GCF of 24 and 30: ________

Practice

Find all factor pairs for each number. Then, answer the questions.

Factor Pairs of 12	Factor Pairs of 15	What factors do 12 and 15 have in common? GCF of 12 and 15: ________
Factor Pairs of 16	**Factor Pairs of 32**	What factors do 16 and 32 have in common? GCF of 16 and 32: ________
Factor Pairs of 25	**Factor Pairs of 45**	What factors do 25 and 45 have in common? GCF of 25 and 45: ________

Find the greatest common factor for each pair of numbers. Make your own lists of factors.

GCF of 8 and 9: ____________________

GCF of 18 and 27: ____________________

Review

Choose the more sensible measurement for each volume.

Volume of a thimble

3 cu. cm | 3 cu. m

Volume of a bathtub

6 cu. in. | 6 cu. ft.

Volume of a small pool

16 cu. km | 16 cu. m

Complete.

240 ÷ 3 = ______

240 ÷ 4 = ______

240 ÷ 6 = ______

2,400 ÷ 3 = ______

2,400 ÷ 4 = ______

2,400 ÷ 6 = ______

Use mental math to find the quotients.

72 ÷ 3 = ______

92 ÷ 2 = ______

72 ÷ 6 = ______

92 ÷ 4 = ______

Circle the word that describes each number.

8: prime | composite

9: prime | composite

12: prime | composite

17: prime | composite

20: prime | composite

21: prime | composite

24: prime | composite

27: prime | composite

29: prime | composite

6.8

Lesson Activities

A

240 ÷ 8 = ______ 300 ÷ 6 = ______ 600 ÷ 3 = ______

800 ÷ 2 = ______ 2,700 ÷ 3 = ______ 4,000 ÷ 2 = ______

B

Mental Division with Trailing Zeros

Cross out the trailing zeros the numbers have in common. Then, divide the other digits.

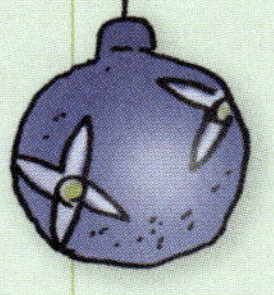

Ex. The winter festival decorating committee wants to buy 1,200 ornaments. The ornaments come in packs of 40. How many packs should the committee buy?

1,200 ÷ 40 = ?

120 tens ÷ 4 tens = 30

1,20~~0~~ ÷ 4~~0~~ = **30**

240 ÷ 80 = ______ 300 ÷ 60 = ______ 600 ÷ 30 = ______

800 ÷ 200 = ______ 2,700 ÷ 300 = ______ 4,000 ÷ 200 = ______

C

Winter Festival Shopping List

- 320 candy canes
- 400 cookies
- 1,500 sheets of sparkly paper (for making snowflakes)

Candy canes come in packs of 40. How many packs should the planning team buy?

Check: ______

Cookies come in boxes of 80. How many boxes should the planning team buy?

Check: ______

Sparkly paper comes in packs of 30 sheets. How many packs should the planning team buy?

Check: ______

Practice

Match.

150 ÷ 30	3	2,400 ÷ 600
210 ÷ 70	4	1,800 ÷ 300
160 ÷ 40	5	2,700 ÷ 900
1,800 ÷ 60	6	1,200 ÷ 40
2,800 ÷ 70	30	3,500 ÷ 700
450 ÷ 9	40	250 ÷ 5
360 ÷ 60	50	2,000 ÷ 50

Solve. Write the equations you use.

Napkins come in packs of 70. How many packs should the planning team buy?

Twinkle lights come in boxes of 200. How many boxes of twinkle lights should the planning team buy?

★ Each tub of cocoa mix makes 80 cups of cocoa. How many tubs should the planning team buy?

Review

Find the greatest common factor for each pair of numbers. Make your own lists of factors.

GCF of 25 and 35: ______________

GCF of 28 and 40: ______________

Circle the numbers that match the description. X the numbers that do not match the description.

Divisible by 3		
120	130	132
144	150	156

Divisible by 4		
120	130	132
144	150	156

Divisible by 6		
120	130	132
144	150	156

Solve. Write the equations you use.

Elizabeth's family has $1\frac{3}{8}$ sausage pizzas and $1\frac{3}{4}$ vegetable pizzas left over after a party. How much more vegetable pizza than sausage pizza do they have?

Preston had 1.36 kg of gummy worms. He ate some of the gummy worms and then he had 0.742 kg left. How many kilograms of gummy worms did he eat?

Unit Wrap-Up

Write the number that makes the statement true. You will use each number once.

2	3	4	5	6	10

A number is divisible by ________ if it is even.

A number is divisible by ________ if it has 0 in its ones-place.

A number is divisible by ________ if you get an even number when you divide the number by 2.

A number is divisible by ________ if it is divisible by 2 and divisible by 3.

A number is divisible by ________ if it has 0 or 5 in its ones-place.

A number is divisible by ________ if the sum of its digits is divisible by 3.

Match.

45 ÷ 15	2	150 ÷ 50
70 ÷ 35	3	320 ÷ 80
100 ÷ 25	4	180 ÷ 90
75 ÷ 15	5	300 ÷ 60

Use mental math to find the quotients.

90 ÷ 3 = ________	100 ÷ 5 = ________	120 ÷ 6 = ________
93 ÷ 3 = ________	95 ÷ 5 = ________	126 ÷ 6 = ________
96 ÷ 3 = ________	90 ÷ 5 = ________	132 ÷ 6 = ________
99 ÷ 3 = ________	85 ÷ 5 = ________	138 ÷ 6 = ________
44 ÷ 2 = ________	96 ÷ 2 = ________	4,800 ÷ 60 = ________
44 ÷ 4 = ________	96 ÷ 4 = ________	4,800 ÷ 600 = ________

6.9

Unit Wrap-Up

Find all factors of each number. Then, answer the questions.

Factor Pairs of 63	Factor Pairs of 75

Is 63 prime or composite?

Is 75 prime or composite?

What factors do 63 and 75 have in common?

GCF of 63 and 75: ____________________

Use the numbers to solve the number riddles. You will use each number once.

65	70	72	81	225	349	357	468

- I am a two-digit number.
- I am divisible by 5.
- I am divisible by 2.

- I am a two-digit number.
- I am divisible by 5.
- I am not divisible by 2.

- I am a two-digit number.
- I am divisible by 6.
- I am divisible by 4.

- I am a two-digit number.
- I am divisible by 3.
- I am not divisible by 2.

- I am a three-digit number.
- I am divisible by 5.

- I am a three-digit number.
- I am divisible by 6.

- I am a three-digit number.
- I am divisible by 3.
- I am not divisible by 5.
- I am not divisible by 4.

- I am a three-digit number.
- I am not divisible by 2.
- I am not divisible by 5.
- I am not divisible by 3.

Lesson Activities

A

LEMONADE STAND EARNINGS

Day 1: $38
Day 2: $88
Day 3: $138
Day 4: $538

$5\overline{)38}$ $5\overline{)88}$ $5\overline{)138}$ $5\overline{)538}$

B

The Quotient Game (2-Player Game)

$2\overline{)196}$

$6\overline{)234}$

$8\overline{)368}$

$4\overline{)424}$

$6\overline{)525}$

$8\overline{)652}$

$4\overline{)788}$

$7\overline{)826}$

$4\overline{)908}$

$5\overline{)935}$

Player 1				Sum of Quotients +
Player 2				Sum of Quotients +

Practice

Describe the mistake in each problem. Then, solve it correctly.

incorrect

```
    73
5 | 374
  - 35 ↓
    24
   -15
     9
```

What is the mistake?

Correct solution:

incorrect

```
   760
3 | 229
  - 21 ↓
    19
   -18
     1
    -0
     1
```

What is the mistake?

Correct solution:

Use long division to solve. Write the equations you use in the work space. Think carefully about how to interpret the remainder.

185 people are in line for the amusement park ride. Each car on the ride holds 4 people. How many cars does it take to hold all the people?

307 visitors are registered to tour the historic village. There are 8 tour guides. The guides try to divide the visitors into groups as evenly as possible. How many visitors will be in each tour group?

WORK SPACE

Review

Match.

Factors of 30	3, 5, 7, 11, 19
Multiples of 30	16, 28, 40, 48, 100
Prime numbers	1, 2, 3, 5, 6, 10, 15, 30
Numbers divisible by 4	30, 60, 90, 120, 150

Complete the chart.

Boxes	10							
Donuts	60	72	78	84	90	102	108	120

Complete.

1 km = ____________ m
1 m = ____________ cm
1 cm = ____________ mm
1 L = ____________ mL
1 kg = ____________ g

1 mi. = ____________ ft.
1 yd. = ____________ ft.
1 ft. = ____________ in.
1 lb. = ____________ oz.
1 c. = ____________ fl. oz.

1 week = ____________ days
1 day = ____________ hr.
1 hr. = ____________ min.
1 min. = ____________ sec.

Solve. Write the equations you use.

Ian had some money. He spent $25, and then he had $35 left. How much money did he start with?

★ Sylvia had $80. She bought 2 lamps at a thrift store, and then she had $36 left. Both lamps cost the same amount. How much did each lamp cost?

Lesson Activities

A

	1	2	3	4	5	6	7	8	9
× 15	15	30	45				105		

B

1. Divide.
2. Multiply.
3. Subtract.

Ex.

1. $15 \overline{)\,94}$, quotient **6**

2. $15 \overline{)\,94}$, quotient 6; **90**

3. $15 \overline{)\,94}$, quotient 6; $- 90$; **4**

$15 \overline{)\,50}$ $15 \overline{)\,97}$ $15 \overline{)\,108}$ $15 \overline{)\,139}$

C

Flip and Divide

(2-Player Game)

Player 1

$15 \overline{)\quad}$ $15 \overline{)\quad}$ $15 \overline{)\quad}$

Sum of remainders

Player 2

$15 \overline{)\quad}$ $15 \overline{)\quad}$ $15 \overline{)\quad}$

Sum of remainders

Practice

Complete the multiplication tables.

	1	2	3	4	5	6	7	8	9
× 70	70	140		280	350		490	560	

	1	2	3	4	5	6	7	8	9
× 25			75		125			200	

Use long division to solve. Use the multiplication tables (above) to help. Then, find the blanks that match the letter for each problem. Write the letter in the matching blanks to solve the riddle.

R: 70 ⟌ 199

H: 70 ⟌ 393

V: 70 ⟌ 432

S: 70 ⟌ 645

N: 25 ⟌ 78

O: 25 ⟌ 80

E: 25 ⟌ 97

D: 25 ⟌ 188

I: 25 ⟌ 206

Why did the student wear glasses for her math lesson?
Because it improves...

					-						
5 R43	3 R22	2 R59	7 R13	8 R6		6 R12	8 R6	9 R15	8 R6	3 R5	3 R3

Review

Find the missing numbers in the equations.

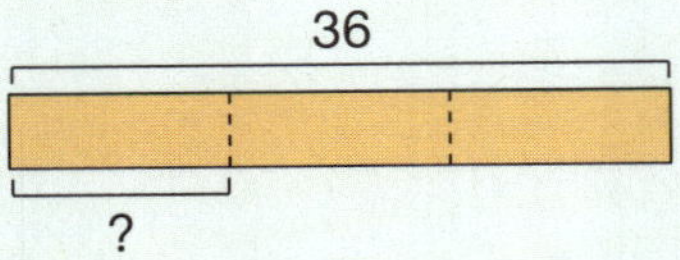

3 × ______ = 36

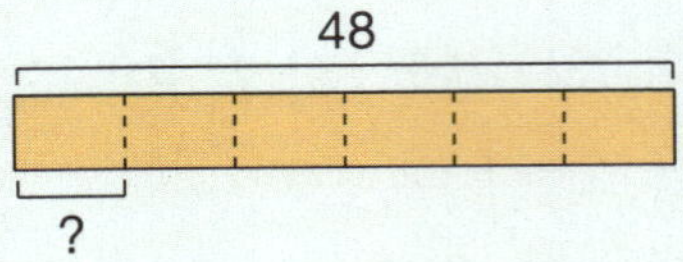

48 ÷ ______ = 6

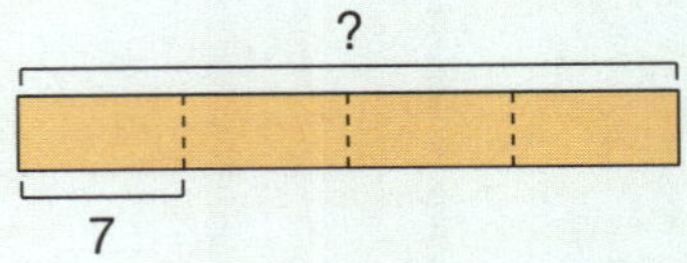

______ ÷ 4 = 7

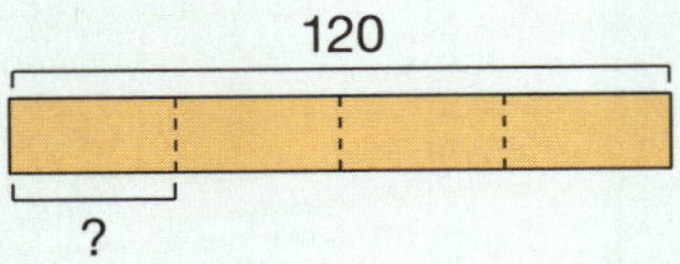

120 ÷ ______ = 4

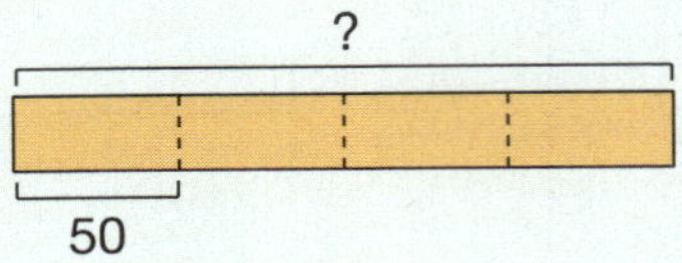

______ ÷ 50 = 4

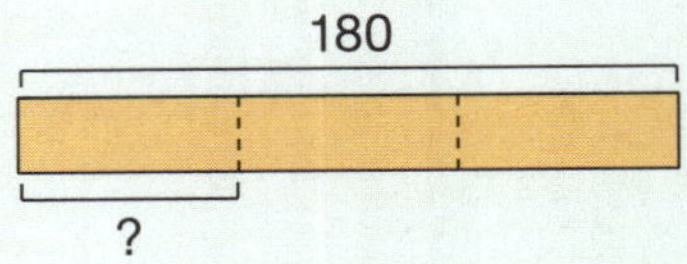

3 × ______ = 180

Complete the chart.

Cups	1							
Fluid Ounces	8	40	64	80	88	160	168	152

Find the average number of children in each cabin at nature camp.

Cabin List

Red Maple: 14 campers

White Oak: 12 campers

Blue Spruce: 9 campers

Silver Birch: 11 campers

White Pine: 14 campers

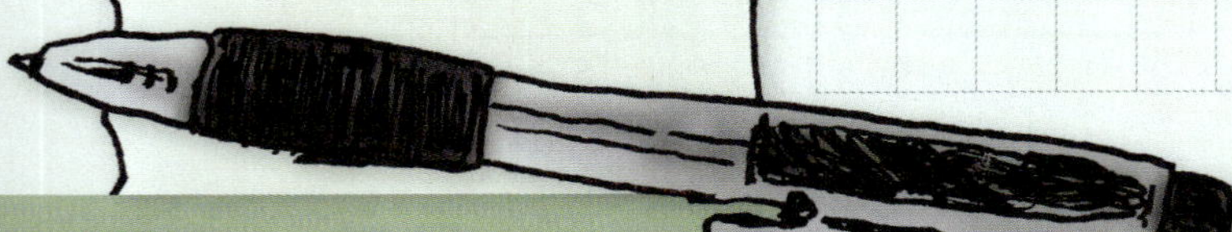

Lesson Activities

A

The party planner has 223 balloons. She wants to arrange them in 30 equal groups. How many balloons should she put in each group?

30 ⟌ 223

Check:

B

Long Division with Two-Digit Divisors

1. Choose how many digits in the dividend to divide.

   Try 1 digit.

   30 ⟌ 518 ✗

   5 is less than 30, so try 2 digits.

   30 ⟌ 518 ✓

   51 is greater than 30, so divide 2 digits.

2. Follow the long division steps for the digits you chose.

```
    1
30⟌518
  - 30↓
   218
```

3. Repeat the long division steps until you have divided all the digits.

```
    17
30⟌518
  - 30↓
   218
 - 210
     8
```

	× 30
1	30
2	60
3	90
4	120
5	150
6	180
7	210
8	240
9	270

30 ⟌ 654

30 ⟌ 245

30 ⟌ 875

7.3

Practice

Use long division to find the quotient. Then, multiply (or multiply and add) to check your answers. Use the multiplication table to help.

	× 40
1	40
2	80
3	120
4	160
5	200
6	240
7	280
8	320
9	360

40) 305

40) 527

40) 999

Check

Check

Check

Use long division to solve. Use the multiplication table to help.

Ella has 837 stickers. She arranges 60 stickers on each page in her sticker book. How many pages does she fill?

After Ella fills as many pages as possible, she puts the leftover stickers on their own page. How many stickers are on this page?

	× 60
1	60
2	120
3	180
4	240
5	300
6	360
7	420
8	480
9	540

Review

Find the greatest common factor for each pair of numbers. Make your own lists of factors.

GCF of 9 and 12: ____________________

GCF of 12 and 16: ____________________

Complete.

360 ÷ 90 = ____________

500 ÷ 50 = ____________

2,400 ÷ 40 = ____________

1,000 ÷ 200 = ____________

3,500 ÷ 700 = ____________

3,000 ÷ 600 = ____________

Use the printed protractors to measure the angles.

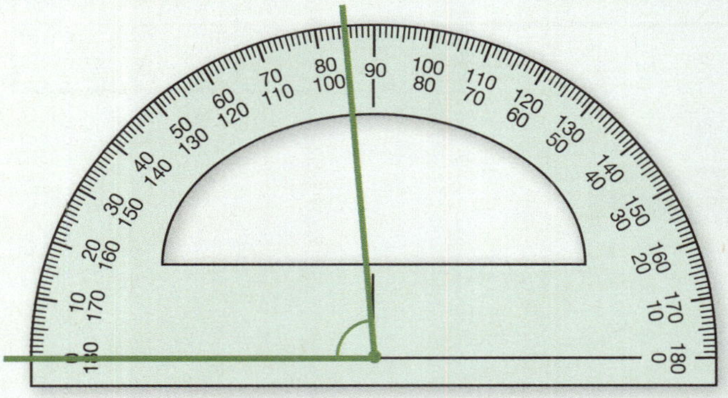

_______°

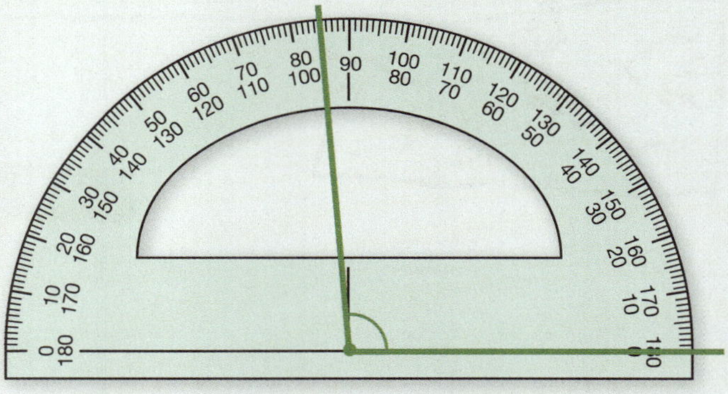

_______°

Solve. Write the equations you use.

Norah read 60 pages on Saturday. She read 3 times as many pages on Saturday as she read on Sunday. How many pages did she read on Sunday?

Shawn practiced the piano for 15 minutes on Monday. He practiced for 3 times as long on Tuesday as he practiced on Monday. How long did he practice the piano on Tuesday?

Lesson Activities

A

	1	2	3	4	5	6	7	8	9
× 24	24		72	96			168	192	216

B

Fundraiser	Total Amount of Money Raised	Amount Raised Per Member	Remainder
Car Wash	$290		
Pancake Breakfast	$570		
Raffle	$230		
Chili Cook-Off	$449		
	Total:		

WORK SPACE

Practice

Use long division to find the quotients. Use the multiplication tables to help.

	× 45
1	45
2	90
3	135
4	180
5	225
6	270
7	315
8	360
9	405

45) 597

	× 67
1	67
2	134
3	201
4	268
5	335
6	402
7	469
8	536
9	603

67) 883

Review

Complete the chart.

Boxes	10						
Cookies	50	65	75	80	90	95	100

Find the missing information for each rectangular prism. Make sure to include the correct units.

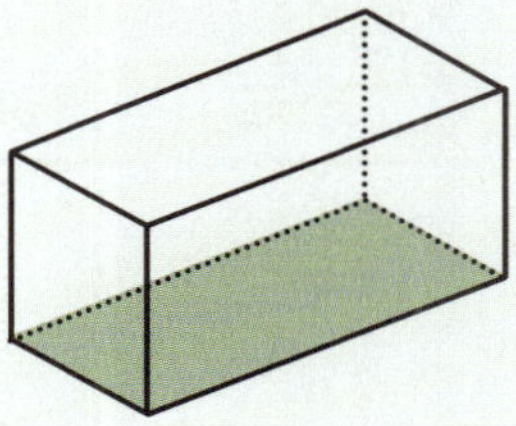

Base area: 10 sq. cm

Height: 3 cm

Volume: ______________

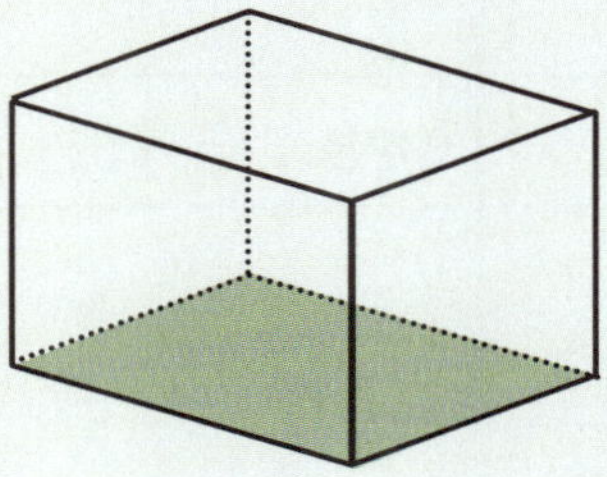

Base area: 20 sq. ft.

Height: ______________

Volume: 80 cu. ft.

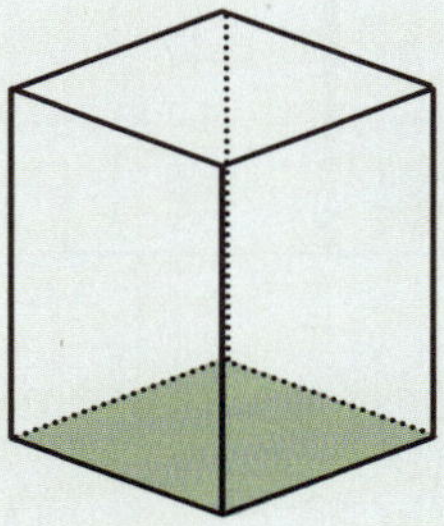

Base area: ______________

Height: 5 m

Volume: 45 cu. m

Lesson Activities

A

How to Divide a Four-Digit Number by a Two-Digit Divisor

1. Choose how many digits in the dividend to divide.
2. Follow the long division steps for the digits you chose.
3. Repeat the long division steps until you have divided all the digits.

Ex.

```
     126
27 | 3,426
   - 27↓
      72
    - 54
     186
    -162
      24
```

B

____________ splits
NAME
4,950 ____________ into
OBJECTS
27 equal groups.

How many are in each group?

How many are left over?

	× 27
1	27
2	54
3	81
4	108
5	135
6	162
7	189
8	216
9	243

	1	2	3	4	5	6	7	8	9
× 82	82	164	246	328	410	492	574	656	738

7,052 people are at the ____________. There are
EVENT
82 ____________ in each
THINGS YOU SIT ON
row for people to sit on.

How many rows are needed so that everyone has a place to sit?

Practice

Complete the multiplication table.

	1	2	3	4	5	6	7	8	9
× 12	12				60		84		108

Use long division to solve the word problems. Use the multiplication table (above) to help.

Ezra's family has 8 chickens. Last year, they gathered 1,980 eggs from their chickens. How many dozens of eggs did they gather? (12 eggs equal 1 dozen.)

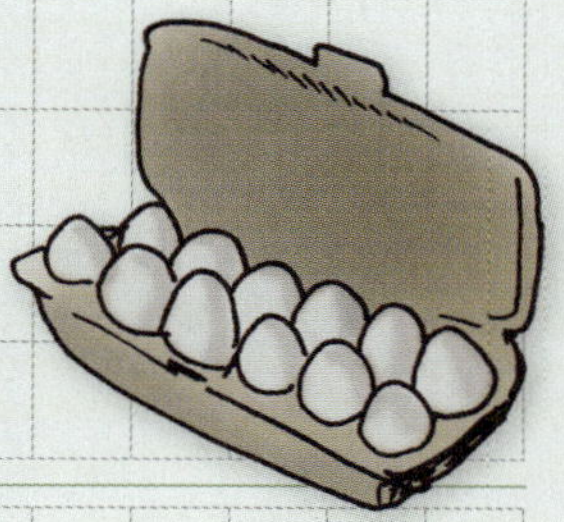

Benjamin Franklin lived for 1,011 months. How many years and months did he live?

The Great Pyramid of Giza is 5,448 inches tall. How many feet tall is it?

7.5

Review

Draw lines to divide the bars into the fractional part listed.

halves

thirds

fourths

sixths

eighths

twelfths

Complete the missing numbers in the equivalent fractions.

$\frac{1}{2} = \frac{4}{\ }$	$\frac{3}{4} = \frac{\ }{8}$	$\frac{1}{4} = \frac{2}{\ }$
$\frac{1}{3} = \frac{\ }{6}$	$\frac{2}{3} = \frac{\ }{6}$	$\frac{3}{3} = \frac{\ }{6}$
$\frac{1}{3} = \frac{\ }{12}$	$\frac{2}{3} = \frac{\ }{12}$	$\frac{3}{3} = \frac{\ }{12}$
$\frac{1}{6} = \frac{\ }{12}$	$\frac{3}{6} = \frac{\ }{12}$	$\frac{5}{6} = \frac{\ }{12}$

Find all factors of each number. Then, answer the questions.

Factors of 23: ____________________

Is 23 prime or composite? ____________

Factors of 25: ____________________

Is 25 prime or composite? ____________

Unit Wrap-Up

Use the words in the word bank to label the numbers in the division problem.

$$\begin{array}{r} 9 \\ 7\,\overline{)\,65} \\ -\,63 \\ \hline 2 \end{array}$$

9 ← ______

7 (______) → 65 ← ______

______ → 2

divisor	remainder
quotient	dividend

Write the long division steps in order.

1. ______
2. ______
3. ______
4. ______

Use long division to find the quotient. Then, multiply (or multiply and add) to check your answers. Use the multiplication table to help.

	× 30
1	30
2	60
3	90
4	120
5	150
6	180
7	210
8	240
9	270

$30\,\overline{)\,286}$ $30\,\overline{)\,480}$ $30\,\overline{)\,565}$

Check Check Check

Unit Wrap-Up

Use long division to solve the word problems. Use the multiplication tables to help.

Charlie has a bracelet-making business. He uses 40 cm of string for each bracelet. How many bracelets can he make from 683 cm of string?

	× 40
1	40
2	80
3	120
4	160
5	200
6	240
7	280
8	320
9	360

Charlie uses 34 beads for each bracelet. How many bracelets can he make from a pack of 1,500 beads?

	× 34
1	34
2	68
3	102
4	136
5	170
6	204
7	238
8	272
9	306

Charlie charges $15 per bracelet. Last year, he earned $1,875. How many bracelets did he sell?

	× 15
1	15
2	30
3	45
4	60
5	75
6	90
7	105
8	120
9	135

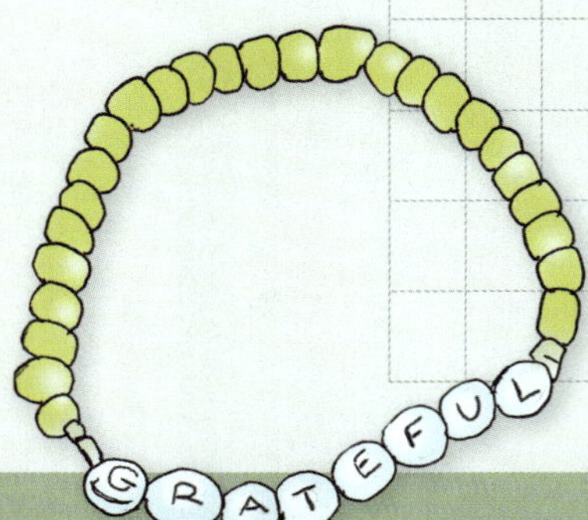

Unit 1 Reference Page

1.1

Mental Multiplication

1. Underline the trailing zeros.
2. Multiply the non-zero digits.
3. Tack on the trailing zeros.

Ex.

$3 \times 500 = ?$

3×5 hundreds $= 15$ hundreds

$3 \times 5\underline{00} = \mathbf{1{,}500}$

Ex.

$30 \times 50 = ?$

3 tens $\times\ 5$ tens $= 15$ hundreds

$3\underline{0} \times 5\underline{0} = \mathbf{1{,}500}$

1.2

1. Multiply 5 ones by 3.
2. Multiply 4 tens by 3. Add 1 ten.
3. Multiply 2 hundreds by 3. Add 1 hundred.

Ex.

$$\begin{array}{r} {}^{1} \\ 245 \\ \times\ \ 3 \\ \hline \mathbf{5} \end{array} \longrightarrow \begin{array}{r} {}^{1\,1} \\ 245 \\ \times\ \ 3 \\ \hline 35 \end{array} \longrightarrow \begin{array}{r} {}^{1\,1} \\ 245 \\ \times\ \ 3 \\ \hline 735 \end{array}$$

1.3

Mental Division

1. Underline the trailing zeros.
2. Divide the other digits.
3. Tack on the underlined trailing zeros.

Ex.

$18{,}000 \div 6 = ?$

18 thousands $\div\ 6 = 3$ thousands

$18{,}\underline{000} \div 6 = \mathbf{3{,}000}$

If the non-zero digits aren't divisible by the divisor, try underlining fewer zeros.

Ex.

$200 \div 4 = ?$

2 hundreds $\div\ 4 = ?$

2 isn't divisible by 4. Try underlining only one zero.

$20\underline{0} \div 4 = ?$

20 tens $\div\ 4 = 5$ tens

$20\underline{0} \div 4 = \mathbf{50}$

1.4

Repeat if needed

1. Divide
2. Multiply
3. Subtract
4. Bring down the next digit (if needed)

Ex.

$$\begin{array}{r} \mathbf{2} \\ 3\overline{)\,85} \\ -\ \mathbf{6}\downarrow \\ \hline \mathbf{25} \end{array} \rightarrow \begin{array}{r} 28 \\ 3\overline{)\,85} \\ -\ 6\downarrow \\ \hline 25 \\ -\ \mathbf{24} \\ \hline \mathbf{1} \end{array}$$

Unit 1 Reference Page

Averages

1.5

The average is one way to describe the "center" of a data set. To find the average:

1. Add up all the values in the data set.
2. Divide by the number of values in the data set.

Ex. What's the average weight of the baskets of apples?

4 lb. 5 lb. 5 lb. 6 lb. 6 lb.
6 lb. 7 lb. 7 lb. 8 lb.

$4 + 5 + 5 + 6 + 6 + 6 + 7 + 7 + 8 = 54$
$54 \div 9 =$ **6 lb.**

Multiply or Divide to Convert Measurements

1.6

To convert from a larger unit to a smaller unit, multiply by the conversion factor. Add on any extra smaller units.

Ex. 4 yd. 1 ft. = _____ ft.

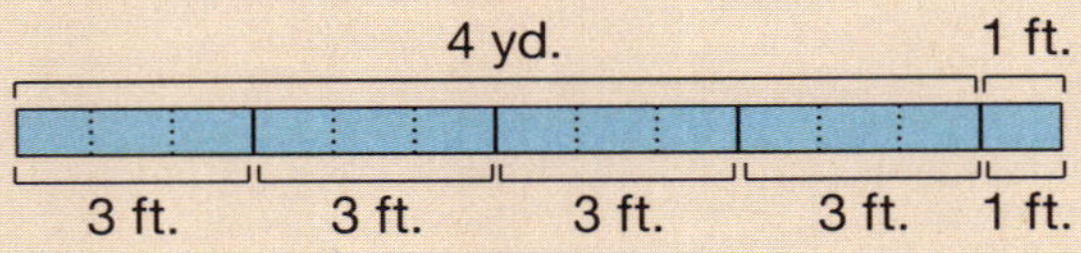

$4 \times 3 = 12$
$12 + 1 = 13$
4 yd. 1 ft. = **13 ft.**

Whole to parts? Multiply to start!

To convert from a smaller unit to a larger unit, divide by the conversion factor.

Ex. 37 mm = _____ cm

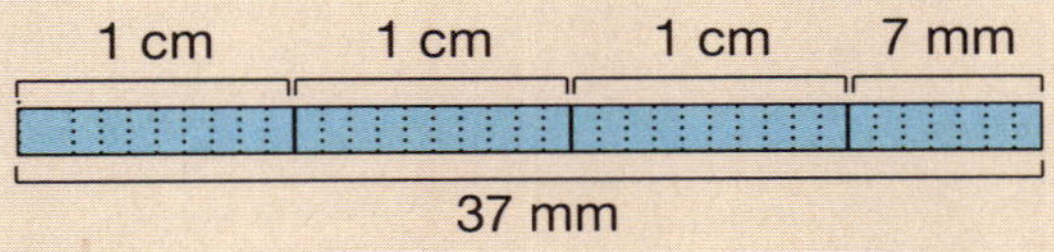

$37 \div 10 = 3$ R7
37 mm = **3 ft. 7 mm**

Parts to whole? Division's in control!

Parentheses

1.8

Parentheses mean "do this first!"

When you see an expression with parentheses, perform the operation in the parentheses before the other operations.

Ex. $7 + (4 \div 2)$
$7 + 2$
9

Ex. $(8 - 3) \times (6 - 4)$
5×2
10

Order of Operations with Parentheses

1.10

1. Complete operations in parentheses.
2. Multiply or divide, from left to right.
3. Add or subtract, from left to right.

Ex. $7 + (5 - 3) \times 4$
$7 + 2 \times 4$
$7 + 8$
15

Unit 2 Reference Page

How to Round Numbers

2.1

1. Underline the digit in the place you are rounding to.
2. Look at the digit in the next-smaller place.
   - If the digit is less than 5, round down. Keep the underlined digit the same, and change all the digits after it to zeros.
   - If the digit is 5 or greater, round up. Increase the underlined digit by 1. Change all the digits after it to zeros.

Ex. Round 12,756 to the nearest thousand.

12,756 ≈ **13,000**

The digit in the next-smaller place is 7.
7 is greater than 5, so you round up.

Ex. Round 12,756 to the nearest ten-thousand.

12,756 ≈ **10,000**

The digit in the next-smaller place is 2.
2 is less than 5, so you round down.

2.2

Distance from the Sun to Pluto:
7,304,326,000 km

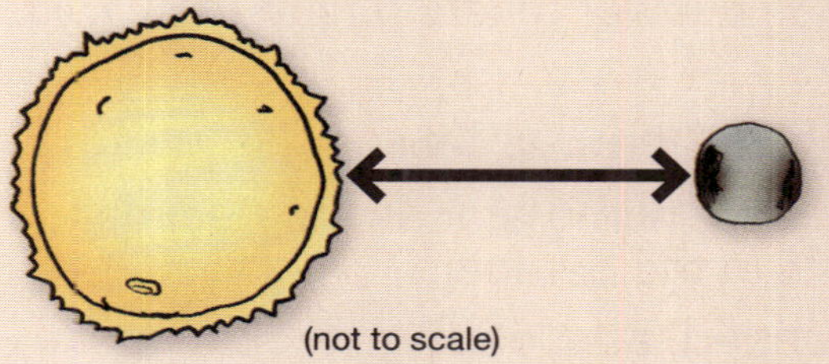
(not to scale)

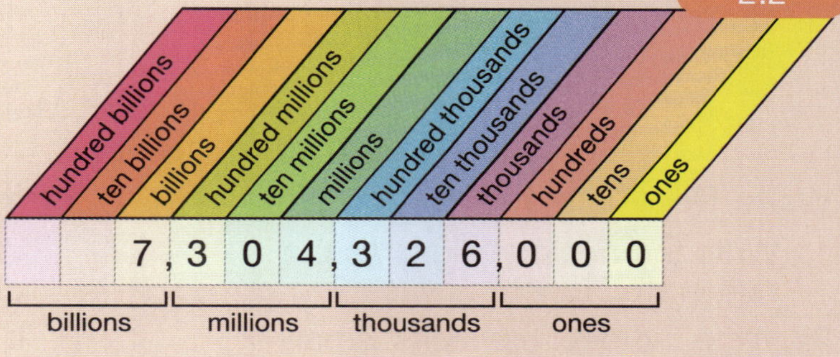

Round Decimals

2.6

Round decimals the same way you round whole numbers.

Ex. Round 1.28 to the nearest whole number.

1.28 ≈ **1**

Ex. Round 1.28 to the nearest tenth.

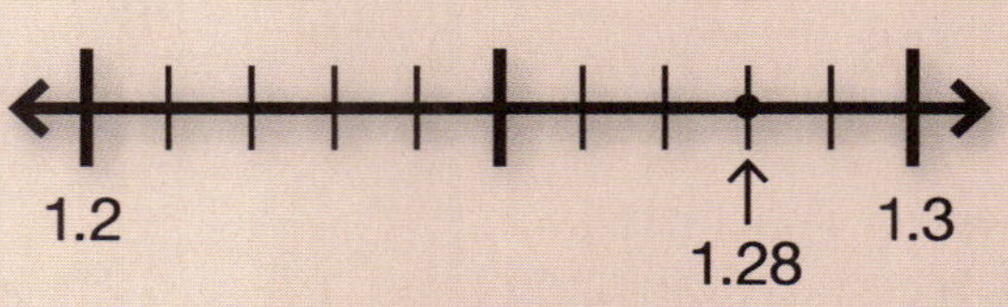

1.28 ≈ **1.3**

Unit 2 Reference Page

Decimals with Thousandths

2.8

Ex. A package of blueberries weighs 0.874 lb. What is the expanded form of 0.874?

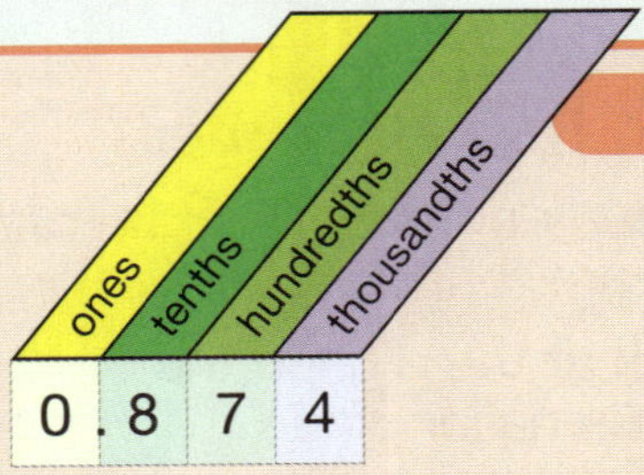

$$\frac{8}{10} + \frac{7}{100} + \frac{4}{1{,}000}$$

Compare Decimals

2.9

We can use place-value thinking or decimal squares to compare decimal numbers.

Ex. Max's reaction time is 0.219 seconds. Yuki's reaction time is 0.27 seconds. Who has the lower reaction time?

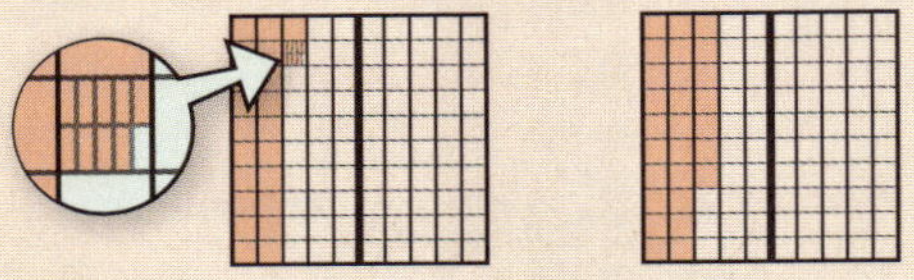

0.219
Max

0.27
Yuki

Max	0 .	2	1	9
Yuki	0 .	2	7	

$0.219 < 0.27$

Max has a lower reaction time than Yuki.

Write Decimals as Fractions

1. Write the decimal digits as the numerator. Ignore any leading zeros.
2. Write the decimal digits' smallest place value as the denominator.

Ex.

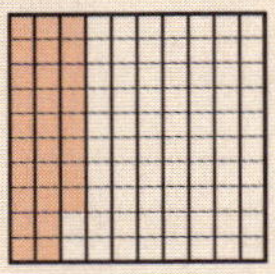

$0.28 = \frac{28}{100}$

Ex.

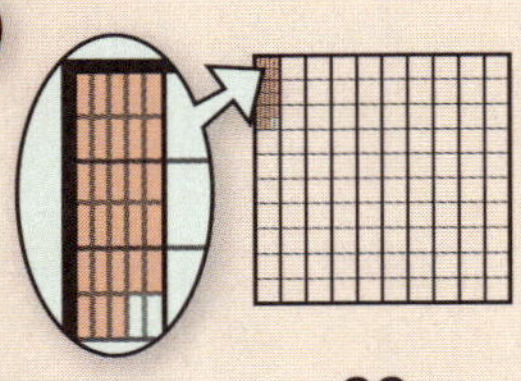

$0.028 = \frac{28}{1{,}000}$

Write Fractions as Decimals

2.10

1. Write the numerator as the decimal digits in the number.
2. If needed, add leading zeros to make the number's smallest place value match the denominator.

Ex.

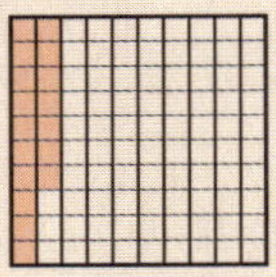

$\frac{17}{100} = 0.17$

Ex.

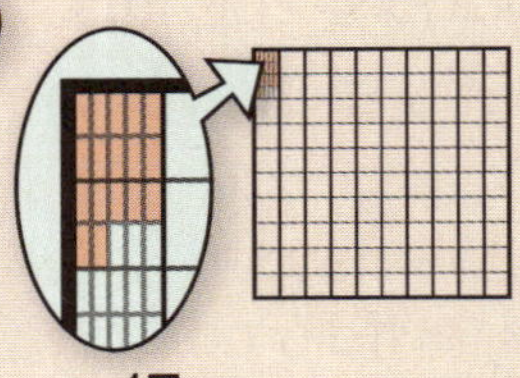

$\frac{17}{1{,}000} = 0.017$

How to Add and Subtract Decimals

1. Line up the decimal points.
2. Tack on zeros until both numbers have the same number of decimal places.
3. Add or subtract like usual. Write a decimal point in the answer below the other decimal points.

2.11

Ex. How far did Nate run on Tuesday and Wednesday?

$$\begin{array}{r} 1.370 \\ +\,3.915 \\ \hline \end{array} \longrightarrow \begin{array}{r} {}^{1} \\ 1.370 \\ +\,3.915 \\ \hline \textbf{5.285} \end{array} \textbf{ miles}$$

Least Common Multiple

3.1

The least common multiple (LCM) of two numbers is the lowest multiple they have in common.

To find the least common multiple:

1. Make a list of the first few multiples of each number.
2. Look for the lowest multiple they have in common.

Ex. Find the least common multiple of 5 and 6.

Multiples of 5: 5, 10, 15, 20, 25, 30, 35...

Multiples of 6: 6, 12, 18, 24, 30, 36, 42...

LCM of 5 and 6: **30**

Two Ways to Mentally Multiply

3.2

Box Method

Ex. There are 6 buns in each pack. How many buns are in 43 packs?

	40	3
6	240	18

240 + 18 = 258

43 × 6 = **258 buns**

Multiply and Adjust

Ex. There are 6 buns in each pack. How many buns are in 43 packs?

40 packs: 40 × 6 = 240
+6
41 packs: 41 × 6 = 246
+6
42 packs: 42 × 6 = 252
+6
43 packs: 43 × 6 = 258

43 × 6 = **258 buns**

Mentally Multiply by 2 or 4

3.3

Multiplying a number by 2 is the same as doubling the number.

1. Break the number into parts.
2. Double each part.
3. Add the doubled parts together.

Ex. 45 × 2 = ?

Double 40 → 80
Double 5 → 10
90

45 × 2 = **90**

Multiplying a number by 4 is the same as doubling the number twice.

Ex. 150 × 4 = ?

Double 100 → 200
Double 50 → 100
300

Double 300 → 600

150 × 4 = **600**

Associative Property

3.4

When you multiply 3 or more numbers, the product remains the same no matter how you group them.

If the only operation in an expression is multiplication, you can multiply the numbers in any order.

Ex. $9 \times 4 \times 5$ → 9×20 → **180**

Multiplying 9 × 20 is easier than 36 × 5, so multiply 4 × 5 first.

Ex. $8 \times 2 \times 9$ → 72×2 → **144**

Multiplying by 2 is the same as doubling, so multiply 8 × 9 first. Then, double the result.

Mental Multiplication

3.5

1. Underline the trailing zeros.
2. Multiply the non-zero digits.
3. Tack on the trailing zeros.

Ex. 300 × 20 = ?

3 hundreds × 2 tens = 6 thousands

3<u>00</u> × 2<u>0</u> = **6,000**

The associative property allows us to break numbers apart in this way to make multiplication easier.

Ex. 300 × 20 = ?

3 × 100 × 2 × 10

6 × 1,000

6,000

How to Multiply Numbers with Trailing Zeros

3.6

1. Stack the numbers vertically. Write the number with trailing zeros on the bottom.
2. Count the number of trailing zeros. Write this number of zeros in the answer.
3. Multiply the non-zero digits like usual.

Ex.

$$\begin{array}{r} 28 \\ \times\ 30 \\ \hline \end{array} \quad \longrightarrow \quad \begin{array}{r} 28 \\ \times\ 30 \\ \hline 0 \end{array} \quad \longrightarrow \quad \begin{array}{r} {}^{2} \\ 28 \\ \times\ 30 \\ \hline 840 \end{array}$$

The Multiplication Algorithm

3.8

The multiplication algorithm breaks multiplication problems into parts. You multiply each part separately. Then, you add the parts to find the final product.

Ex.

$$\begin{array}{rl} 42 & \\ \times\ 38 & \\ \hline 336 & \leftarrow 42 \times 8 \\ +\ 1{,}260 & \leftarrow 42 \times 30 \\ \hline 1{,}596 & \leftarrow 42 \times 38 \end{array}$$

1. Multiply the top number by the bottom number's ones-place.
2. Write a place-holder zero.
3. Multiply the top number by the bottom number's tens-place.
4. Add.

Ex.

$$\begin{array}{r} {\scriptstyle 1} \\ 42 \\ \times\ 38 \\ \hline \mathbf{336} \end{array} \rightarrow \begin{array}{r} {\scriptstyle 1} \\ 42 \\ \times\ 38 \\ \hline 336 \\ \mathbf{0} \end{array} \rightarrow \begin{array}{r} {\scriptstyle 1} \\ 42 \\ \times\ 38 \\ \hline 336 \\ \mathbf{1{,}26}0 \end{array} \rightarrow \begin{array}{r} {\scriptstyle 1} \\ 42 \\ \times\ 38 \\ \hline 336 \\ +\ 1{,}260 \\ \hline \mathbf{1{,}596} \end{array}$$

Extending the Multiplication Algorithm

3.9

You can use the multiplication algorithm to multiply numbers with any number of digits.

Write the number with more digits on top. Then, multiply the top number by each digit in the bottom number.

Write as many place-holder zeros as you need to put the digits in the correct place.

Ex.

$$\begin{array}{rl} {\scriptstyle 2} & \\ {\scriptstyle 1\ 41} & \\ 4{,}172 & \\ \times\ \ \ 36 & \\ \hline 25{,}032 & \leftarrow 4{,}172 \times 6 \\ +\ 125{,}160 & \leftarrow 4{,}172 \times 30 \\ \hline 150{,}192 & \leftarrow 4{,}172 \times 36 \end{array}$$

Ex.

$$\begin{array}{rl} {\scriptstyle 3} & \\ {\scriptstyle 2} & \\ 209 & \\ \times\ 143 & \\ \hline 627 & \leftarrow 209 \times 3 \\ 8{,}360 & \leftarrow 209 \times 40 \\ +\ 20{,}900 & \leftarrow 209 \times 100 \\ \hline 29{,}887 & \leftarrow 209 \times 143 \end{array}$$

Unit 4 Reference Page

Volume

The volume of a three-dimensional solid is the amount of space the solid takes up.

We measure volume with cubic units. A cube that is 1 centimeter on each side has a volume of 1 cubic centimeter.

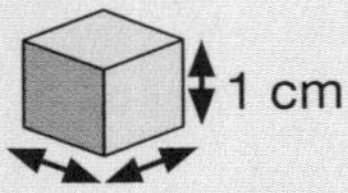

4.1

Ex. What is the volume of this solid?

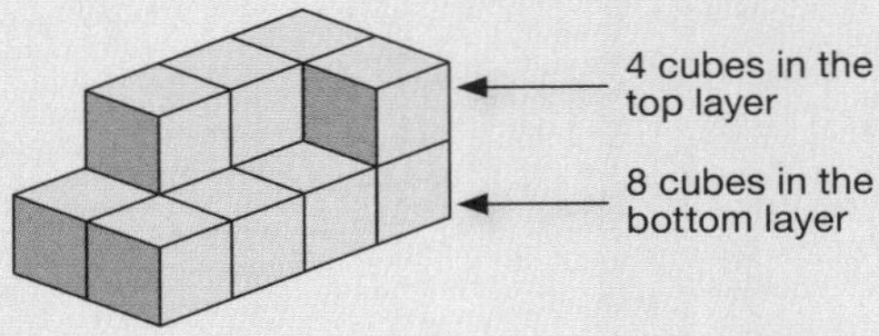

This solid is made from 12 cubes, so it has a volume of 12 cubic cm.

Volume of a Rectangular Prism

To find the volume of a rectangular prism, we multiply its length times its width times its height.

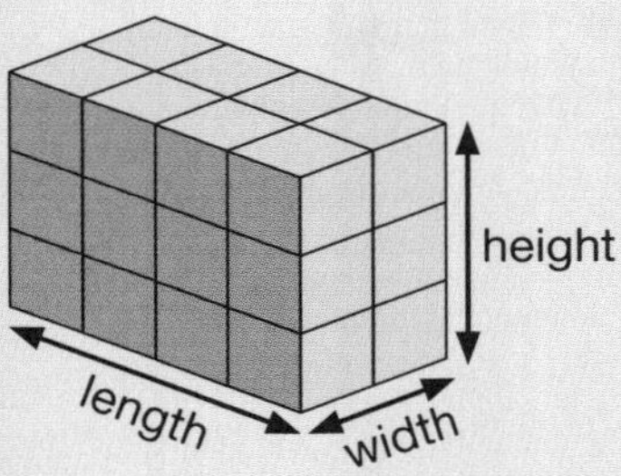

length × width × height = volume

4.2

Ex. What is the volume of a 4 cm by 2 cm by 3 cm rectangular prism?

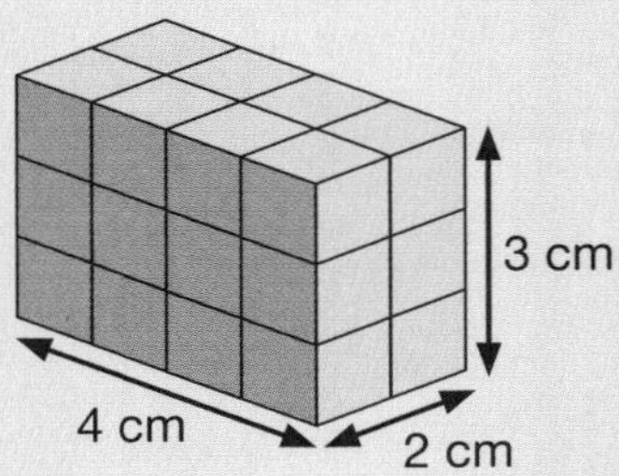

4 × 2 × 3 = **24 cubic cm**

How to Find a Missing Dimension

If you know the volume of a rectangular prism and two of its dimensions, you can use the volume formula to find the missing dimension.

1. Use the volume formula to write an equation. Write a blank for the missing dimension.
2. Multiply the two dimensions you know.
3. Divide the volume by the product of the two dimensions you know.

4.4

Ex. The box's volume is 30 cubic cm. What is its height?

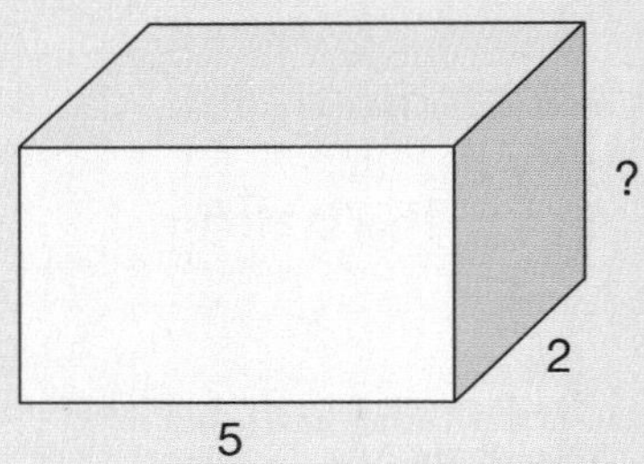

length × width × height = volume

5 × 2 × ____ = 30

10 × ____ = 30

30 ÷ 10 = **3 cm**

Area and Volume

If you know the area of the base of a rectangular prism, you've already found its length times its width.

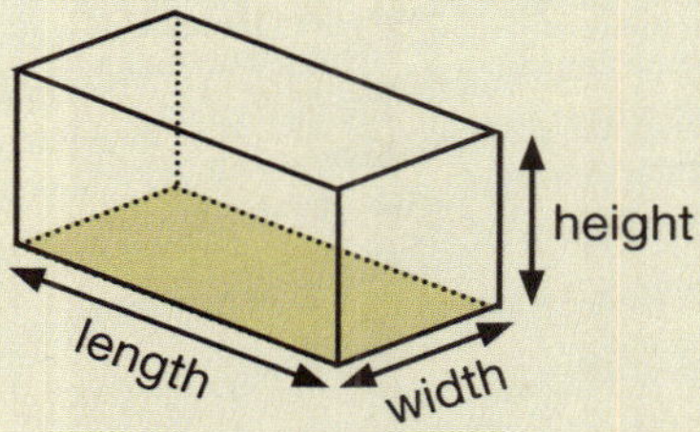

So, you can multiply the base area times its height to find its volume.

length × width × height = volume

base area × height = volume

4.7

Ex. The bathroom floor has an area of 54 sq. ft. The ceilings in the bathroom are 8 ft. high. What is the volume of the bathroom?

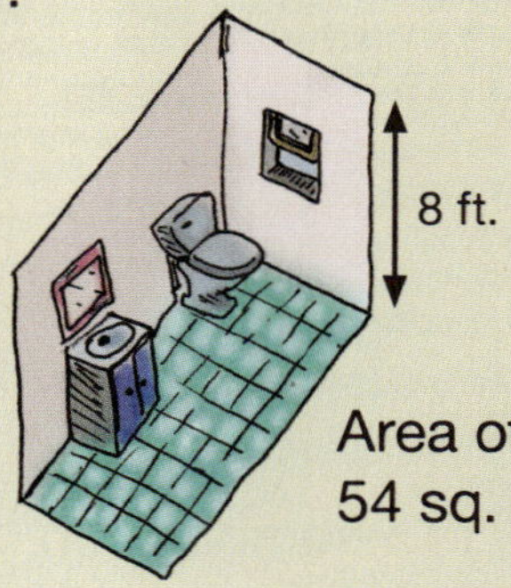

base area × height = volume

54 × 8 = **432 cu. feet**

How to use Volume to Find Base Area or Height

If you know the volume of a rectangular prism and its height, you can divide the volume by the height to find the area of the base.

4.8

Ex. The box's volume is 20 cu. cm. Its height is 5 cm. What is the area of its base?

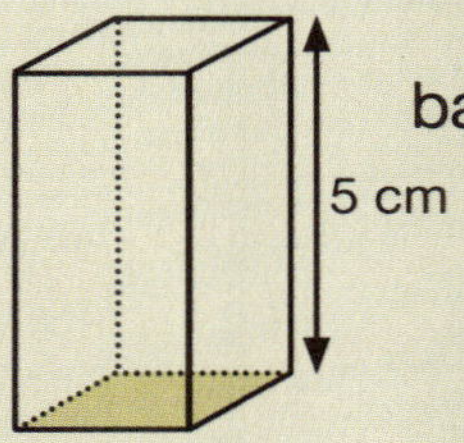

base area × height = volume

______ × 5 = 20

20 ÷ 5 = **4 sq. cm**

If you know the volume of a rectangular prism and the area of its base, you can divide the volume by the area of the base to find the height.

Ex. The box's volume is 40 cu. cm. Its base has an area of 8 sq. cm. What is its height?

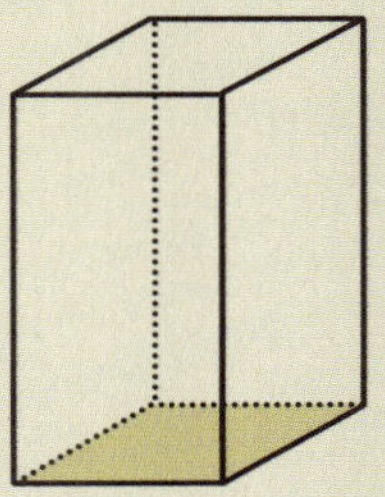

base area × height = volume

8 × ______ = 40

40 ÷ 8 = **5 cm**

Fractions

5.1

Fractions are numbers that represent part of a whole.

The numerator tells the number of parts. The denominator tells how many equal parts the whole was split into.

Ex. What fraction of the cake has green frosting?

$\frac{2}{5}$

Numerator Number of parts

Denominator How many equal parts the whole was split into

Mixed Numbers

5.2

A mixed number is a combination of a whole number and a fraction.

To convert a fraction to a mixed number, divide the numerator by the denominator.

Ex. Write $\frac{9}{4}$ as a mixed number.

$9 \div 4 = 2 \text{ R}1$

$\div \; \frac{9}{4} = \mathbf{2\frac{1}{4}}$

To convert a mixed number to a fraction, multiply the denominator by the whole number and add the numerator.

Ex. Write $2\frac{3}{5}$ as a fraction.

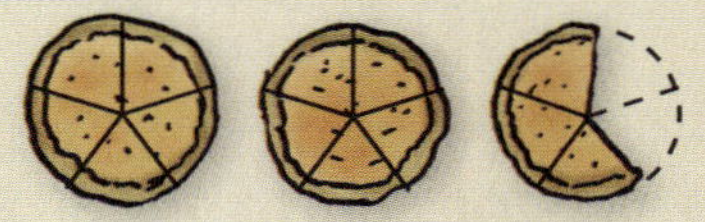

$5 \times 2 + 3 = 13$

$+$

$2\frac{3}{5} = \mathbf{\frac{13}{5}}$

$\times$

Equivalent Fractions

5.3

Equivalent fractions are fractions that have different numerators and denominators but are equal to the same value.

One way to create an equivalent fraction is to make each fractional part into more equal parts. Multiply the numerator and denominator by the same number to find the equivalent fraction.

Ex. Trina has $\frac{1}{2}$ of a pizza. She cuts the pizza into 4 equal slices. What equivalent fraction does she create?

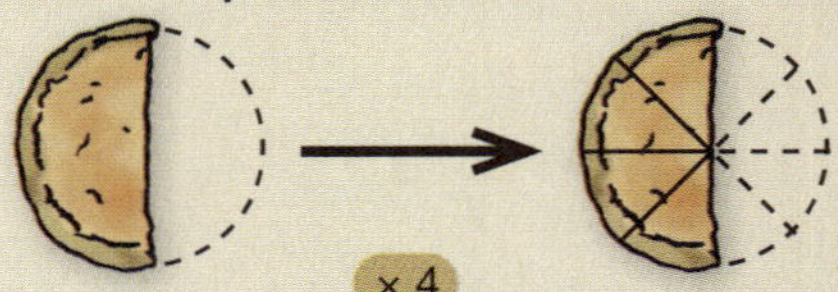

$\times 4$

$\frac{1}{2} = \frac{4}{8}$

$\times 4$

Unit 5 Reference Page

Use Common Denominators to Compare Fractions

When fractions have different denominators, we first find a common denominator. Then, it's easier to compare the fractions.

1. Find the least common multiple of both denominators.
2. Write an equivalent fraction for each fraction you are comparing. Use the LCM as the denominator for both equivalent fractions.
3. Compare the equivalent fractions.

5.4

Ex. Which is greater, $\frac{2}{3}$ or $\frac{3}{4}$?

The denominators are 3 and 4.

The LCM of 3 and 4 is 12. Use 12 as the common denominator.

$$\frac{2 \times 4}{3 \times 4} = \frac{8}{12} \qquad \frac{3 \times 3}{4 \times 3} = \frac{9}{12}$$

$\frac{9}{12}$ is greater than $\frac{8}{12}$, so $\frac{3}{4}$ is greater than $\frac{2}{3}$.

How to Use Common Denominators to Add Fractions

1. Find the least common multiple (LCM) of both denominators. You will use this number for the common denominator.
2. Rewrite each fraction as an equivalent fraction with the common denominator.
3. Add the fractions.

5.5

Ex. $\frac{2}{3} + \frac{1}{6} = ?$

The denominators are 3 and 6.

The LCM of 3 and 6 is 6.

So, use 6 as the common denominator.

$$\frac{2}{3} + \frac{1}{6} \;\rightarrow\; \frac{4}{6} + \frac{1}{6} = \frac{5}{6}$$

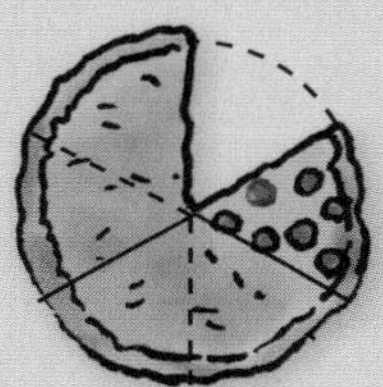

How to Use Common Denominators to Subtract Fractions

1. Find the least common multiple (LCM) of both denominators. You will use this number for the common denominator.
2. Rewrite each fraction as an equivalent fraction with the common denominator.
3. Subtract the fractions.

5.6

Ex. $\frac{7}{8} - \frac{1}{4} = ?$

The denominators are 8 and 4.

The LCM of 8 and 4 is 8.

So, use 8 as the common denominator.

$$\frac{7}{8} - \frac{1}{4} \;\rightarrow\; \frac{7}{8} - \frac{2}{8} = \frac{5}{8}$$

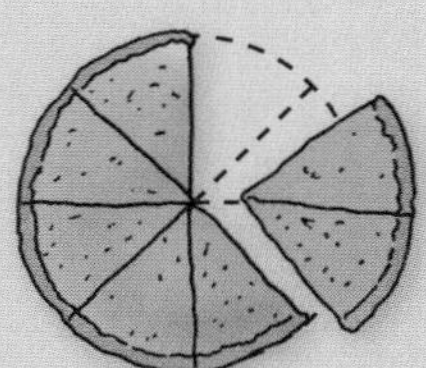

Unit 5 Reference Page

Use Common Denominators to Add Mixed Numbers

5.8

1. Rewrite the problem. Keep the whole numbers the same. Write the fractions as equivalent fractions with common denominators.
2. Add the fractions. Then, add the whole numbers.
3. If you have an improper fraction in the sum, convert the improper fraction to a mixed number. Add it to the whole number.

Ex.

$$\begin{array}{r} 1\frac{2}{3} = 1\frac{4}{6} \\ +\,2\frac{1}{2} = 2\frac{3}{6} \\ \hline \end{array} \longrightarrow \begin{array}{r} 1\frac{2}{3} = 1\frac{4}{6} \\ +\,2\frac{1}{2} = 2\frac{3}{6} \\ \hline 3\frac{7}{6} \end{array} \longrightarrow \begin{array}{r} 1\frac{2}{3} = 1\frac{4}{6} \\ +\,2\frac{1}{2} = 2\frac{3}{6} \\ \hline 3\frac{7}{6} = 4\frac{1}{6} \end{array}$$

Use Common Denominators to Subtract Mixed Numbers

5.9

1. Rewrite the problem. Keep the whole numbers the same. Write the fractions as equivalent fractions with common denominators.
2. If the top fraction is less than the bottom fraction, trade 1 whole for fractional parts.
3. Subtract the fractions. Then, subtract the whole numbers.

Ex.

$$\begin{array}{r} 3\frac{1}{2} = 3\frac{3}{6} \\ -\,1\frac{5}{6} = 1\frac{5}{6} \\ \hline \end{array} \longrightarrow \begin{array}{r} 2\frac{9}{6} \\ 3\frac{1}{2} = \cancel{3}\frac{\cancel{3}}{6} \\ -\,1\frac{5}{6} = 1\frac{5}{6} \\ \hline \end{array} \longrightarrow \begin{array}{r} 2\frac{9}{6} \\ 3\frac{1}{2} = \cancel{3}\frac{\cancel{3}}{6} \\ -\,1\frac{5}{6} = 1\frac{5}{6} \\ \hline 1\frac{4}{6} \end{array}$$

Unit 6 Reference Page

Divide by 2 or 5

6.2

A number is divisible by 2 if it is even.

To mentally divide a number by 2, break the number into parts and split each part in half.

Ex. Simon won 38 tickets at the arcade. He shared the tickets equally with his brother. How many did they each get?

$38 \div 2 = ?$

Half of 30 → 15

Half of 8 → 4

19

$38 \div 2 =$ **19 tickets**

A number is divisible by 5 if it has 0 or 5 in its ones-place.

To mentally divide a number by 5, write the problem as a missing factor problem. Then, multiply and adjust to find the missing factor.

Ex. Isabella won 65 tickets at the arcade. Each bracelet costs 5 tickets. How many bracelets can she buy?

$65 \div 5 = ?$ → _____ $\times 5 = 65$

$10 \times 5 = 50$. Too low.
$11 \times 5 = 55$. Too low.
$12 \times 5 = 60$. Too low.
$13 \times 5 = 65$. Just right!

$65 \div 5 =$ **13 bracelets**

Divide by 3

6.3

A number is divisible by 3 if the sum of its digits is divisible by 3.

Ex. Is 96 divisible by 3?

$9 + 6 = 15$

15 is divisible by 3, so 96 is divisible by 3.

To mentally divide a number by 3, write the problem as a missing factor problem. Then, multiply and adjust to find the missing factor.

Ex. Sasha has 57 tickets. Each game at the fair costs 3 tickets. How many games can he play?

$57 \div 3 = ?$ → _____ $\times 3 = 57$

$20 \times 3 = 60$. Too high.
$19 \times 3 = 57$. Just right!

$57 \div 3 =$ **19 games**

Unit 6 Reference Page

6.4

Divide by 6

A number is divisible by 6 if it is divisible by 2 and divisible by 3.

Ex. Is 78 divisible by 6?

78 is an even number, so it is divisible by 2.

7 + 8 = 15. 15 is divisible by 3, so 78 is divisible by 3.

78 is divisible by both 2 and 3, so it is divisible by 6.

To mentally divide a number by 6, write the problem as a missing factor problem. Then, multiply and adjust to find the missing factor.

Ex. The bakery packs its products in boxes of 6. If they pack 78 donuts, how many boxes of donuts do they fill?

$78 \div 6 = ?$ ➔ $\_\_\_\_ \times 6 = 78$

$10 \times 6 = 60$. Too low.
$11 \times 6 = 66$. Too low.
$12 \times 6 = 72$. Too low.
$13 \times 6 = 78$. Just right!

$78 \div 6 =$ **13**

6.5

Divide by 4

To mentally divide a number by 4, divide by 2 twice.

Ex. There are 60 children at lacrosse camp. The coaches split the children into 4 equal groups. How many children are in each group?

$60 \div 4 = ?$

$60 \div 2 = 30$

$30 \div 2 = 15$

$60 \div 4 =$ **15 children**

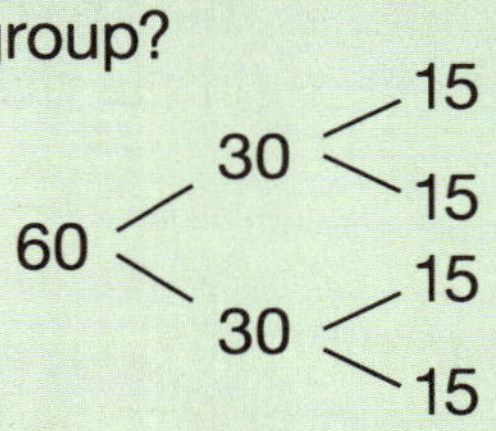

A number is divisible by 4 if you get an even number when you divide the number by 2.

Ex. Is 60 divisible by 4?

$60 \div 2 = 30$

30 is an even number. That means you can divide it by 2 and get another whole number.

So, 60 is divisible by 4.

Unit 6 Reference Page

How to Find All Factors of a Number Less Than 100

To find all factors of a number less than 100, check to see whether the target number is divisible by the numbers 1 to 9.

If the target number is divisible by one of the numbers, write the matching factor pair.

Once you find all the factor pairs, write all the factors in order from least to greatest.

6.6

Ex. Find all the factors of 68.

$68 \div 1 = 68$. 1×68 is a factor pair.

$68 \div 2 = 34$. 2×34 is a factor pair.

68 is not divisible by 3, so 3 is not a factor of 68.

$68 \div 4 = 17$. 4×17 is a factor pair.

68 is not divisible by 5, 6, 7, 8, or 9. So, 5, 6, 7, 8, and 9 are not factors of 68.

Factors of 68: **1, 2, 4, 17, 34, and 68.**

Prime numbers have exactly 2 factors: 1 and the number itself.

Composite numbers have more than 2 factors.

Ex. Is 68 prime or composite?

68 has more than 2 factors, so it is composite.

Ex. Is 23 prime or composite?

23 has exactly 2 factors, so it is prime.

Greatest Common Factor

The greatest common factor (GCF) of two numbers is the highest factor they have in common.

To find the greatest common factor:

1. Make a list of the factors of each number.
2. Look for the greatest factor they have in common.

6.7

Ex. Find the greatest common factor of 10 and 15.

Factor pairs of 10:	Factor pairs of 15:
1×10	1×15
2×5	3×5

The common factors of 10 and 15 are 1 and 5.

So, the greatest common factor of 10 and 15 is **5**.

Mental Division with Trailing Zeros

Cross out the trailing zeros the numbers have in common. Then, divide the other digits.

6.8

Ex. The winter festival decorating committee wants to buy 1,200 ornaments. The ornaments come in packs of 40. How many packs should the committee buy?

$1{,}200 \div 40 = ?$

$120 \text{ tens} \div 4 \text{ tens} = 30$

$1{,}20\not{0} \div 4\not{0} = \mathbf{30}$

7.2

1. Divide.
2. Multiply.
3. Subtract.

Ex.

```
     6              6              6
15)94   →     15)94   →     15)94
                 90            -90
                               ---
                                 4
```

Long Division with Two-Digit Divisors

7.3

1. Choose how many digits in the dividend to divide.

Try 1 digit.

```
30)518  ✗
```

5 is less than 30, so try 2 digits.

```
30)518  ✓
```

51 is greater than 30, so divide 2 digits.

2. Follow the long division steps for the digits you chose.

```
     1
30)518
  -30↓
   218
```

3. Repeat the long division steps until you have divided all the digits.

```
    17
30)518
  -30↓
   218
  -210
     8
```

How to Divide a Four-Digit Number by a Two-Digit Divisor

7.5

1. Choose how many digits in the dividend to divide.
2. Follow the long division steps for the digits you chose.
3. Repeat the long division steps until you have divided all the digits.

Ex.

```
      126
27)3,426
   -27↓
     72
    -54
    186
   -162
     24
```